Translator - Youngju Ryu
English Adaptation - Jake Forbes
Copy Editor - Carol Fox
Cover Artist - Raymond Swanland
Retouch and Lettering - Eric Pineda

Editor - Jake Forbes
Managing Editor - Jill Freshney
Production Coordinator - Antonio DePietro
Production Manager - Jennifer Miller
Art Director - Matthew Alford
Editorial Director - Jeremy Ross
VP of Production - Ron Klamert
President & C.O.O. - John Parker
Publisher & C.E.O. - Stuart Levy

Email: editor@TOKYOPOP.com
Come visit us online at www.TOKYOPOP.com

A  Manga

TOKYOPOP Inc.
5900 Wilshire Blvd. Suite 2000
Los Angeles, CA 90036

ISBN: 1-59182-511-3

First TOKYOPOP printing: January 2004

10 9 8 7 6 5 4 3 2
Printed in the USA

VOLUME 10

BY

MIN-Woo HYUNG

LOS ANGELES ★ TOKYO ★ LONDON

THE CAST OF CHARACTERS

During the war against Lucifer, the archangel Temozarela led the agents of light. In the years that followed, Temozarela watched as God's attention shifted from his seraphim to his new creation—man. Jealousy caused Temozarela and his disciples to abandon their heavenly post and attempt to corrupt humanity to prove the superiority of the seraphim to God. During the Crusades he attempted to begin his plan, but Belial sealed him in the Domas Porada for 500 years. Now, released by Ivan Isaacs, Temozarela is free again, but too weak to carry out his dark designs. His disciples have begun to sanctify the ground in the American West, spreading plague and death in preparation for the Unholy Sabbath.

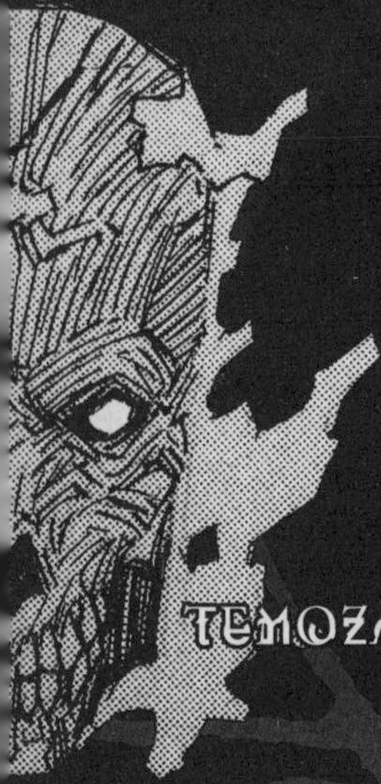

TEMOZARELA

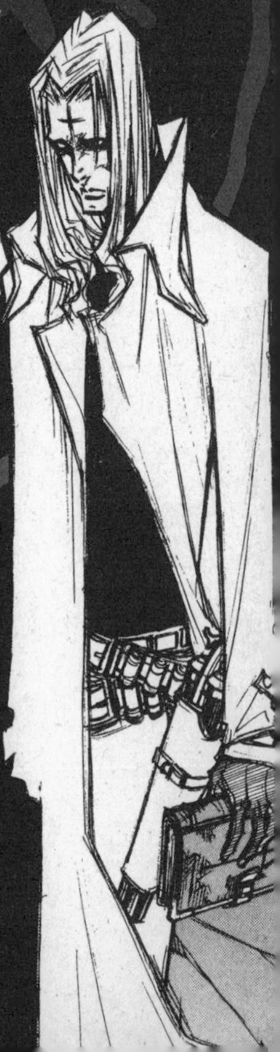

FATHER IVAN ISAACS

Ivan Isaacs was a young priest with a passion for ancient cultures when he was recruited to study the Domas Porada. Little did he know that this mission would be his last—at least his last in life. After helping revive an ancient battle for Heaven and Earth, Ivan and his beloved Gena were slain. In order to get revenge and atone for endangering the world, Ivan made a pact with the devil Belial: his soul in exchange for a second chance at life...and superhuman strength. Now Ivan wanders the old west, hunting down Temozarela's disciples and keeping a journal of his tragic tale.

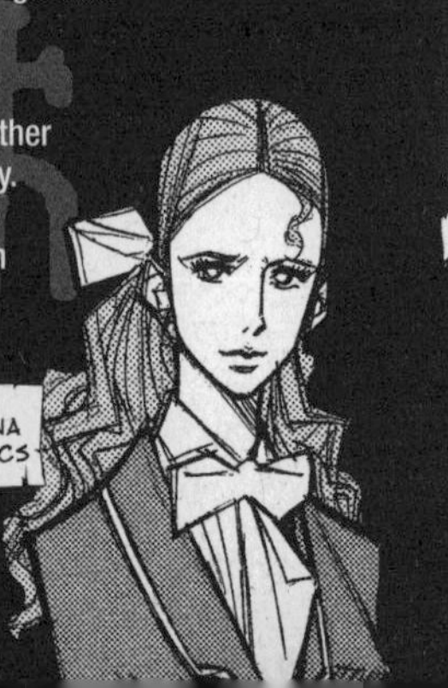

GENA ISAACS

Gena Isaacs was an only child, so her father Jacob adopted Ivan to keep her company. In time the two developed a mutual love that went beyond sibling affection, much to their father's dismay. Jacob sent Ivan to seminary, but the young would-be lovers' feelings remained. Before Ivan could act on his feelings, Gena was captured and killed by agents of Temozarela.

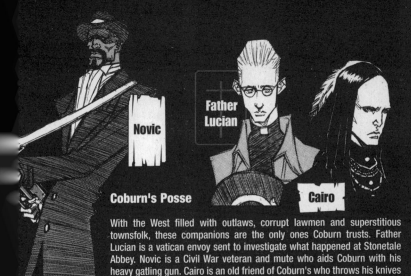

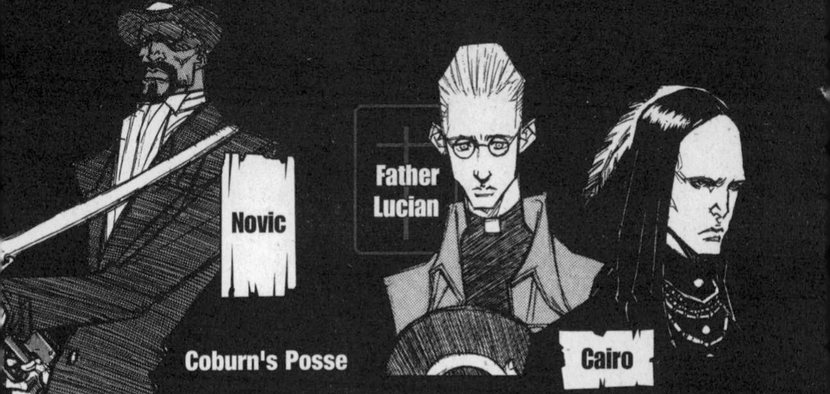
Novic
Father Lucian
Cairo

Coburn's Posse

With the West filled with outlaws, corrupt lawmen and superstitious townsfolk, these companions are the only ones Coburn trusts. Father Lucian is a vatican envoy sent to investigate what happened at Stonetale Abbey. Novic is a Civil War veteran and mute who aids Coburn with his heavy gatling gun. Cairo is an old friend of Coburn's who throws his knives with deadly accuracy.

Lizzie inherited leadership of the Angel Gang from her father. She's loved by her men, and feared by everyone else. She has more of a conscience than some of her fellow outlaws, but her hands are not clean of blood. Her rational world was shattered when her path crossed that of Ivan Isaacs. Now trouble seems to be her only friend. A hanging, a lynching, even a zombie curse—she just can't seem to get a break these days. During the St. Baldlas massacre, she was bitten by one of Temozarela's zombies and her blood now bears his curse.

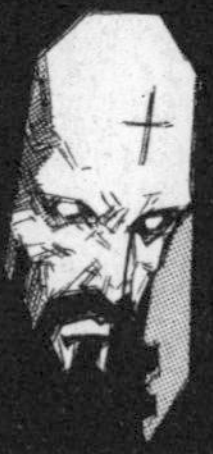

BELIAL

The devil Belial makes Ivan his agent in the mortal world so that he may battle the agents of the fallen Arch-Angel Temozarela, who is planning an upheaval of Heaven and Hell. Belial used to be Betheal, a Catholic priest in the Middle Ages when he we was a prosecutor in trials of heresy. After Temozarela shattered his faith, Betheal turned himself into the demon Belial in order to get his revenge.

Coburn is the only federal marshal investigating possible links between an outbreak of plague and other mysterious events happening around the Old West. After Lizzie is found to be the only survivor of the St. Baldlas massacre, Coburn takes her into custody. Together they follow Ivan Isaacs, the only one who knows the truth about what's going on.

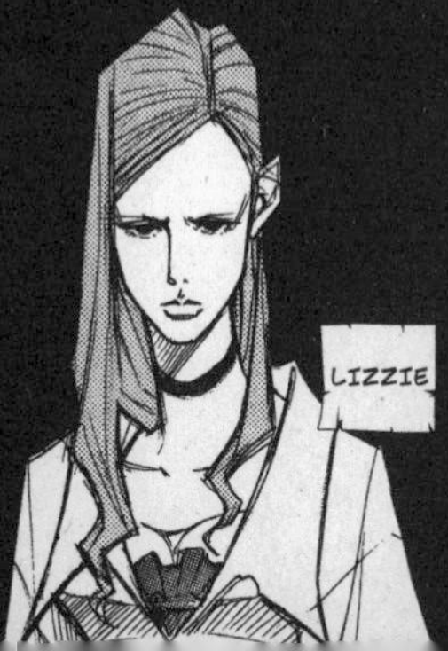
LIZZIE

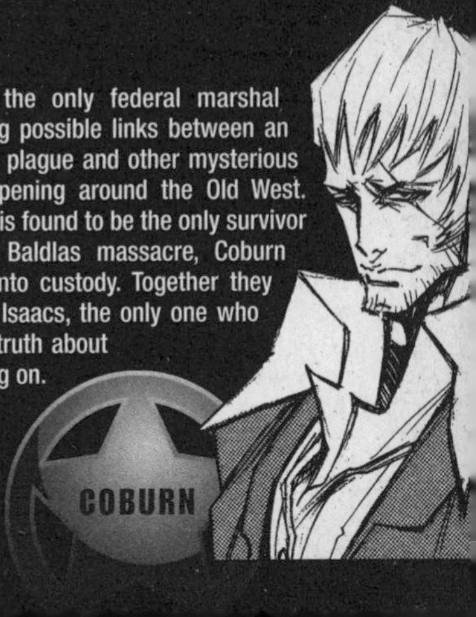
COBURN

THE STORY SO FAR...

Ivan's journey of revenge has led him to the fortress of Achmode, one of Temozarela's fallen angels. During his centuries of exile, Achmode has turned his palace into a twisted mockery of heaven, complete with angels of his own design. After battling his way through the unheavenly host, Ivan reached their master.

Meanwhile, Coburn, a federal marshal, is hot on Ivan's trail. An unexplained series of incidents has left several frontier towns ravaged, and a mysterious "plague" has created widespread panic in the West. Now that earthly explanations have failed him, only the pale-faced Priest can help. Coburn and his posse were last seen crossing the desert en route to Bosack.

Now let us watch as two great men cross swords with the forces of darkness, and cross paths with each other at long last.

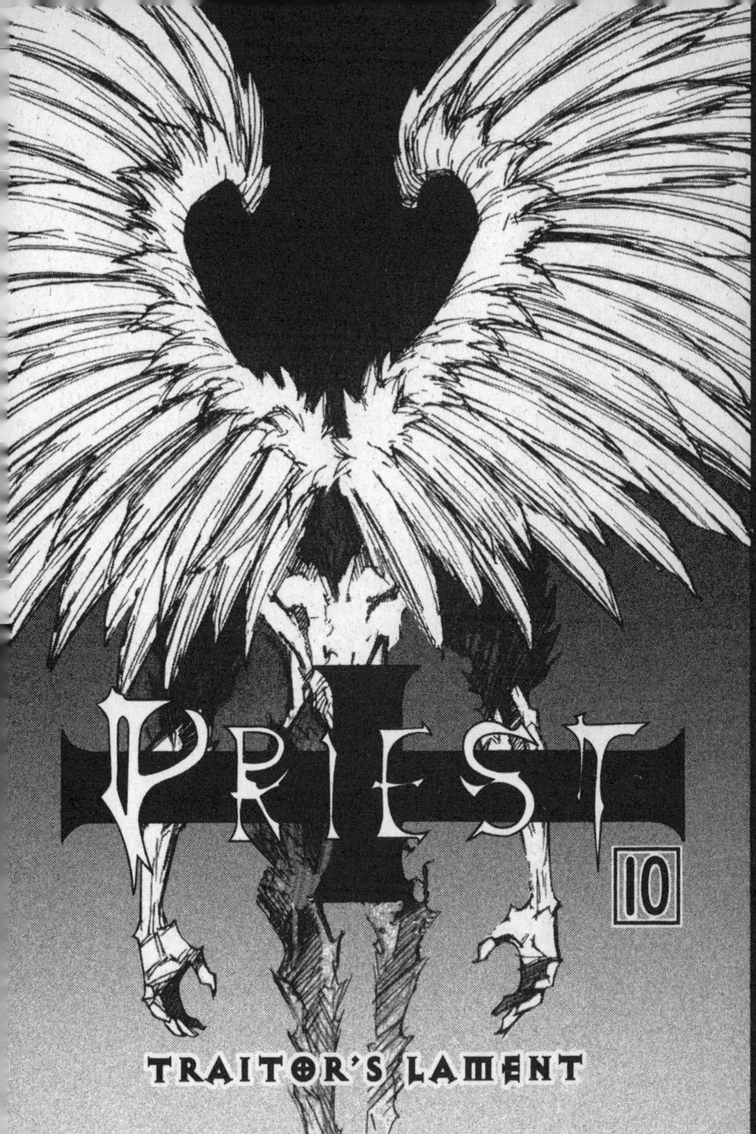
PRIEST
10
TRAITOR'S LAMENT

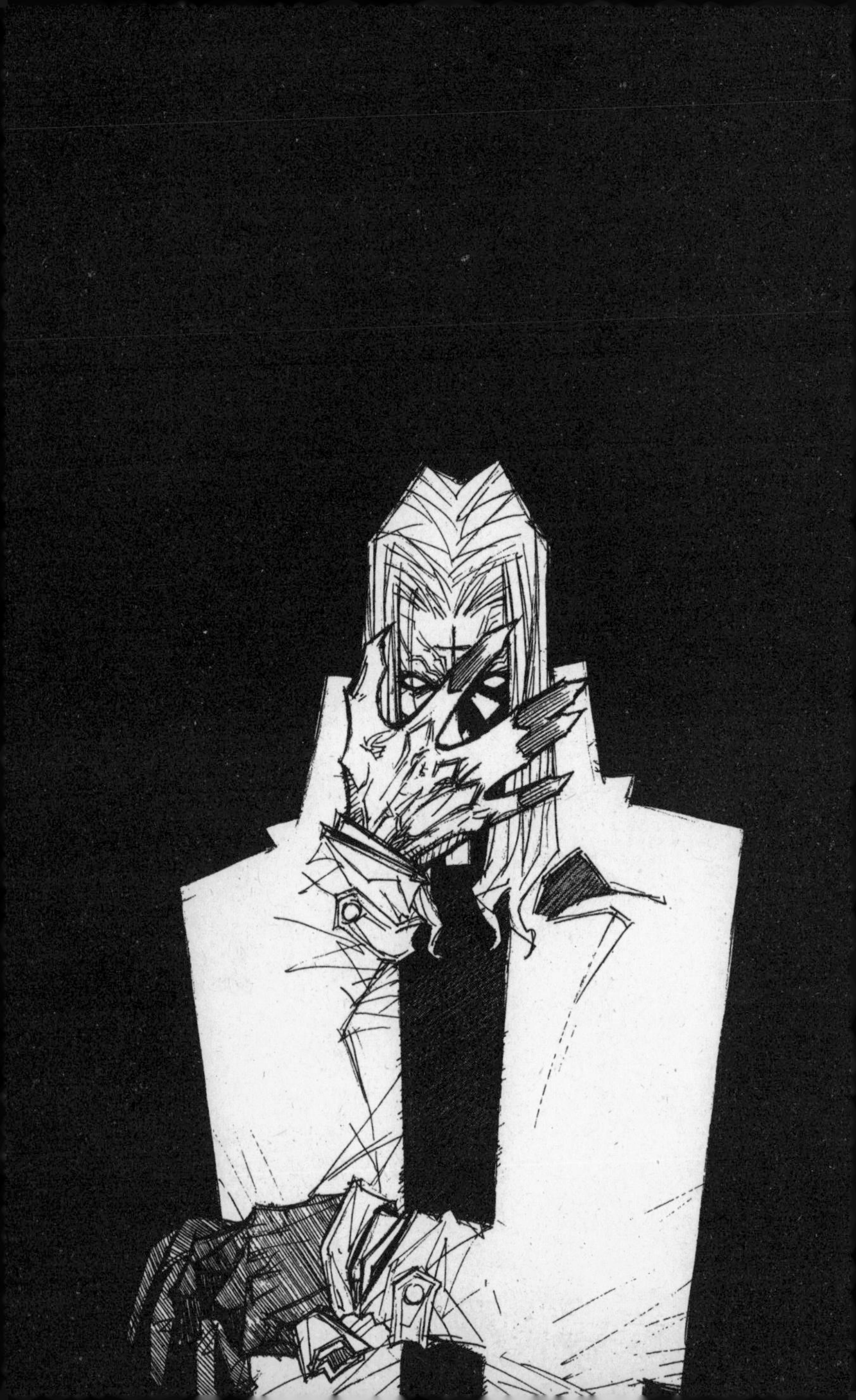

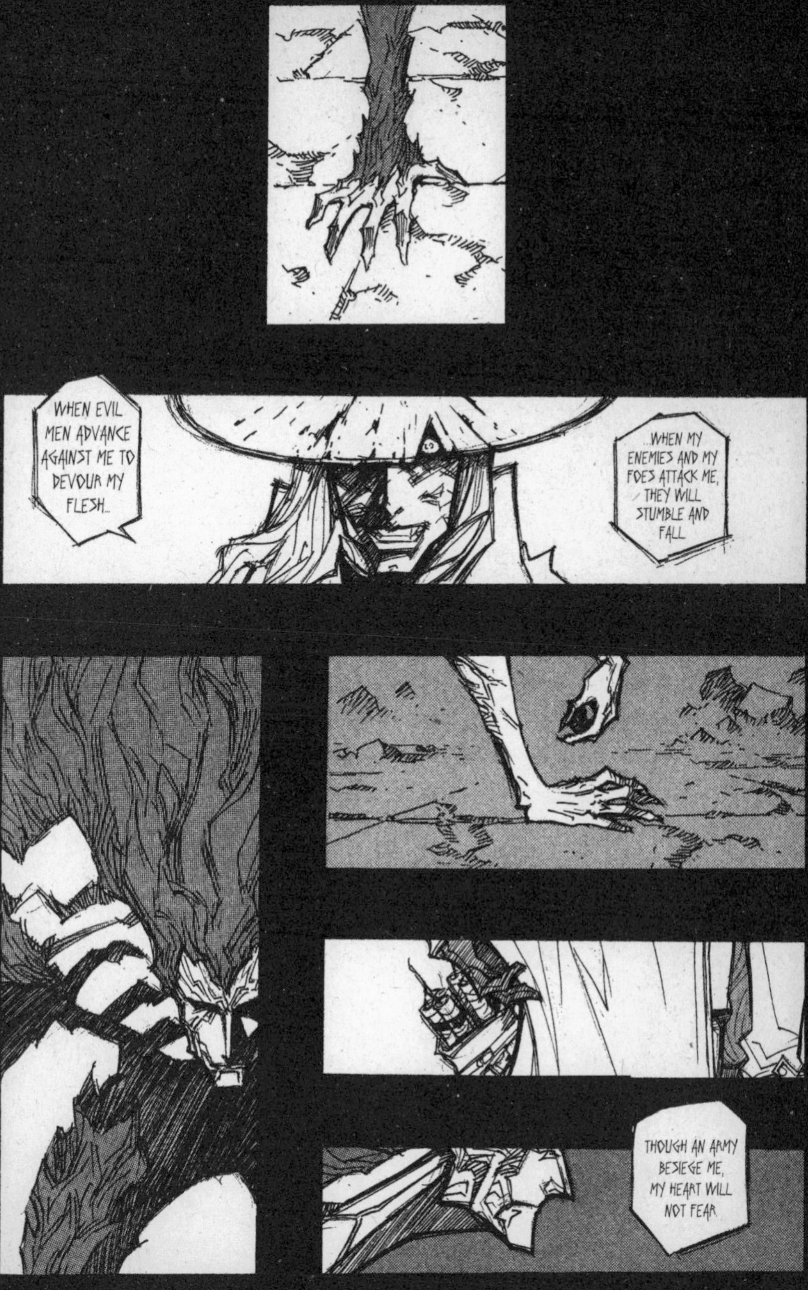
WHEN EVIL MEN ADVANCE AGAINST ME TO DEVOUR MY FLESH...
...WHEN MY ENEMIES AND MY FOES ATTACK ME, THEY WILL STUMBLE AND FALL
THOUGH AN ARMY BESIEGE ME, MY HEART WILL NOT FEAR.

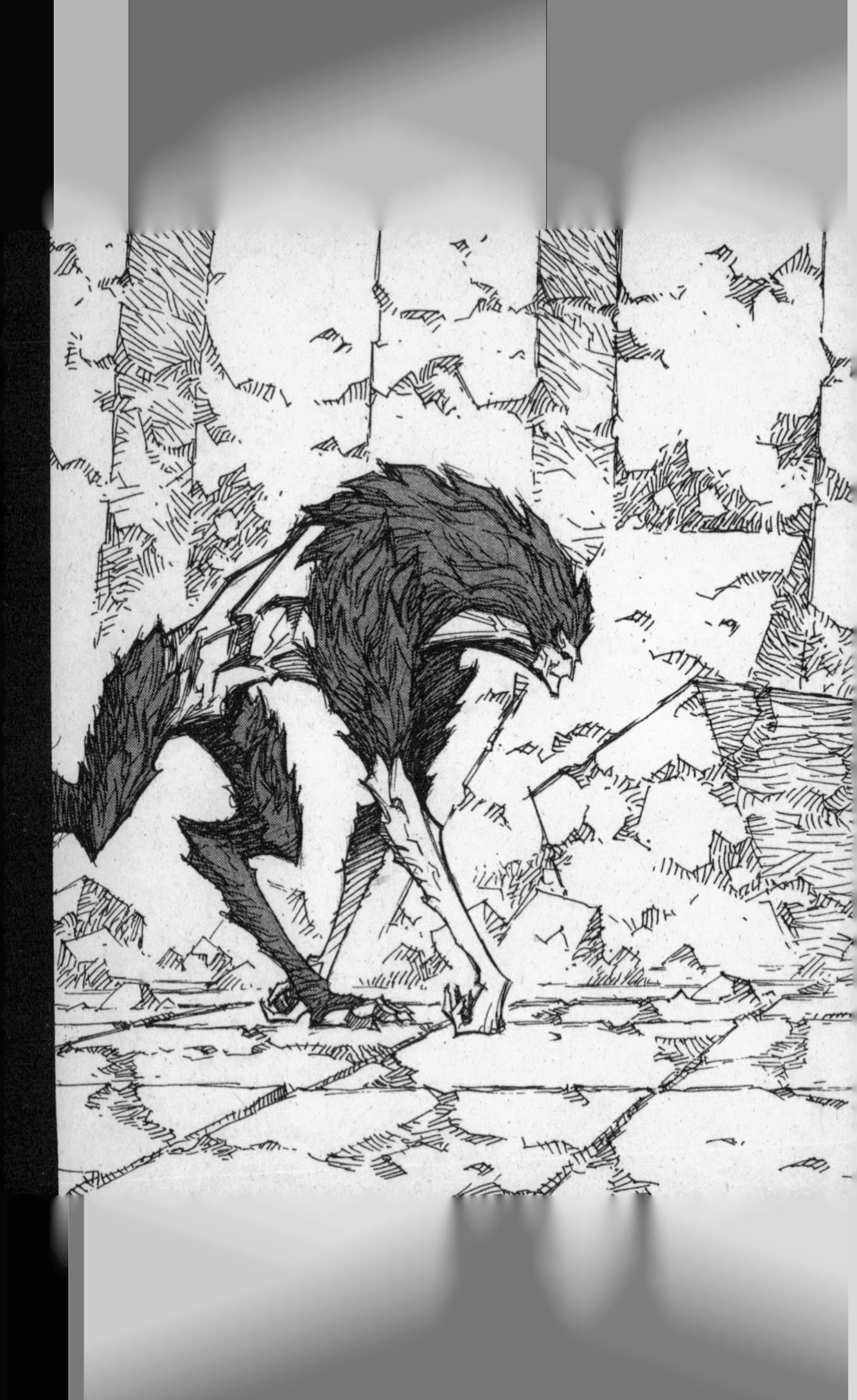

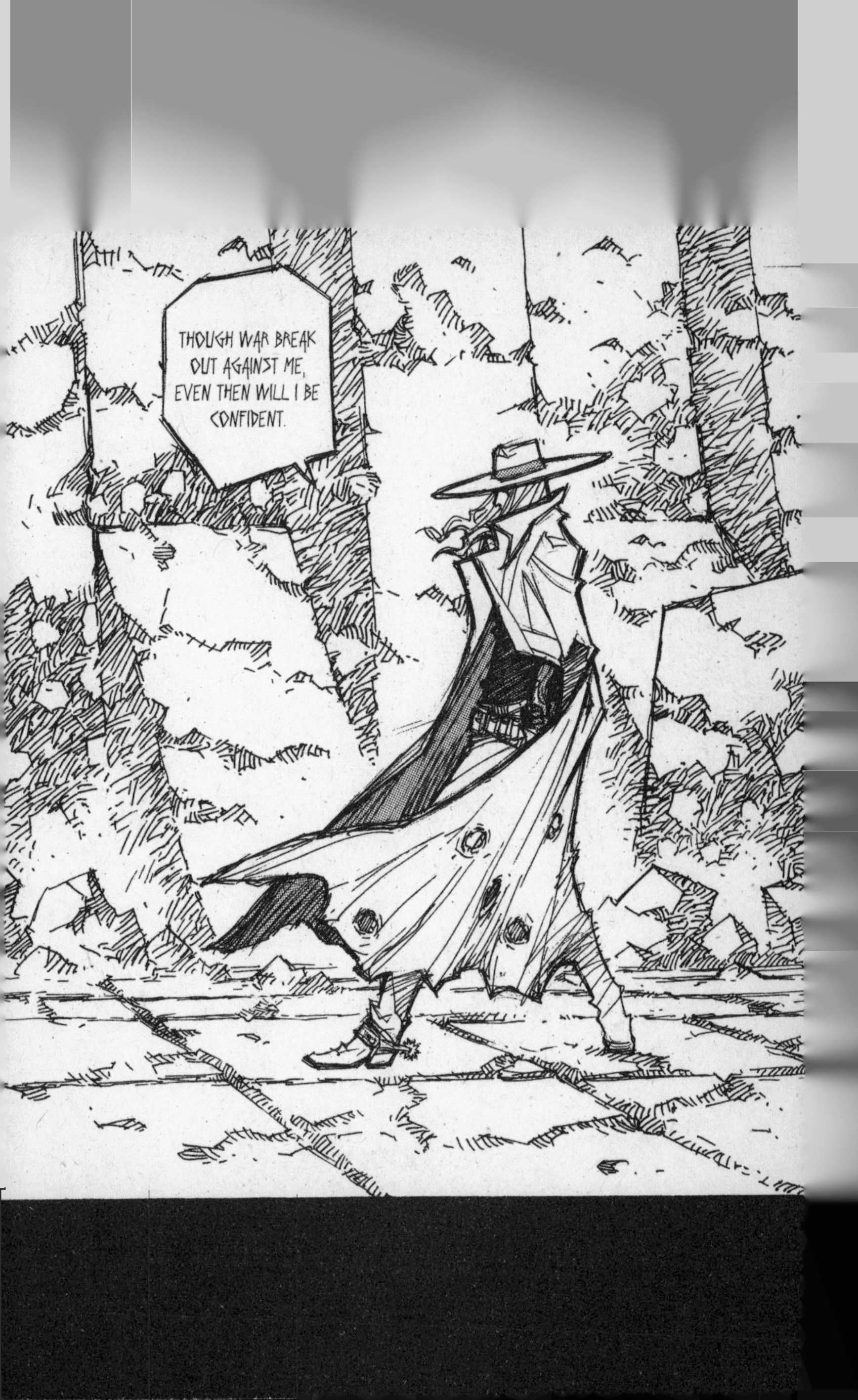
THOUGH WAR BREAK OUT AGAINST ME, EVEN THEN WILL I BE CONFIDENT.

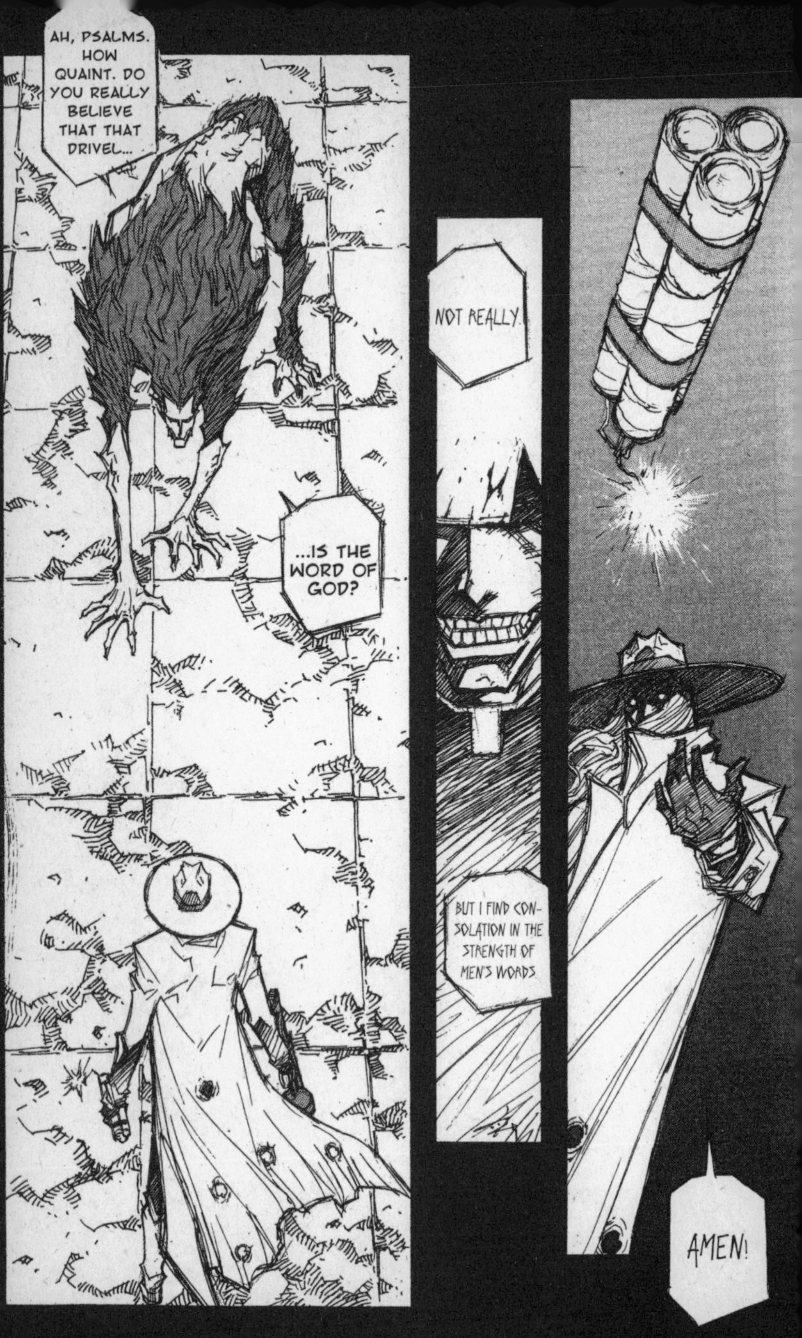
AH, PSALMS. HOW QUAINT. DO YOU REALLY BELIEVE THAT THAT DRIVEL...
...IS THE WORD OF GOD?
NOT REALLY.
BUT I FIND CONSOLATION IN THE STRENGTH OF MEN'S WORDS.
AMEN!

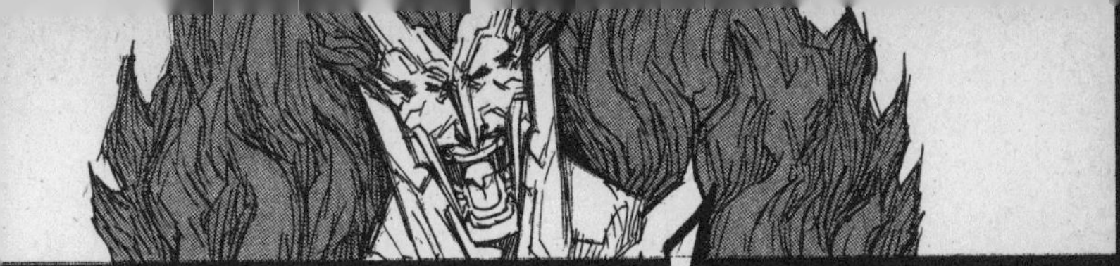

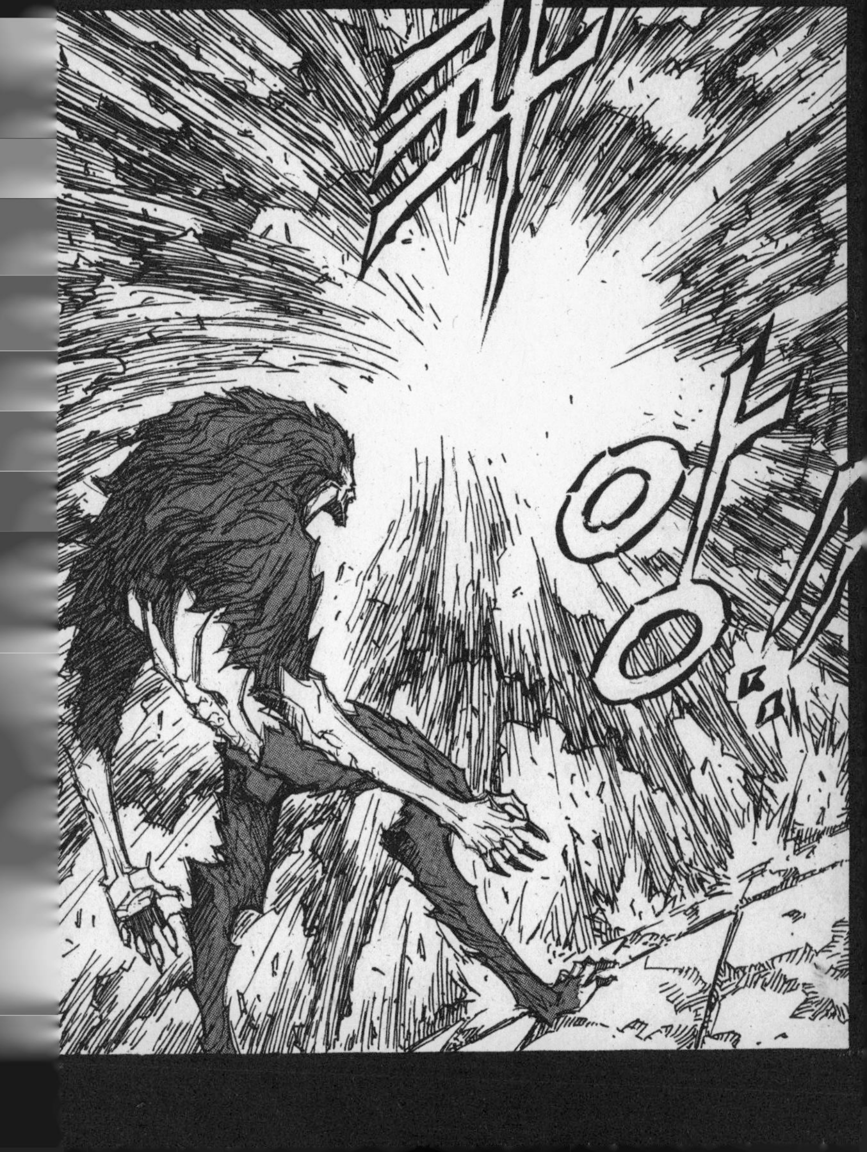
콰앙!!

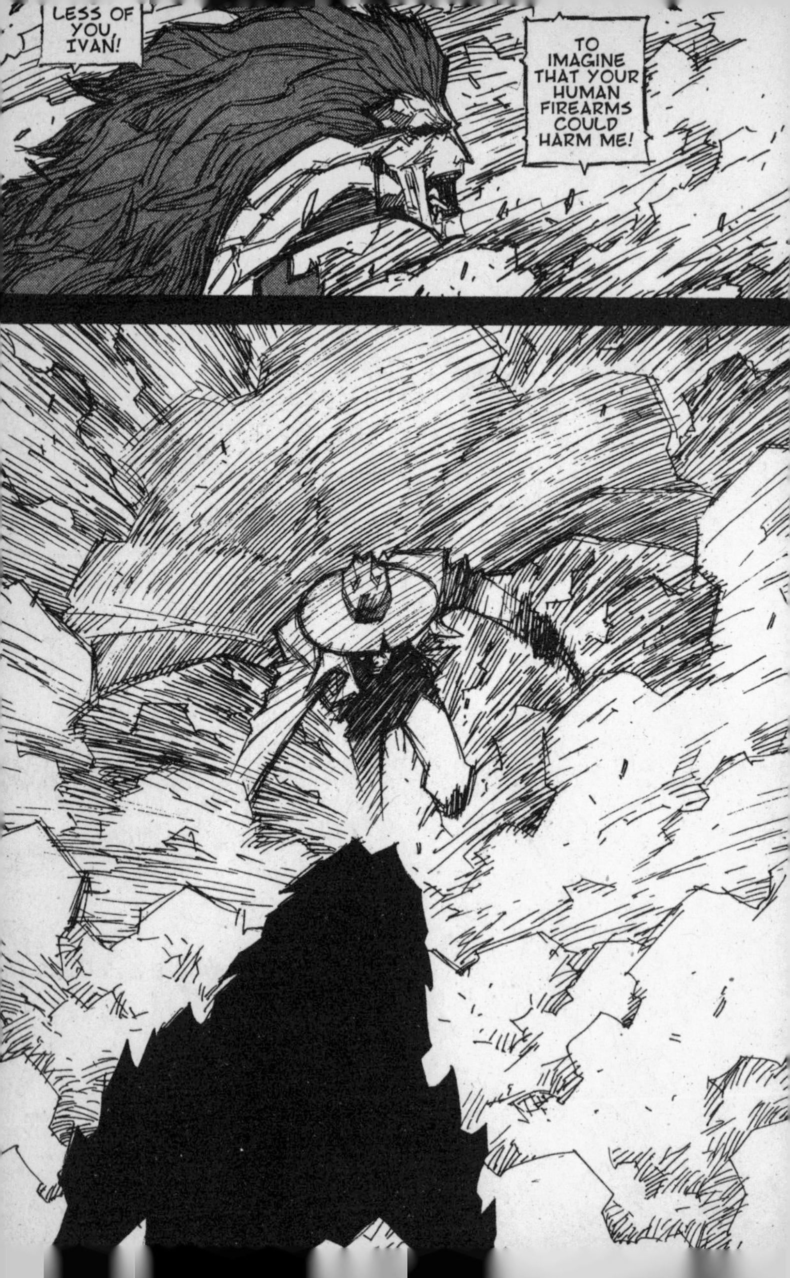
TO IMAGINE THAT YOUR HUMAN FIREARMS COULD HARM ME!
LESS OF YOU, IVAN!

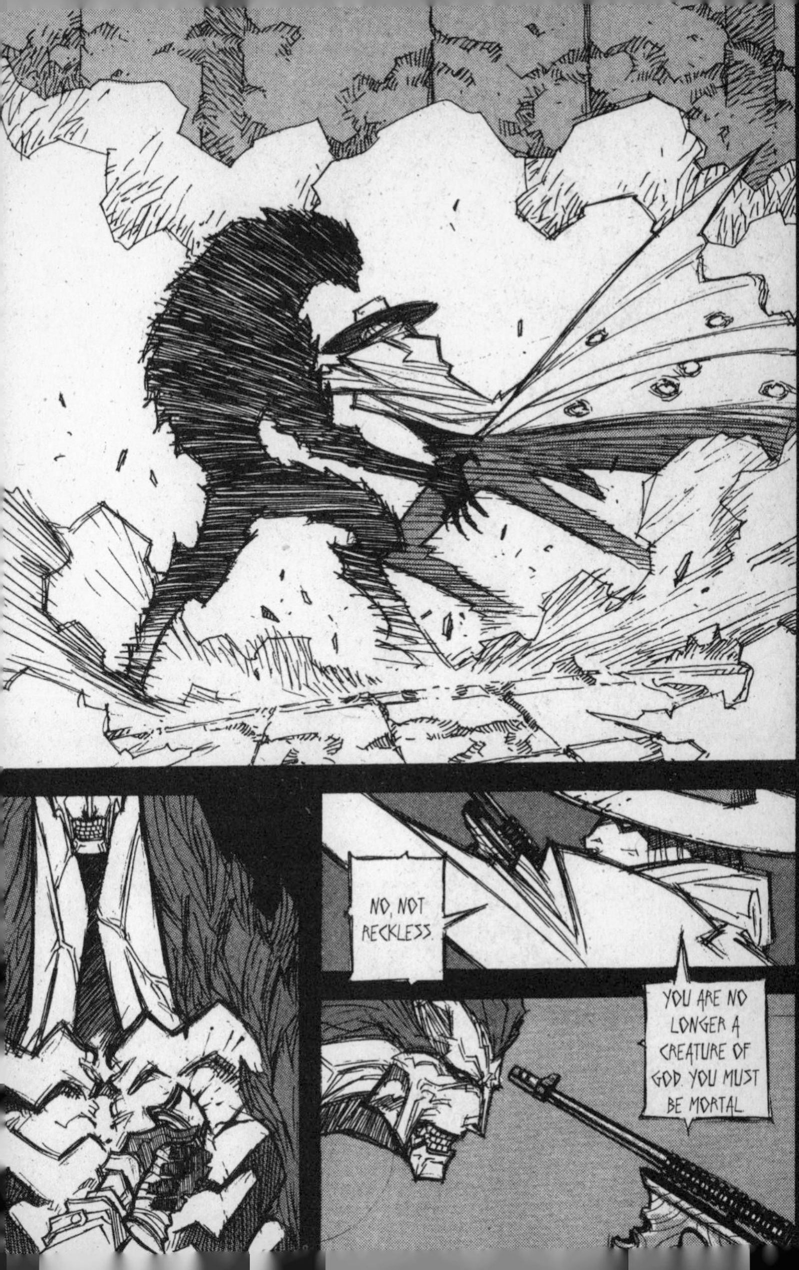
NO, NOT RECKLESS.
YOU ARE NO LONGER A CREATURE OF GOD. YOU MUST BE MORTAL.

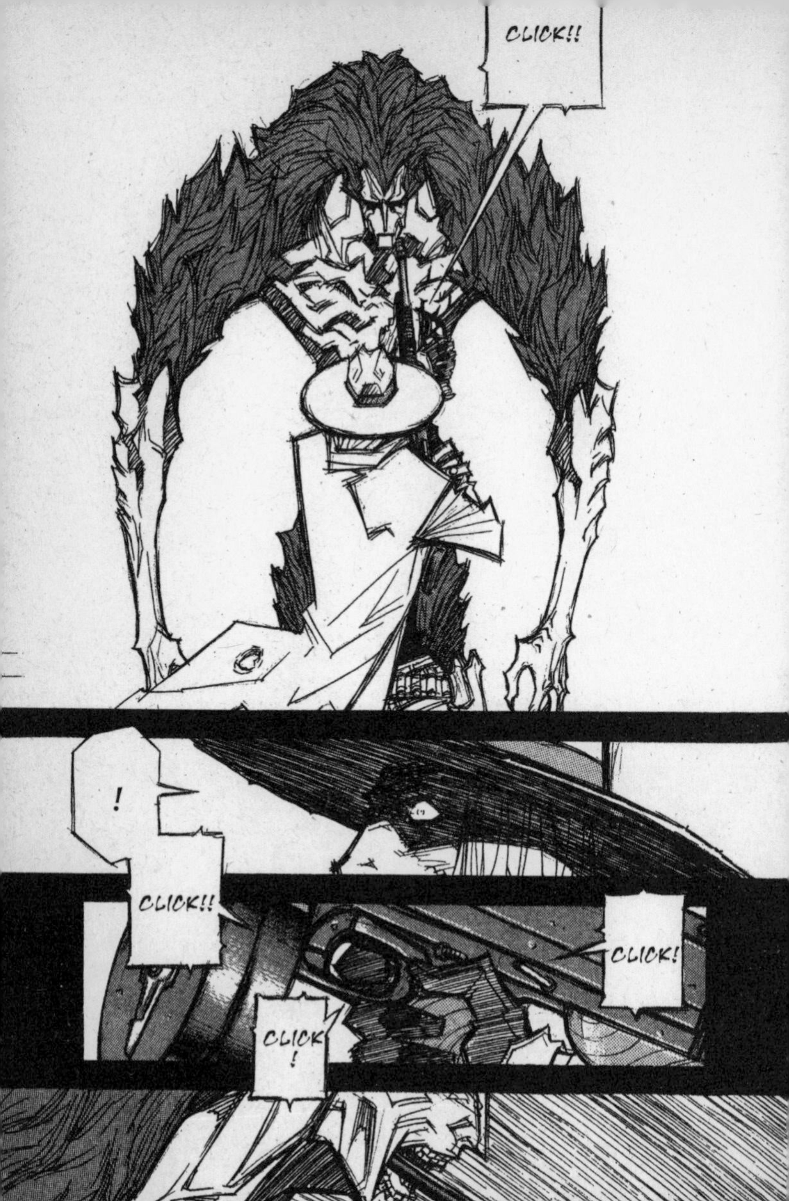
CLICK!!
!
CLICK!
CLICK!!
CLICK !

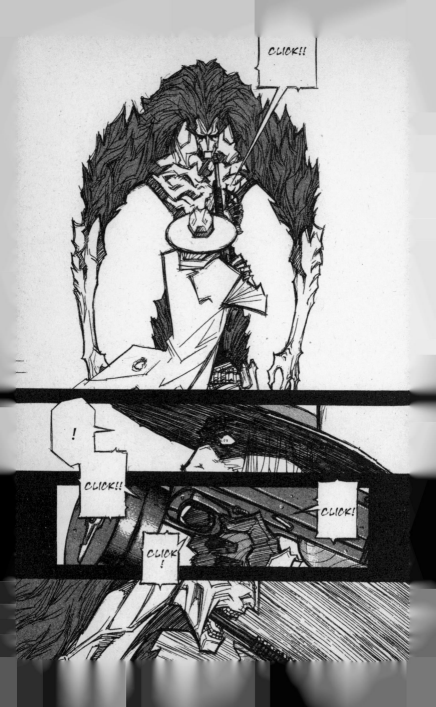

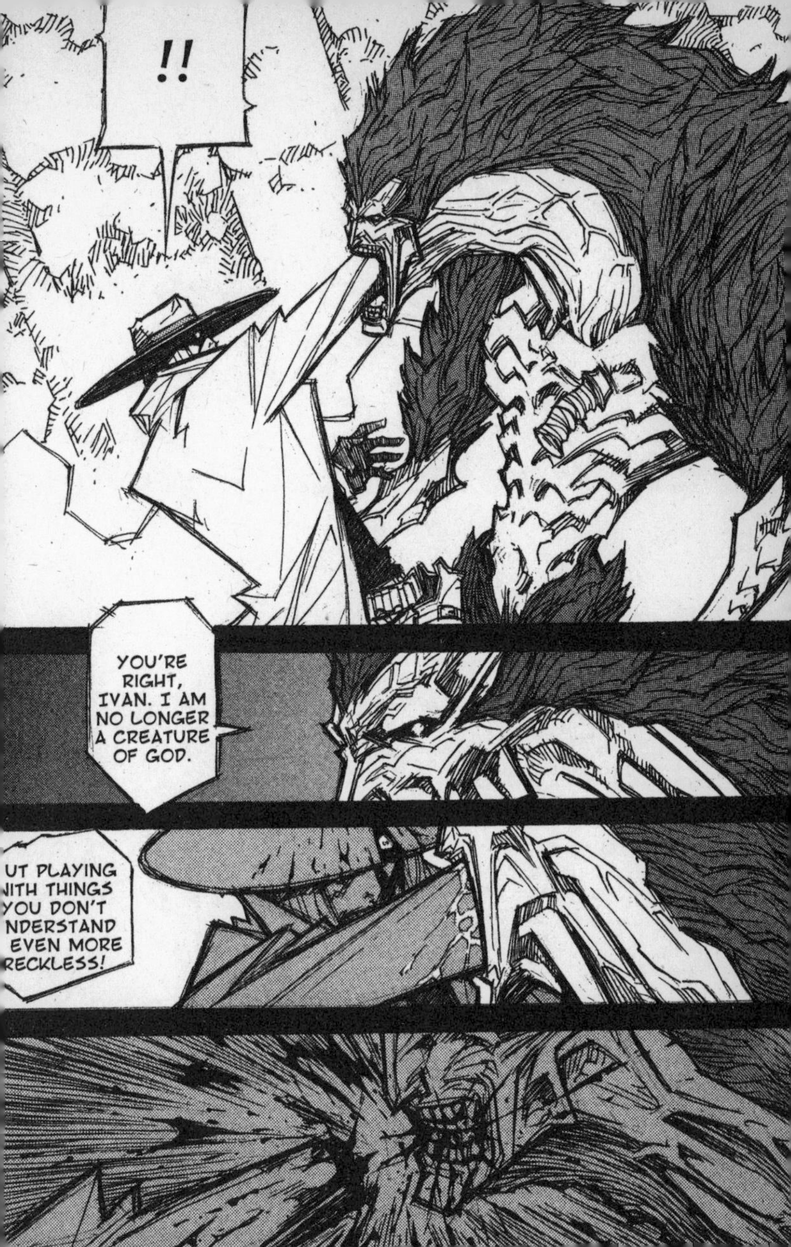
!!
YOU'RE RIGHT, IVAN. I AM NO LONGER A CREATURE OF GOD.
UT PLAYING NITH THINGS YOU DON'T NDERSTAND EVEN MORE RECKLESS!

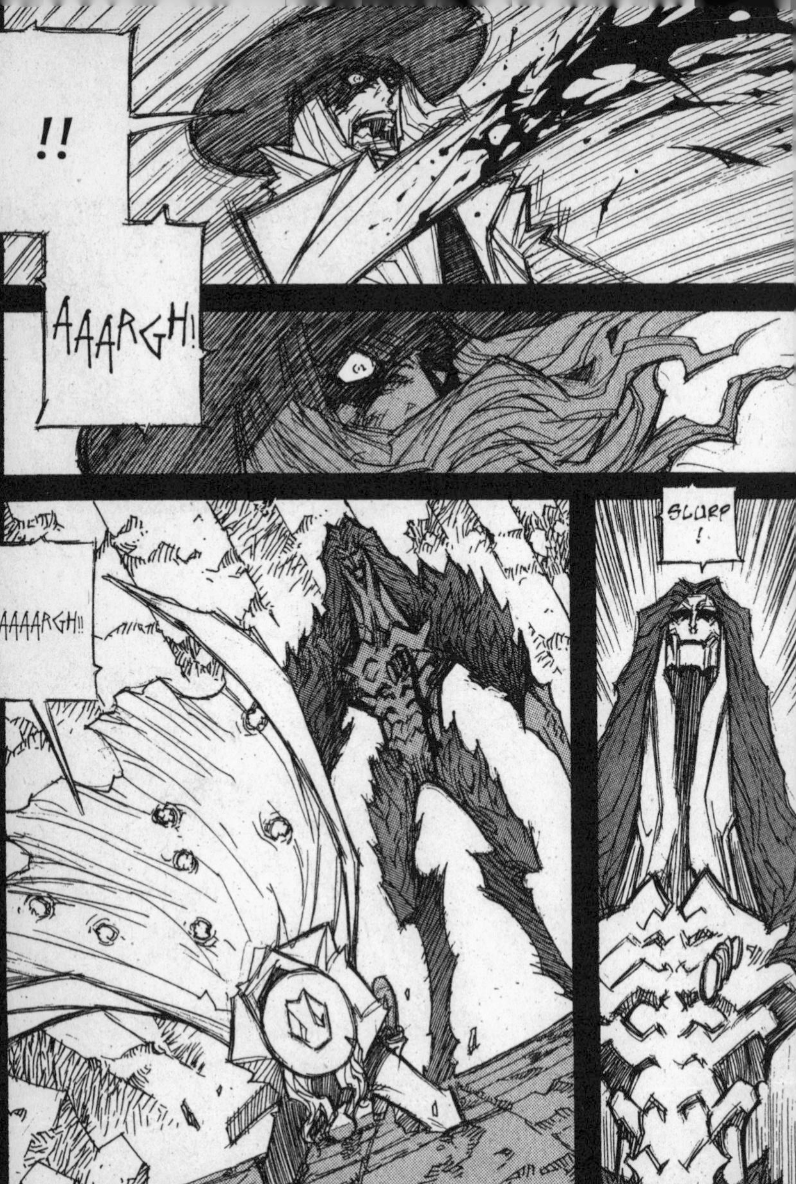
!!
AAARGH!
SLURP !
AAAARGH!!

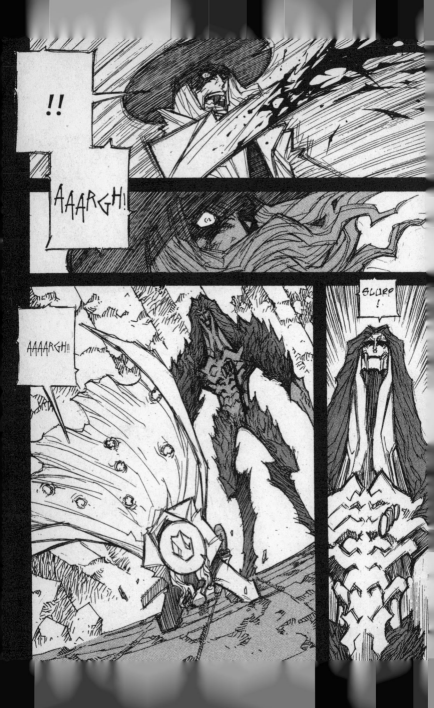

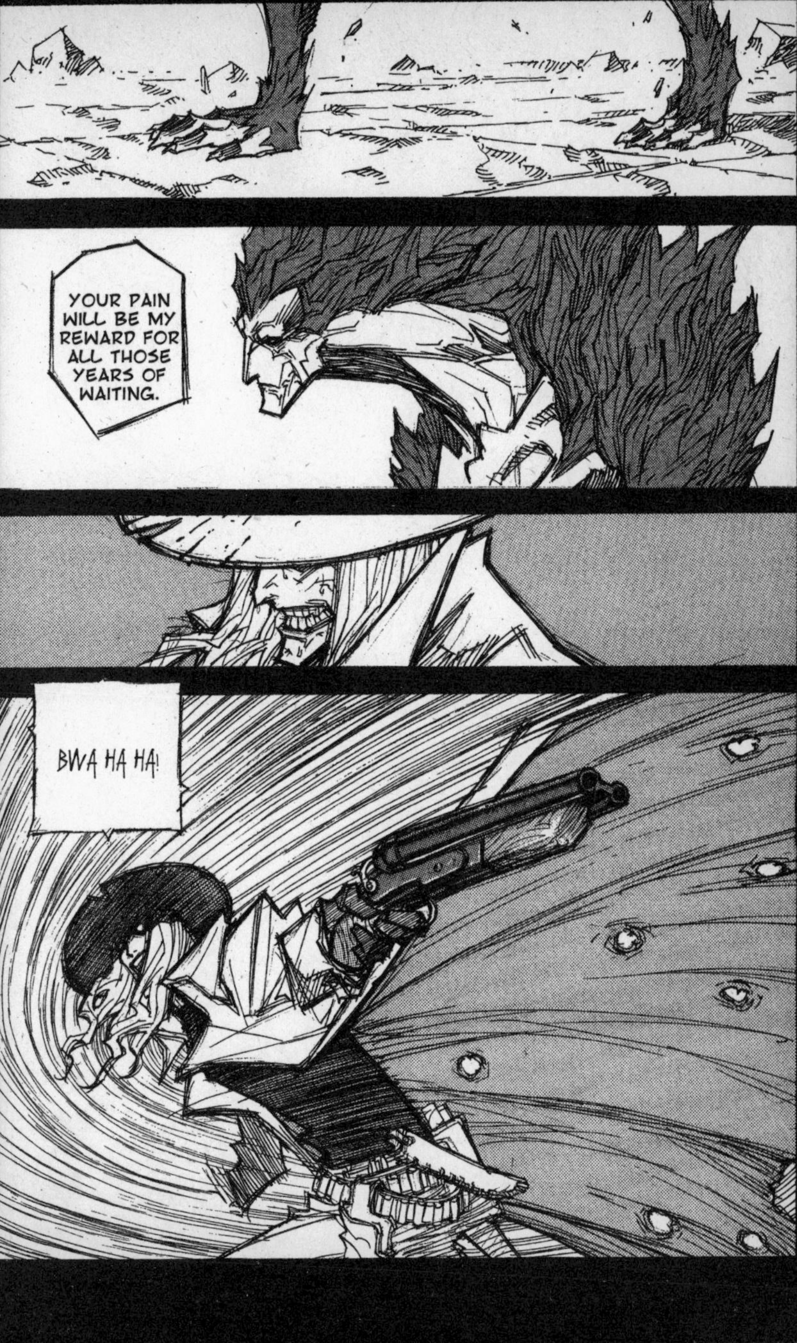
YOUR PAIN WILL BE MY REWARD FOR ALL THOSE YEARS OF WAITING.
BWA HA HA!

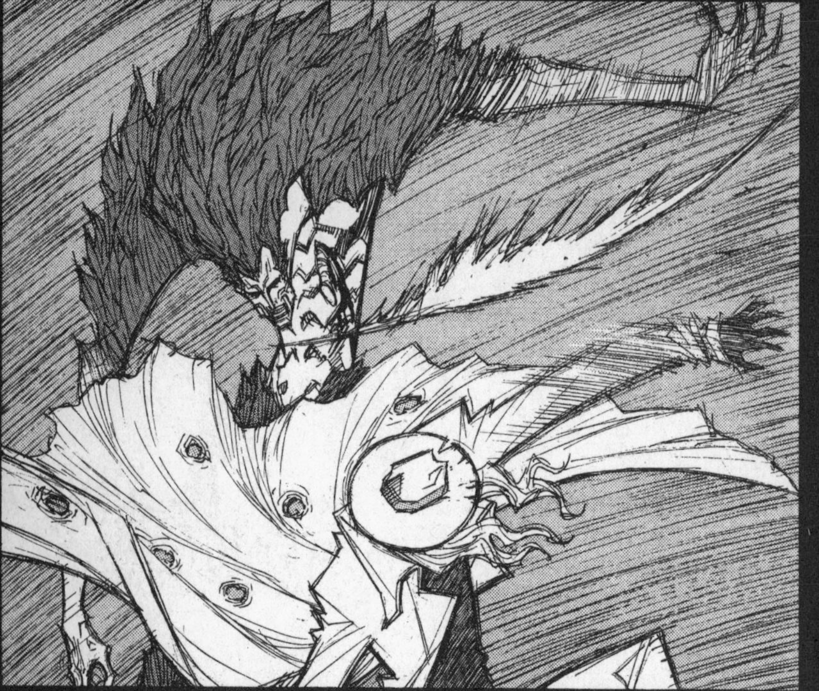

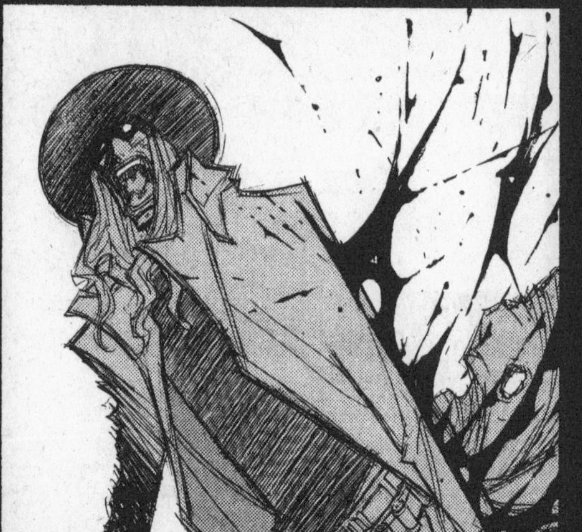

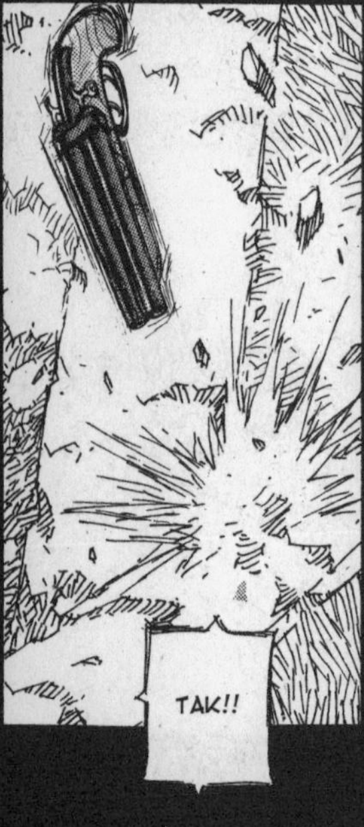
TAK!!

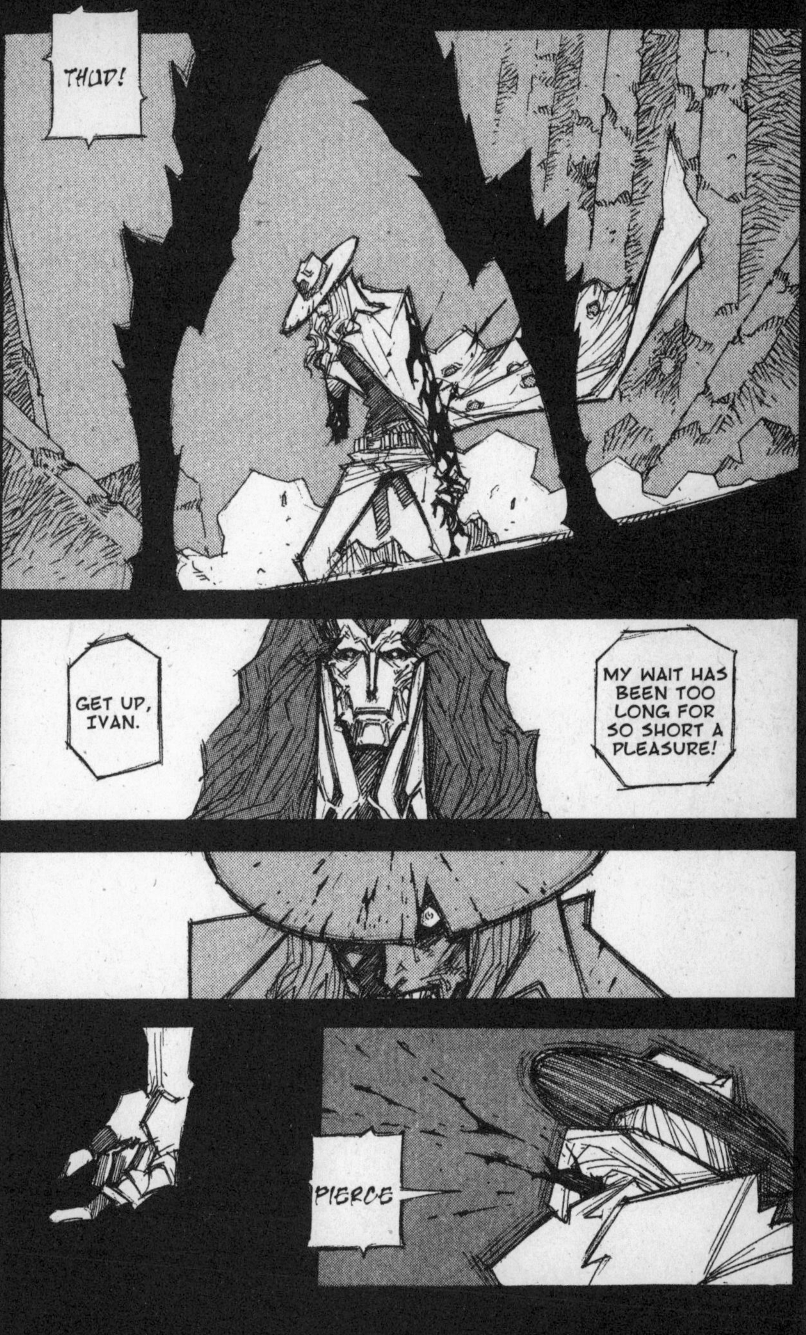
THUD!
MY WAIT HAS BEEN TOO LONG FOR SO SHORT A PLEASURE!
GET UP, IVAN.
PIERCE

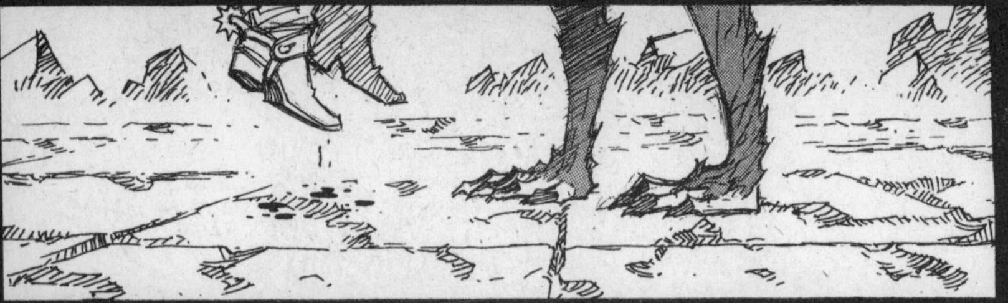

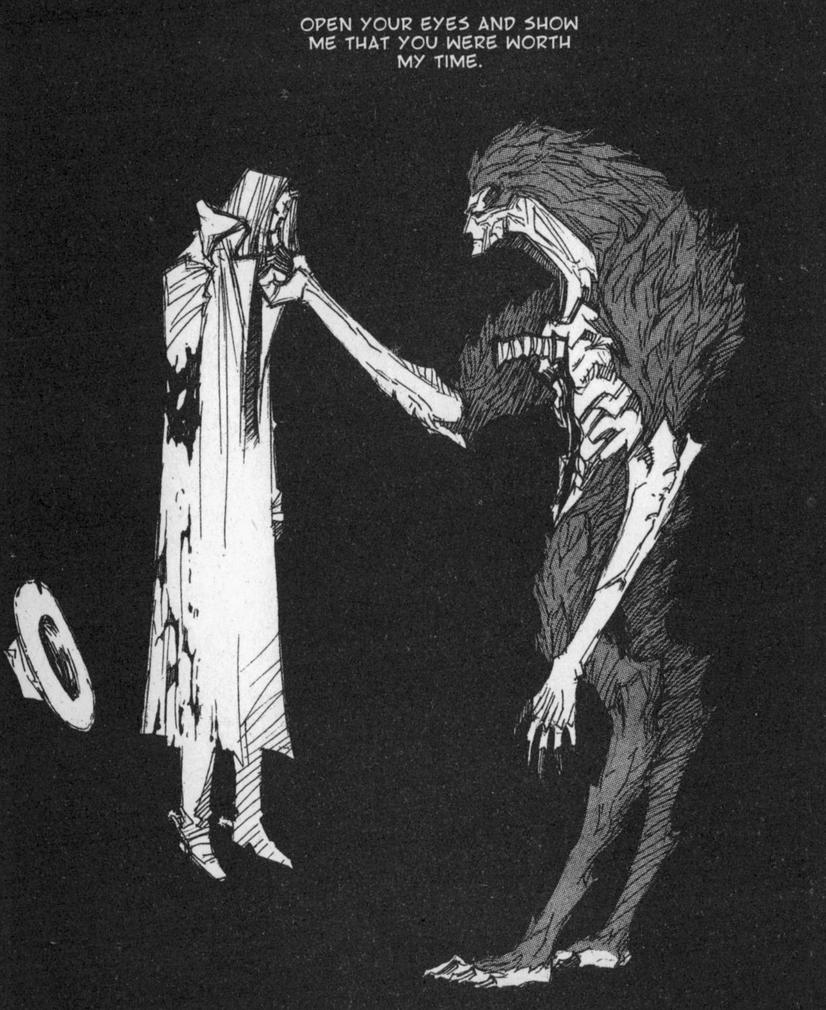
OPEN YOUR EYES AND SHOW ME THAT YOU WERE WORTH MY TIME.

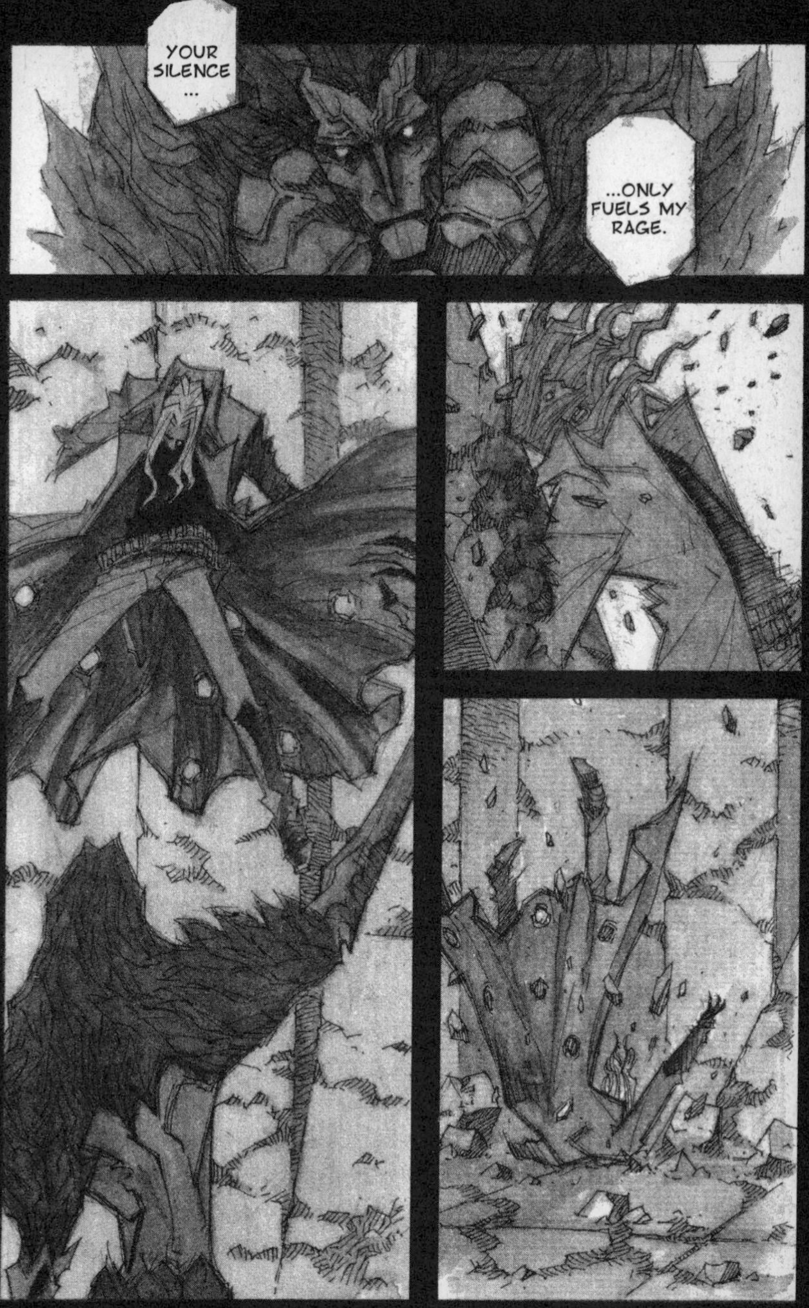
YOUR SILENCE ...
...ONLY FUELS MY RAGE.

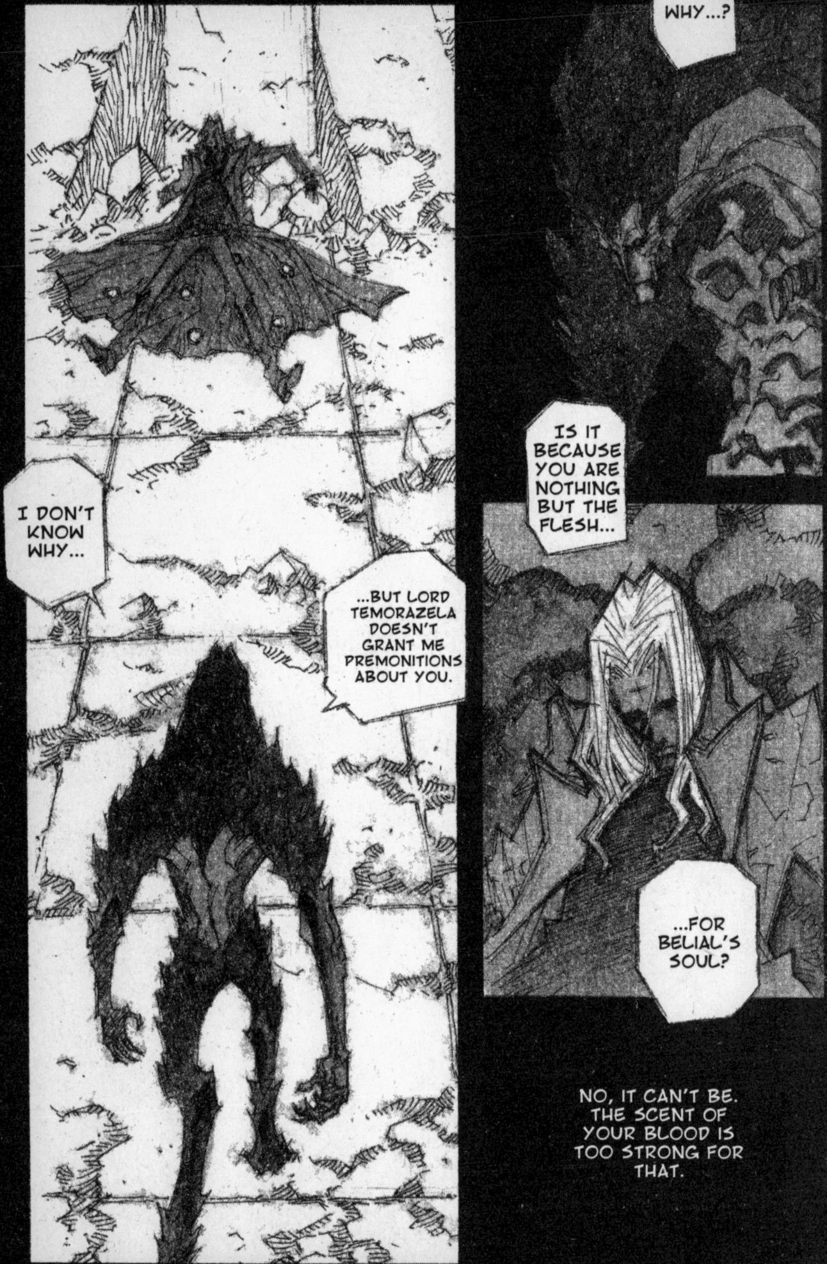

I DON'T KNOW WHY...
...BUT LORD TEMORAZELA DOESN'T GRANT ME PREMONITIONS ABOUT YOU.
WHY...?
IS IT BECAUSE YOU ARE NOTHING BUT THE FLESH...
...FOR BELIAL'S SOUL?
NO, IT CAN'T BE. THE SCENT OF YOUR BLOOD IS TOO STRONG FOR THAT.

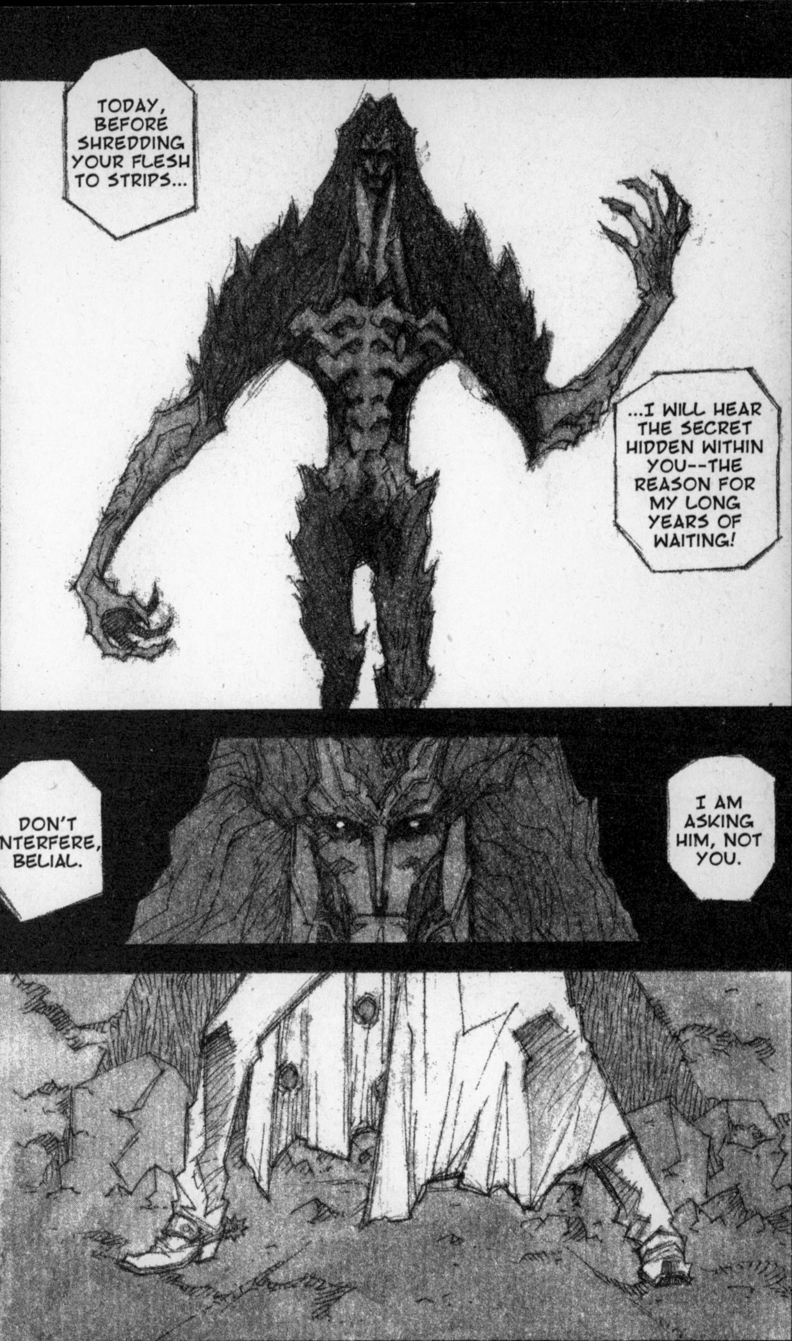
TODAY, BEFORE SHREDDING YOUR FLESH TO STRIPS...
...I WILL HEAR THE SECRET HIDDEN WITHIN YOU--THE REASON FOR MY LONG YEARS OF WAITING!
DON'T NTERFERE, BELIAL.
I AM ASKING HIM, NOT YOU.

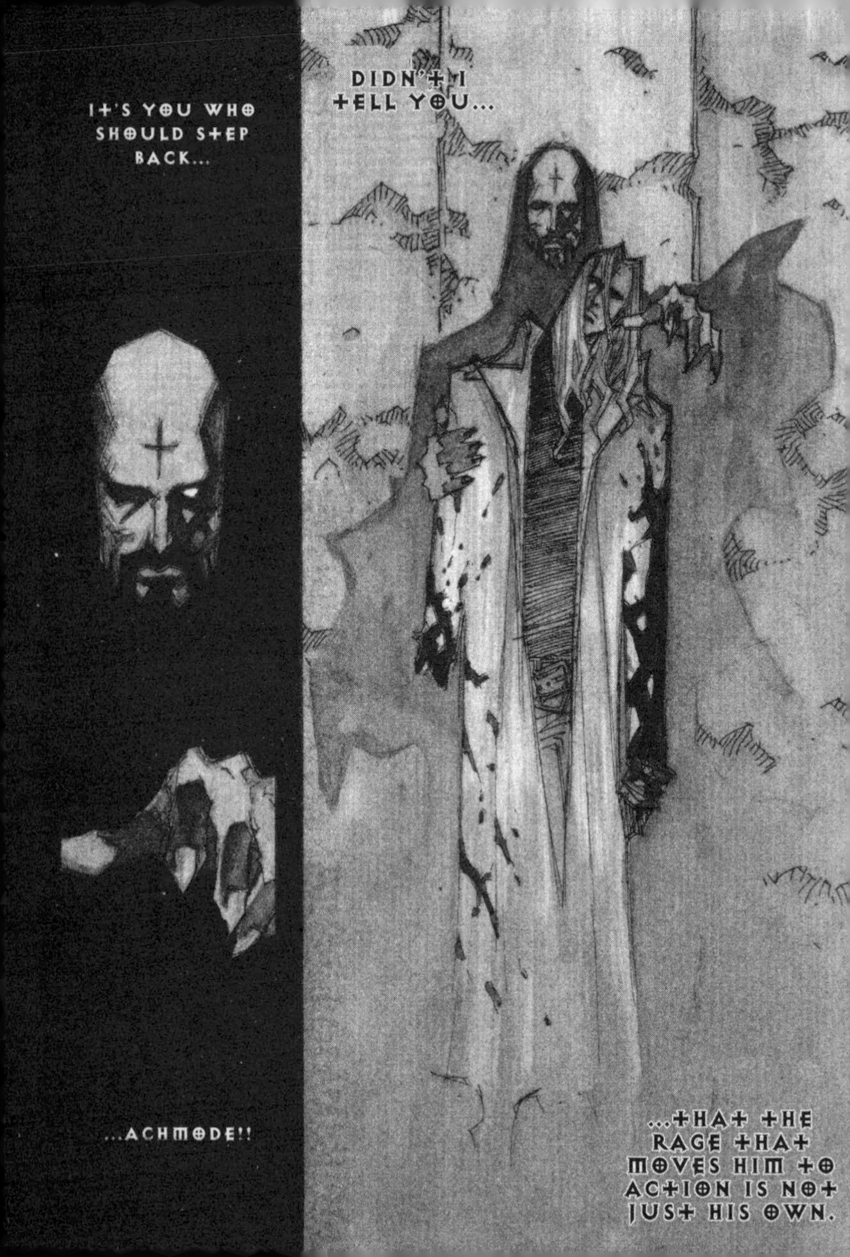
IT'S YOU WHO SHOULD STEP BACK...
...ACHMODE!!
DIDN'T I TELL YOU...
...THAT THE RAGE THAT MOVES HIM TO ACTION IS NOT JUST HIS OWN.

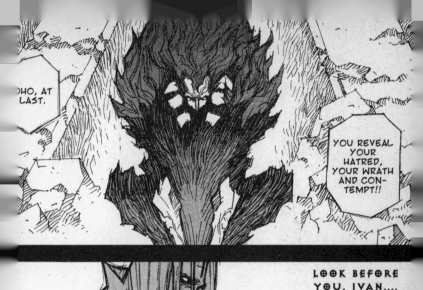

HO, AT LAST.

YOU REVEAL YOUR HATRED, YOUR WRATH AND CONTEMPT!!

LOOK BEFORE YOU, IVAN....

HE'S ONE OF THEM.

ONE OF THOSE WHO TOOK EVERYTHING FROM YOU...

...BEFORE YOU COULD REPENT OF YOUR MISTAKE.

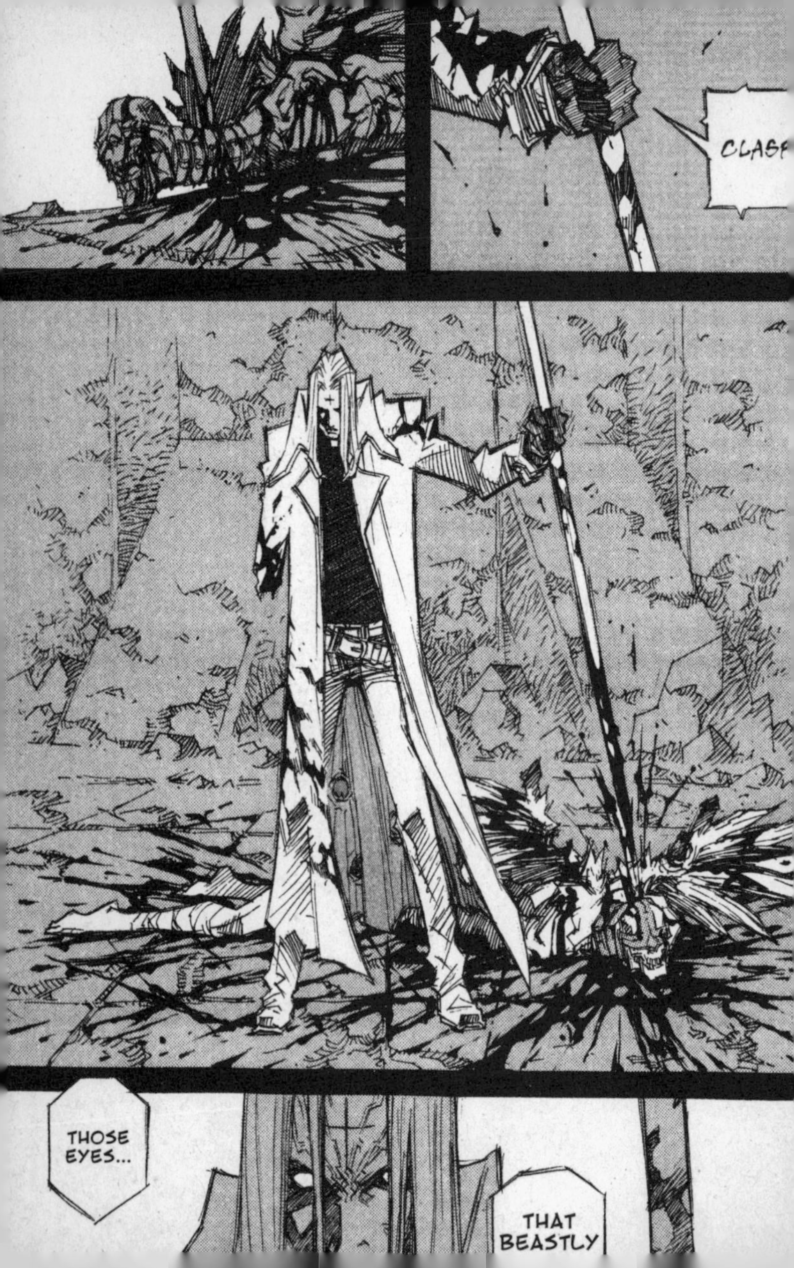
CLAS
THOSE EYES...
THAT BEASTLY

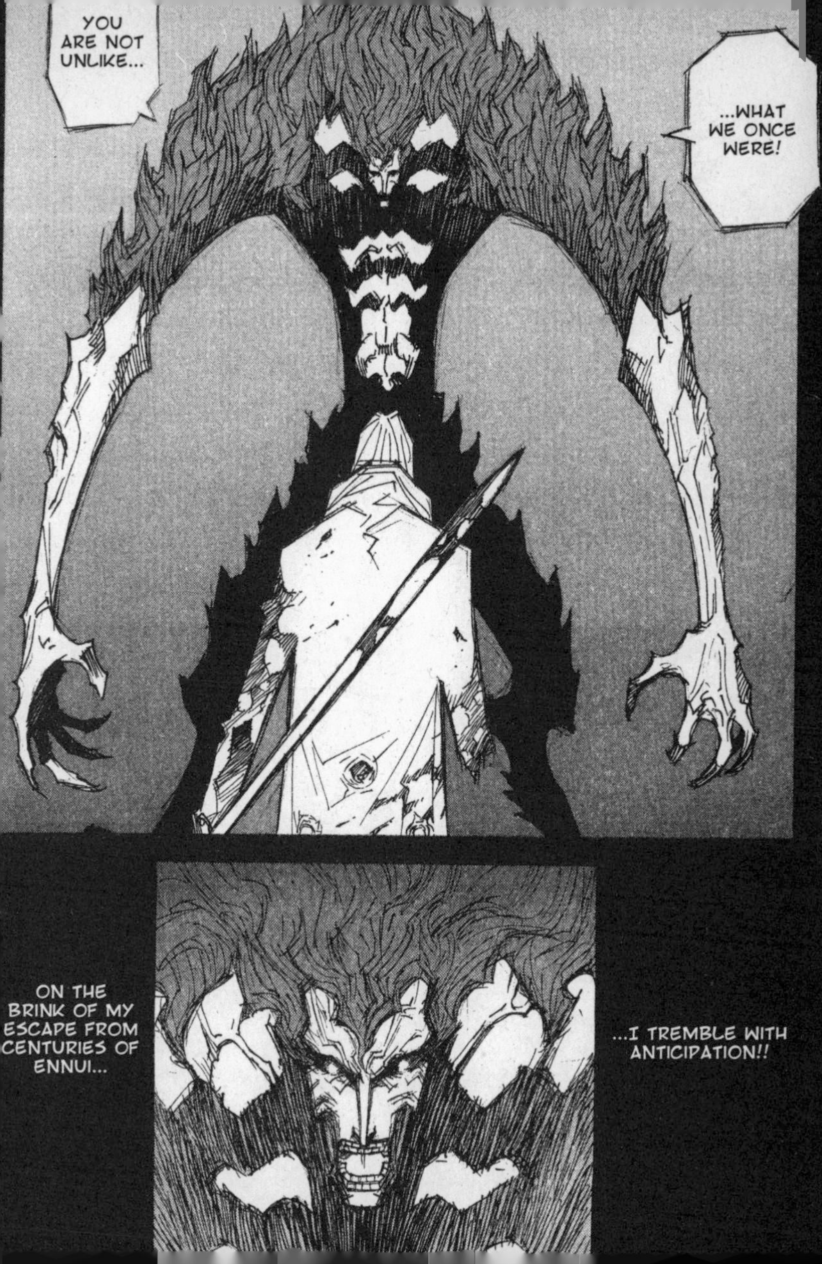
YOU ARE NOT UNLIKE...
...WHAT WE ONCE WERE!
ON THE BRINK OF MY ESCAPE FROM CENTURIES OF ENNUI...
...I TREMBLE WITH ANTICIPATION!!

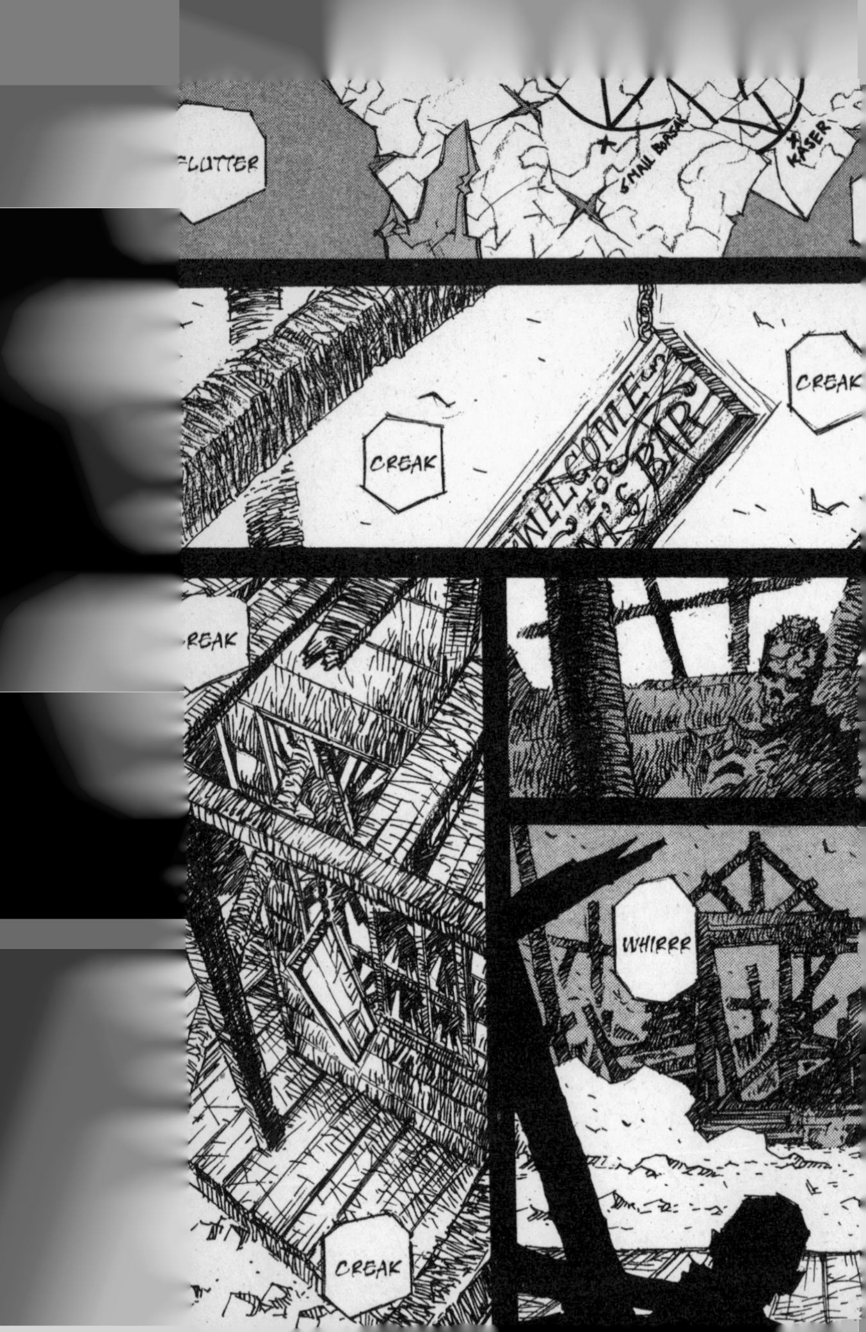
KASER
SMALL BOASAL
FLUTTER
CREAK
WELCOME TO
'S BAR
CREAK
WHIRRR
CREAK

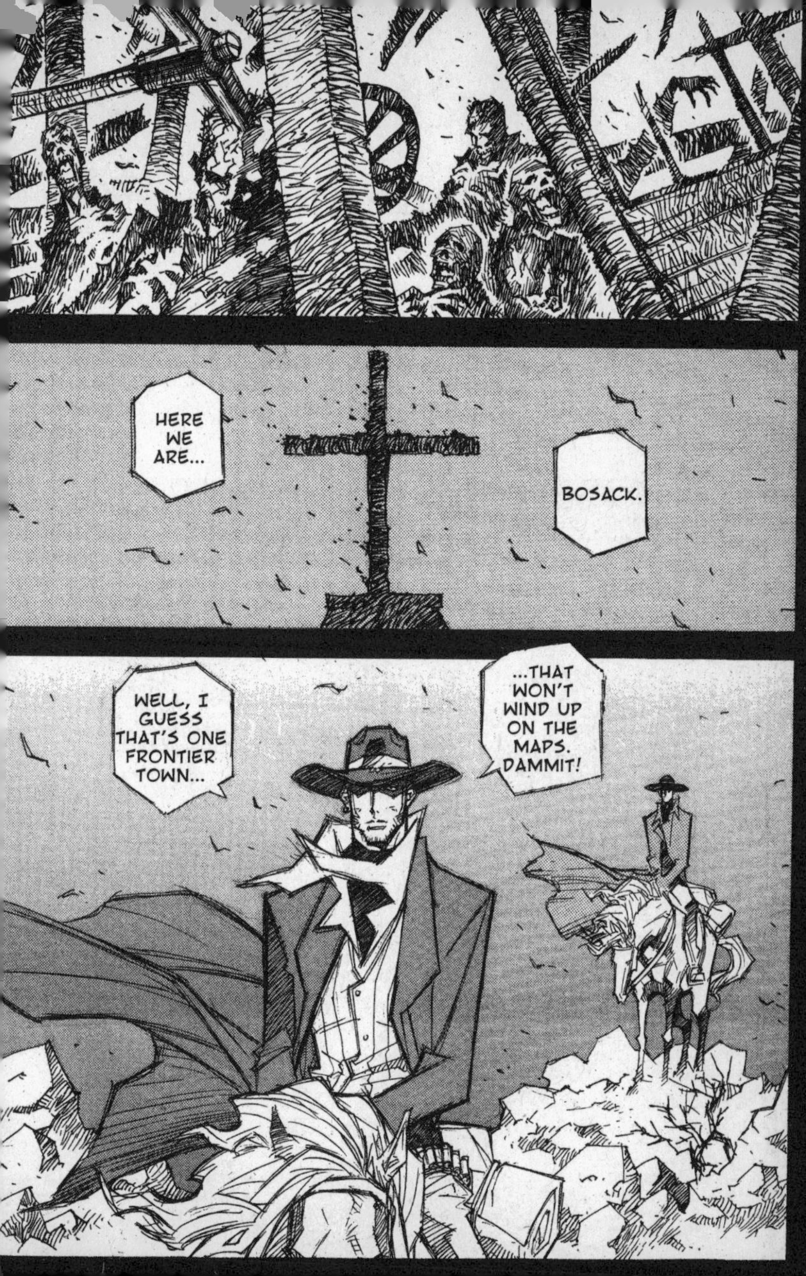
HERE WE ARE...
BOSACK.
WELL, I GUESS THAT'S ONE FRONTIER TOWN...
...THAT WON'T WIND UP ON THE MAPS. DAMMIT!

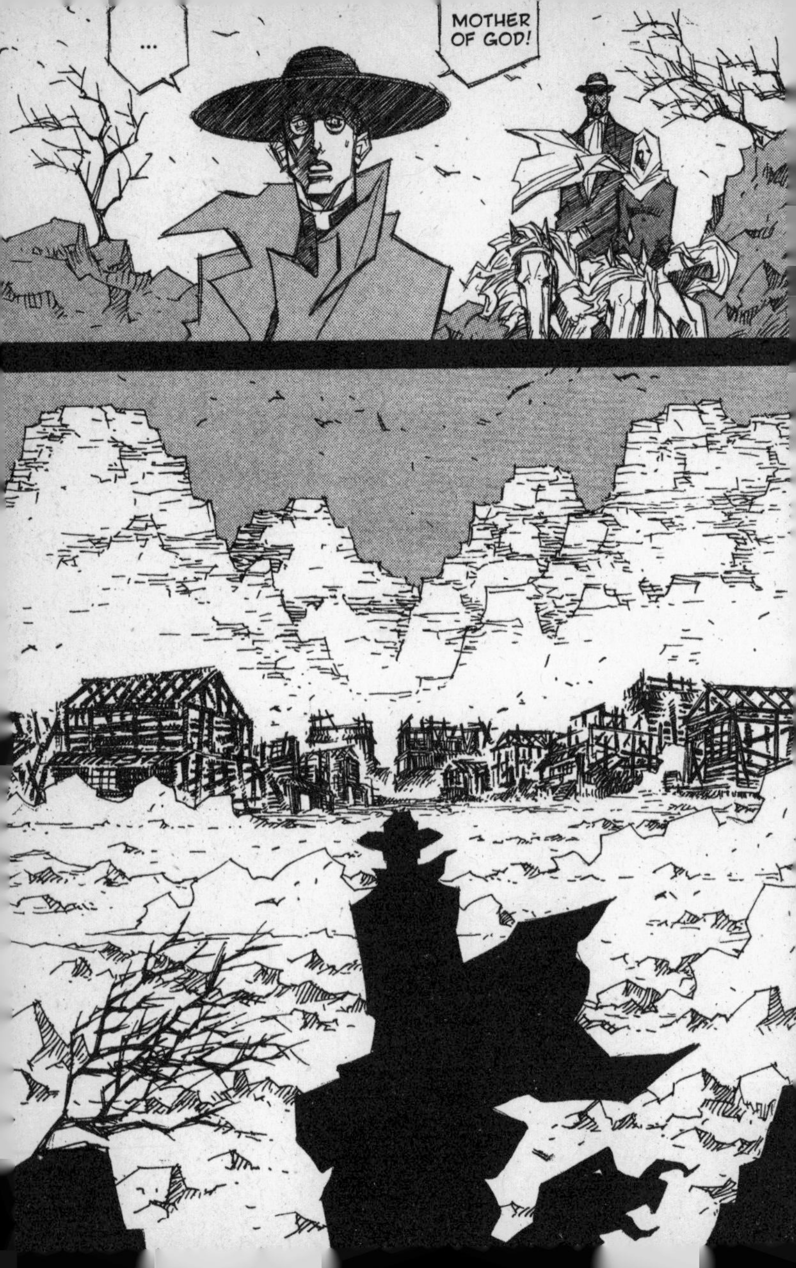
MOTHER OF GOD!
...

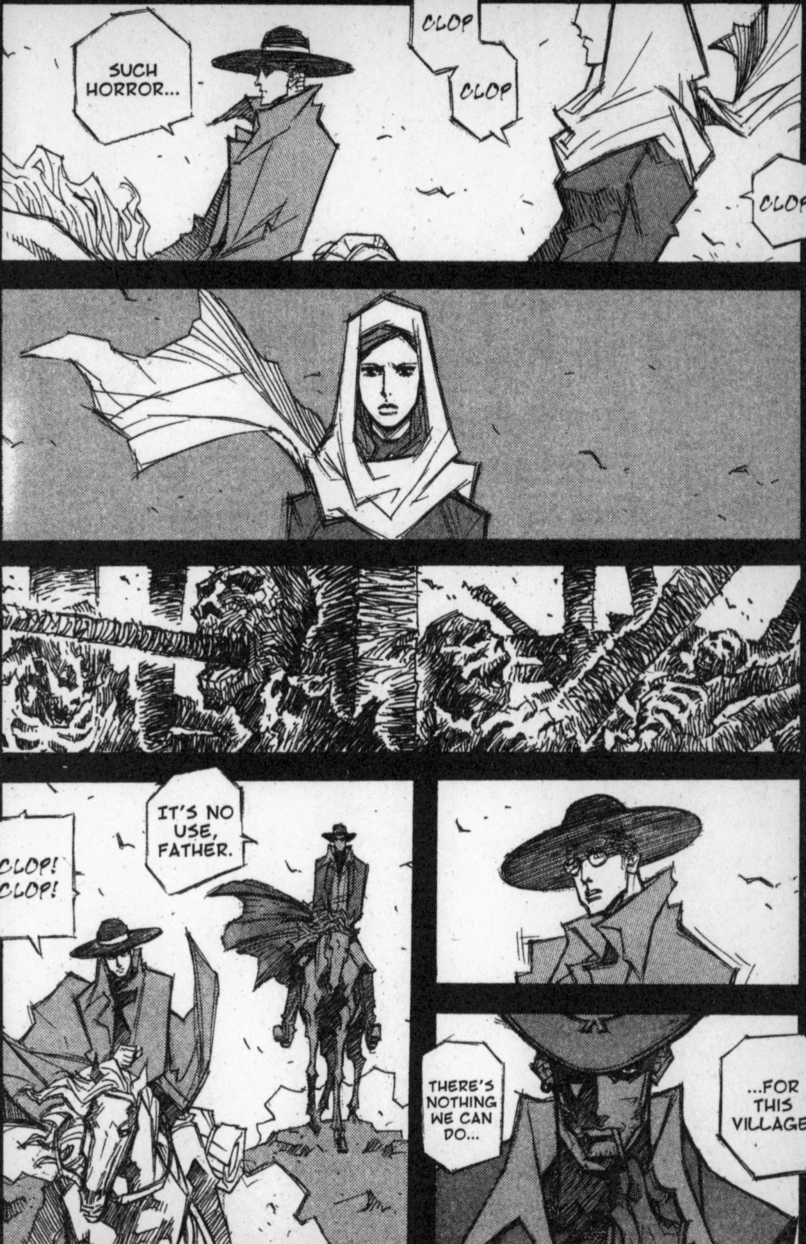
SUCH HORROR...
CLOP
CLOP
CLOP
CLOP! CLOP!
IT'S NO USE, FATHER.
THERE'S NOTHING WE CAN DO...
...FOR THIS VILLAGE.

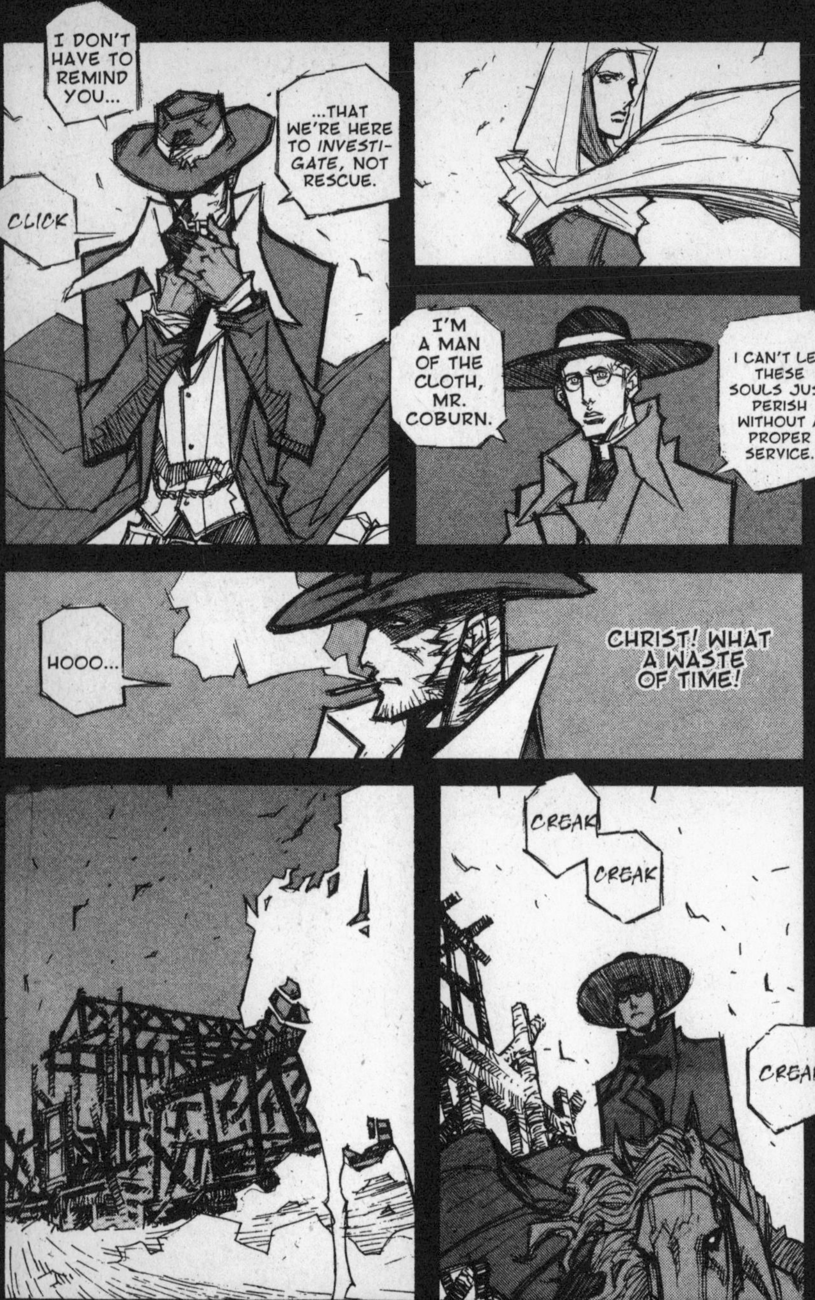
I DON'T HAVE TO REMIND YOU...
...THAT WE'RE HERE TO INVESTIGATE, NOT RESCUE.
CLICK
I'M A MAN OF THE CLOTH, MR. COBURN.
I CAN'T LET THESE SOULS JUST PERISH WITHOUT A PROPER SERVICE.
HOOO...
CHRIST! WHAT A WASTE OF TIME!
CREAK
CREAK
CREAK

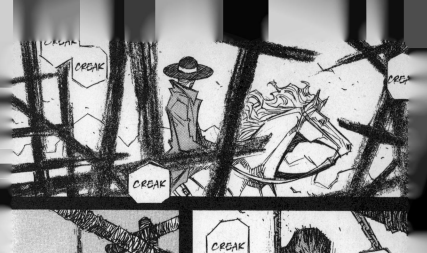

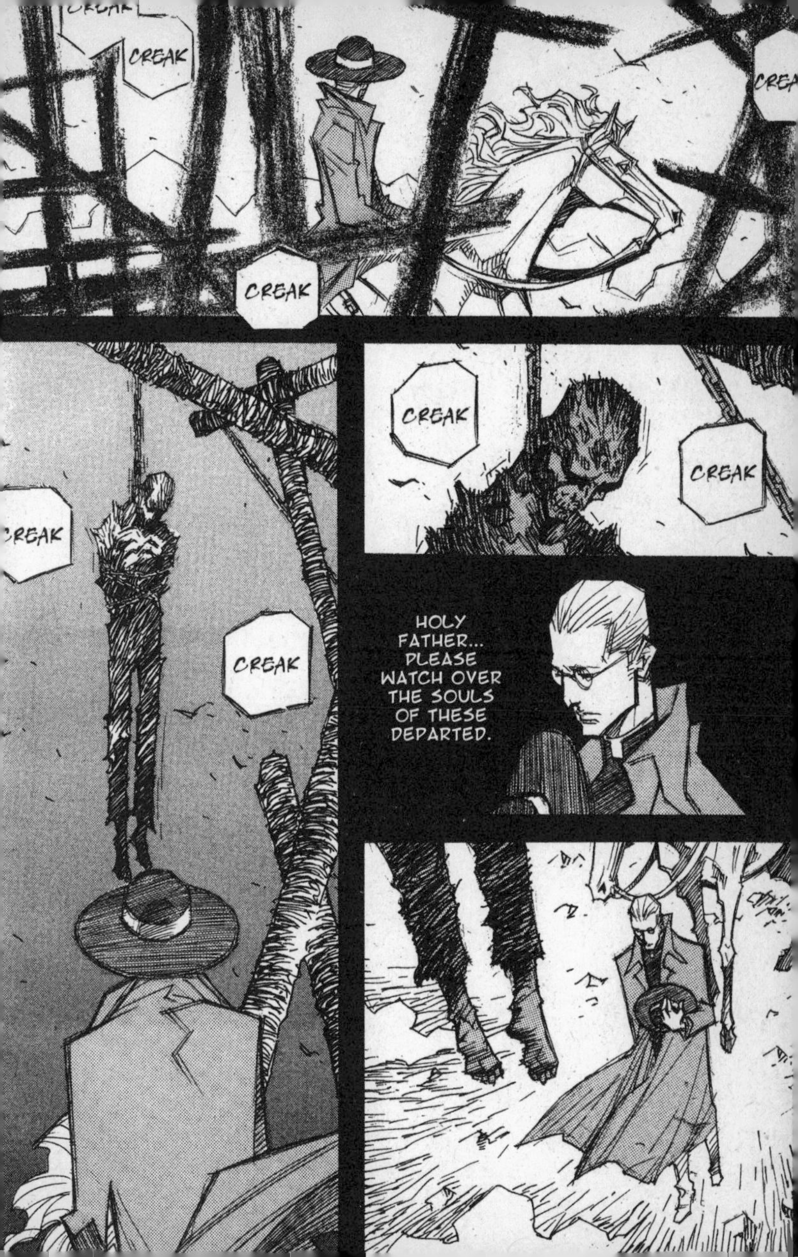
CREAK
CREAK
CREAK
CREAK
HOLY FATHER... PLEASE WATCH OVER THE SOULS OF THESE DEPARTED.
CREAK

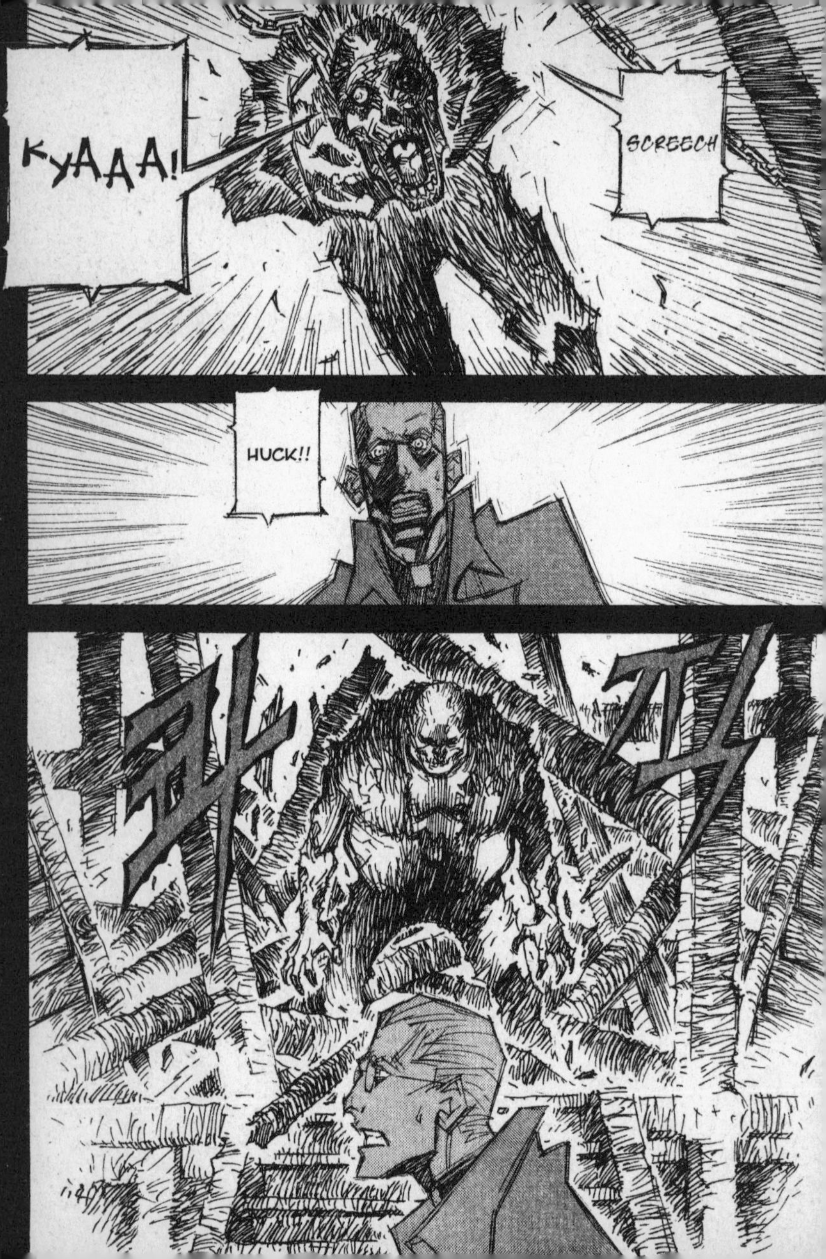
SCREECH
KYAAA!
HUCK!!

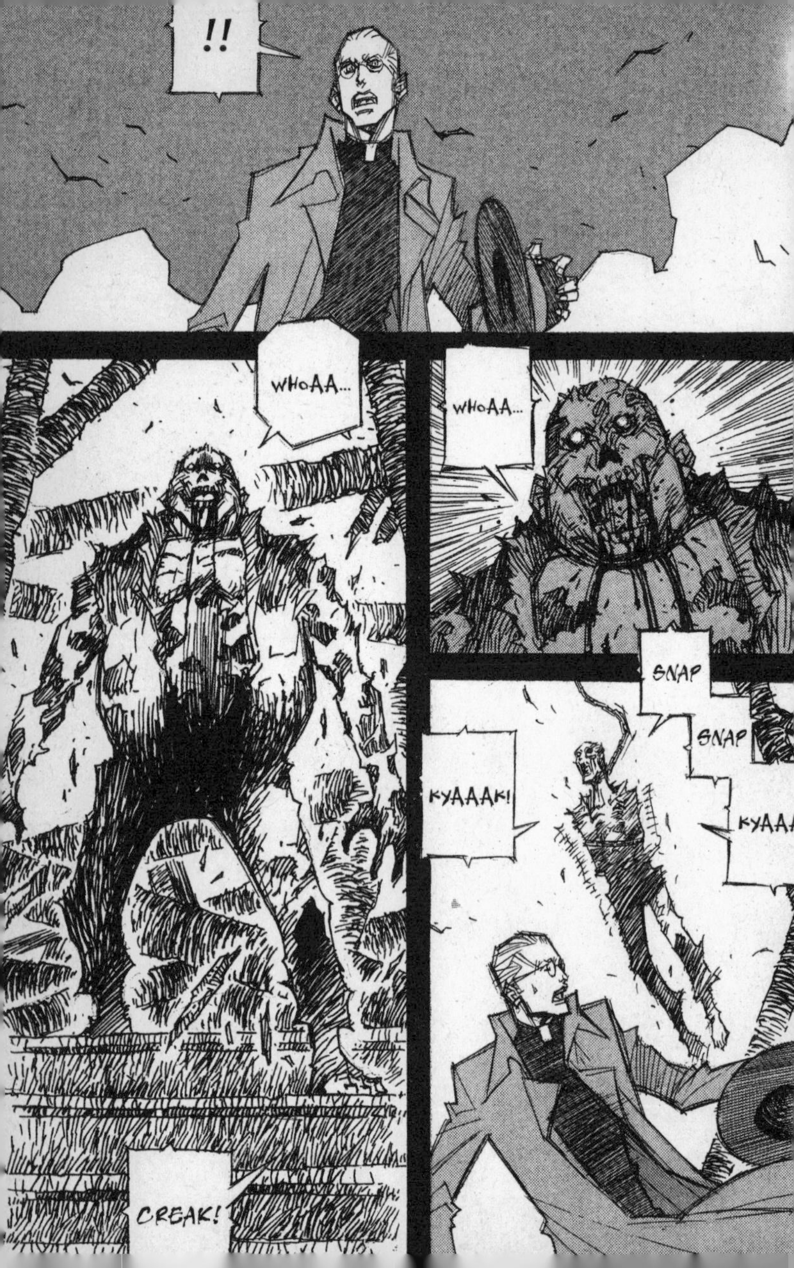
!!
WHOAA...
SNAP
SNAP
KYAA
KYAAAK!
WHOAA...
CREAK!

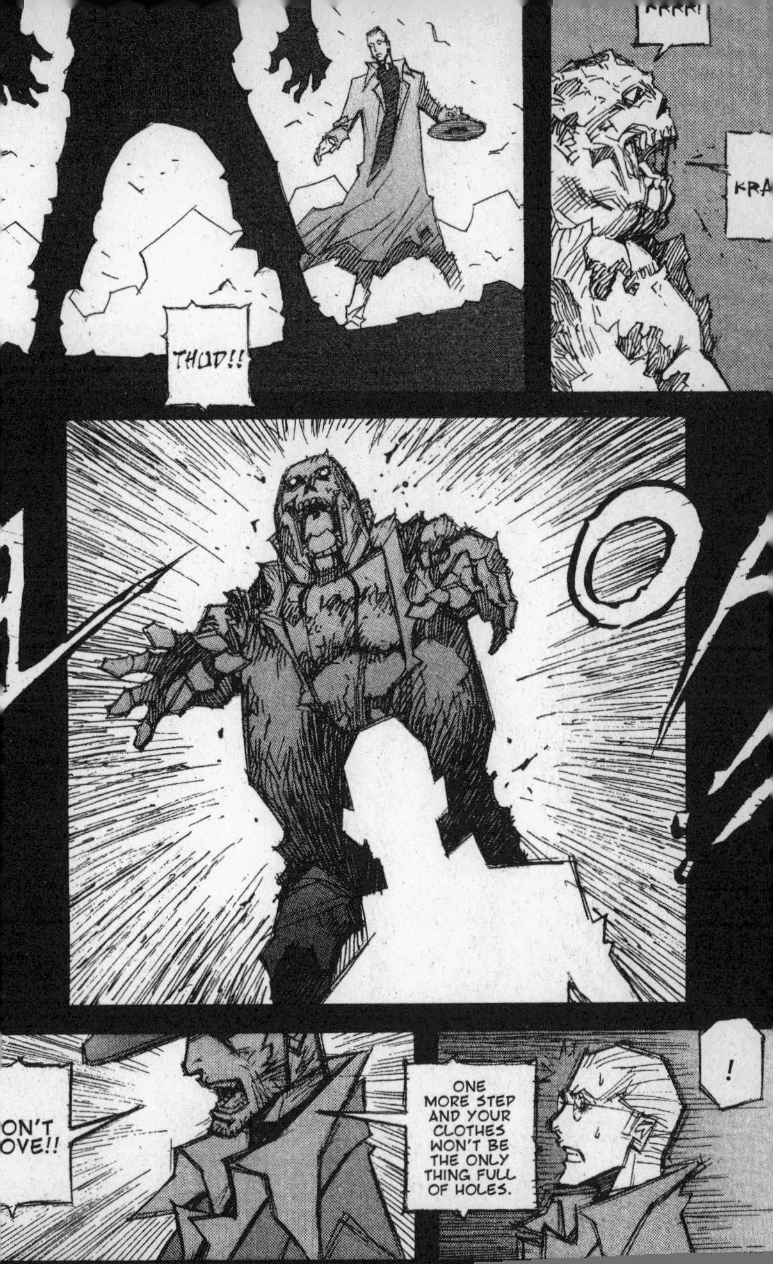
KRA
THUD!!
!
ONE MORE STEP AND YOUR CLOTHES WON'T BE THE ONLY THING FULL OF HOLES.
ON'T
OVE!!

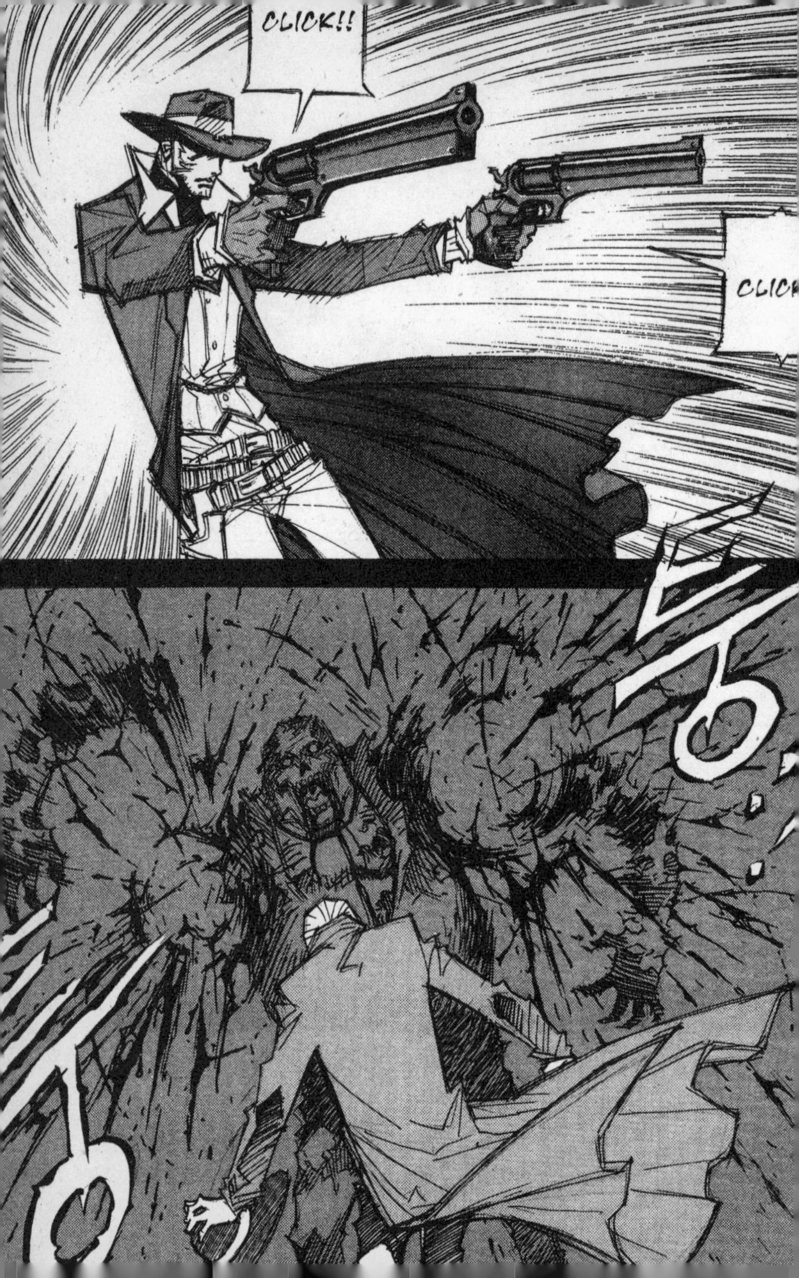
CLICK!!
CLICK

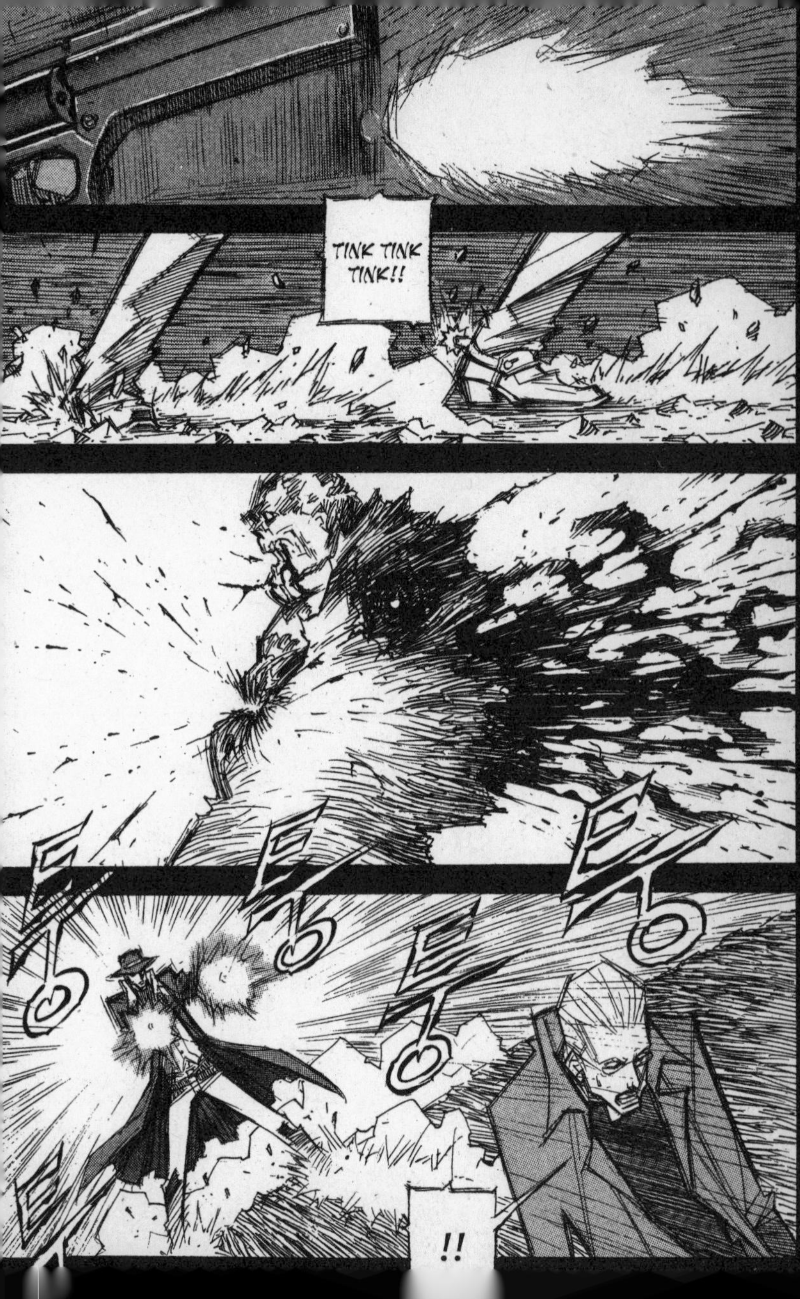
TINK TINK
TINK!!
!!

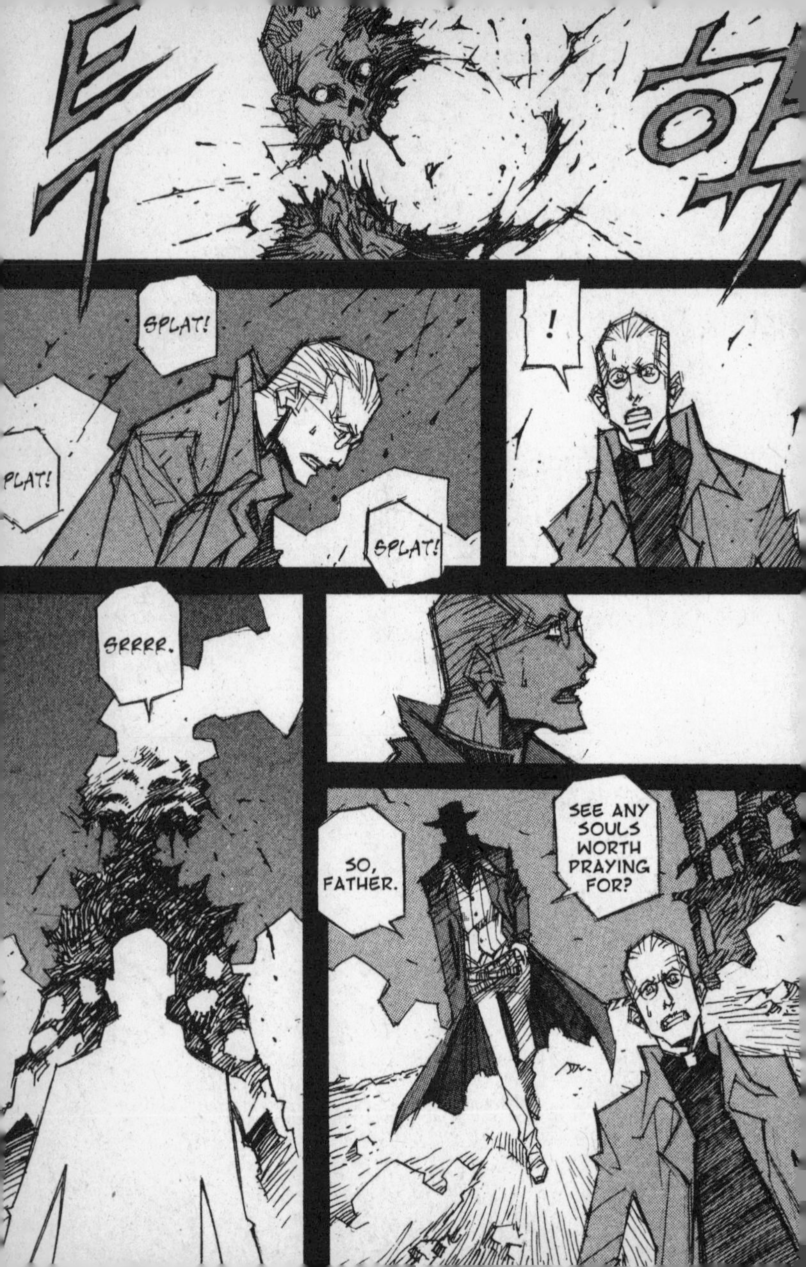
SPLAT!
SPLAT!
SPLAT!
!
SRRRR.
SO, FATHER.
SEE ANY SOULS WORTH PRAYING FOR?

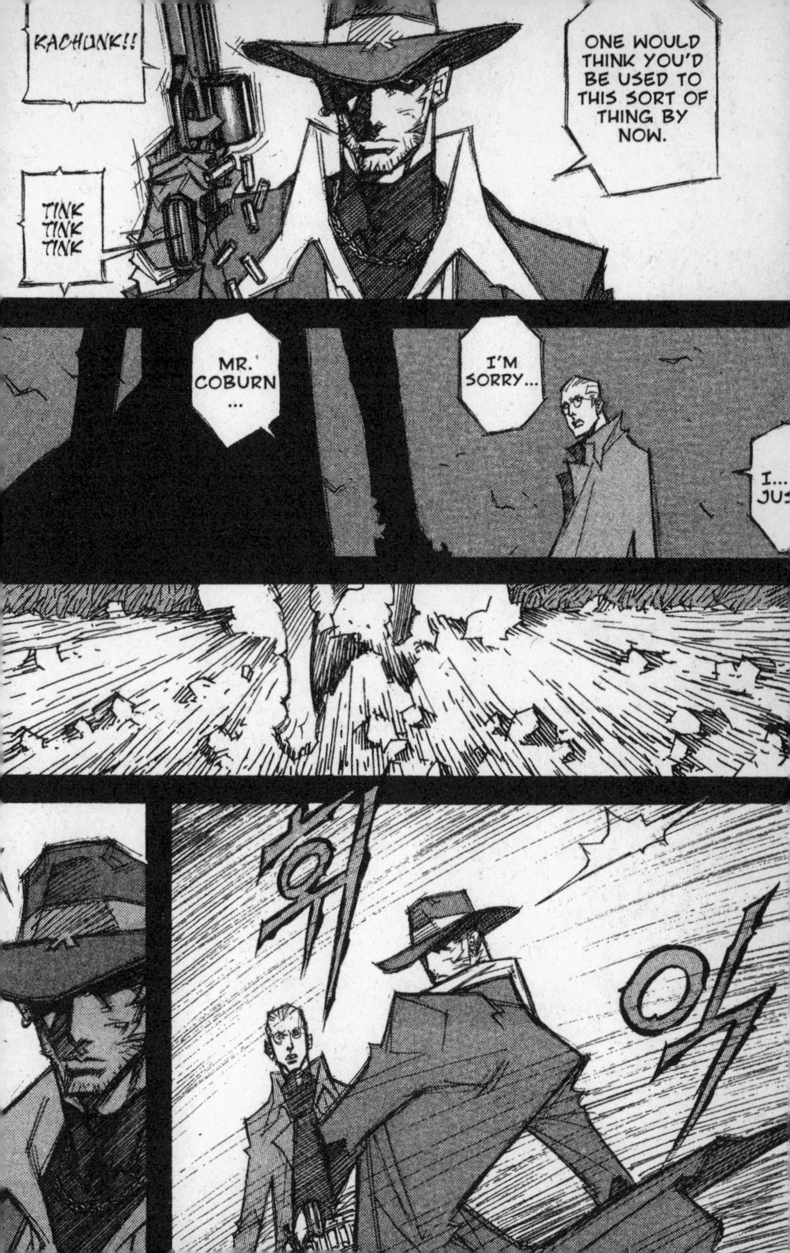
KACHUNK!!
TINK TINK TINK
ONE WOULD THINK YOU'D BE USED TO THIS SORT OF THING BY NOW.
MR. COBURN ...
I'M SORRY...
I... JU

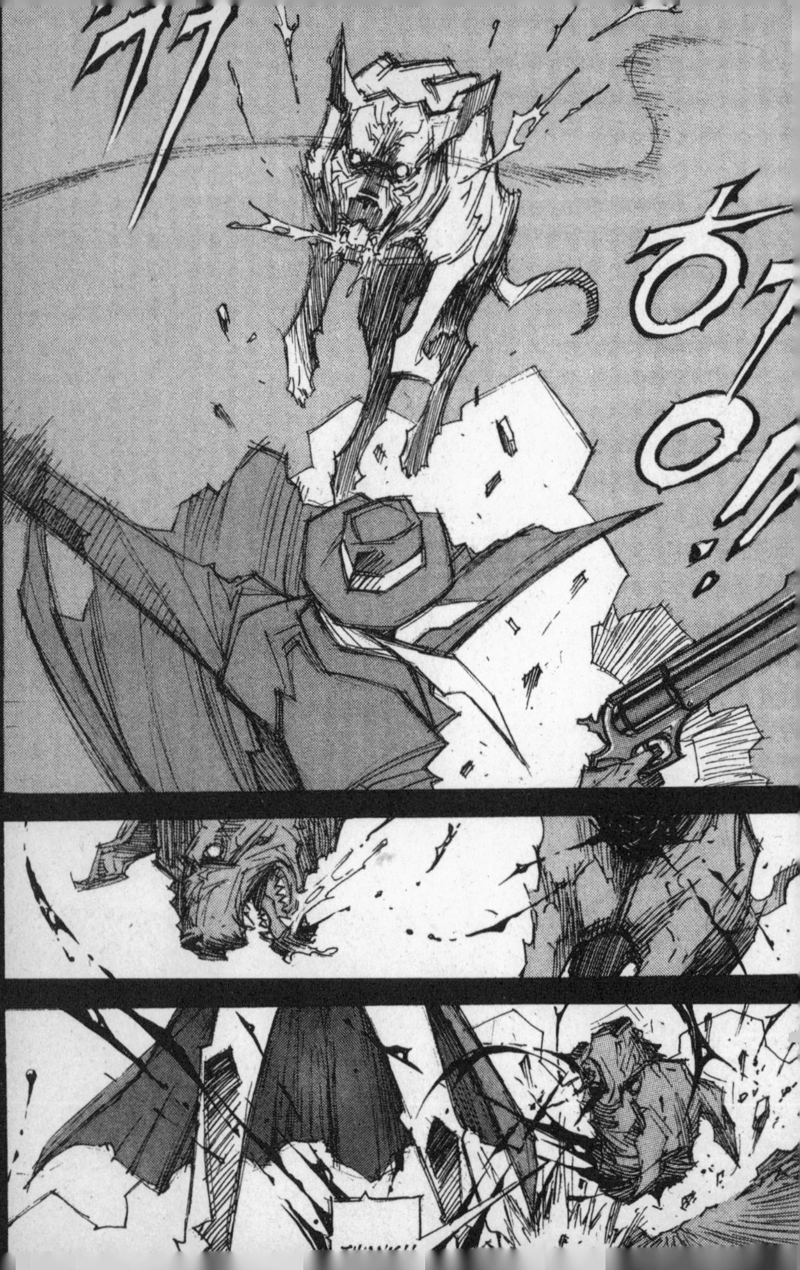

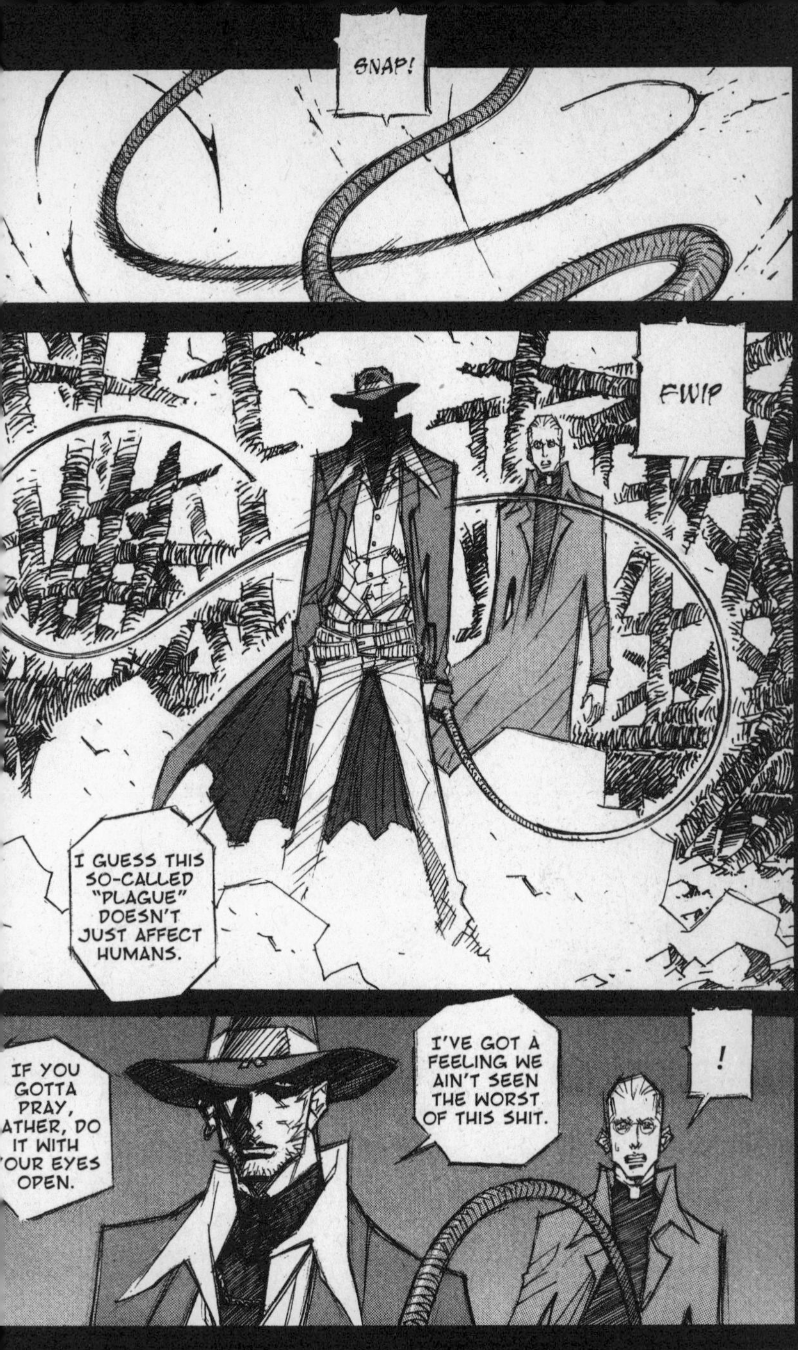
SNAP!
FWIP
I GUESS THIS SO-CALLED "PLAGUE" DOESN'T JUST AFFECT HUMANS.
!
I'VE GOT A FEELING WE AIN'T SEEN THE WORST OF THIS SHIT.
IF YOU GOTTA PRAY, ATHER, DO IT WITH OUR EYES OPEN.

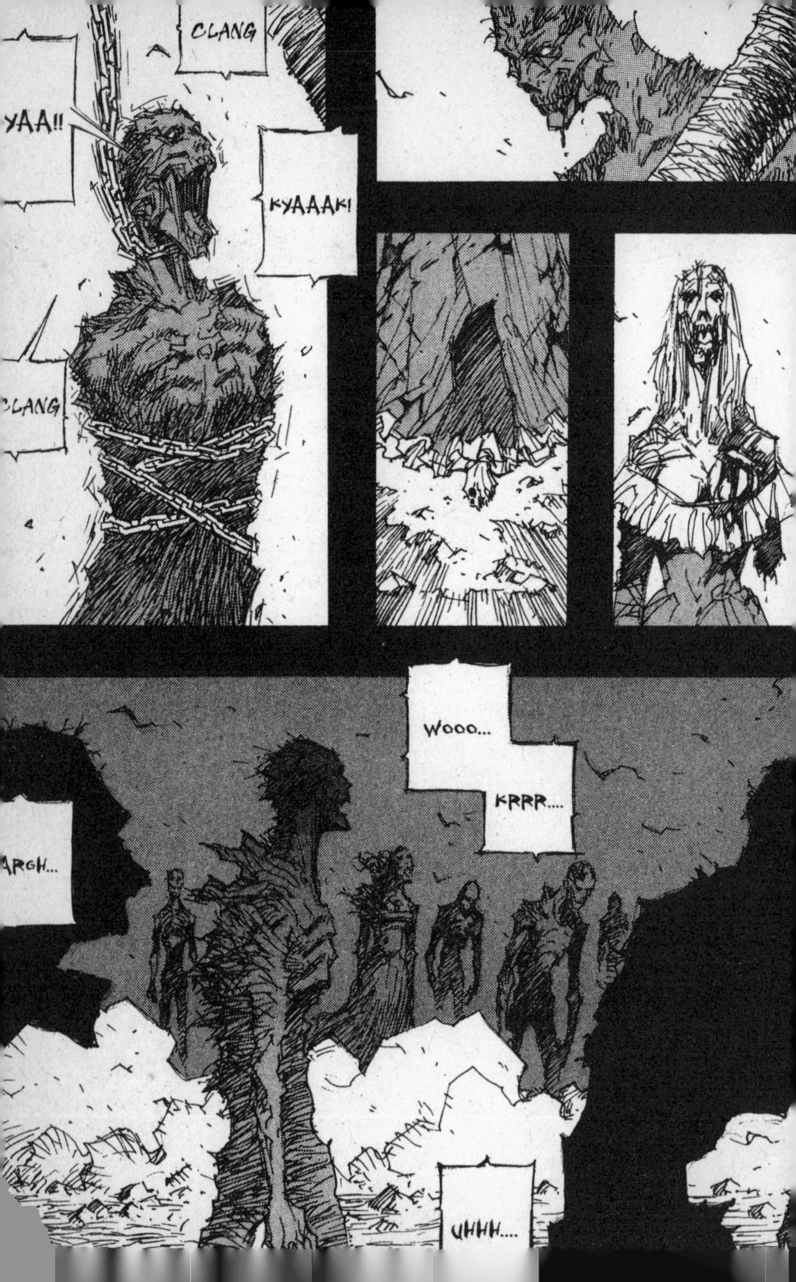
CLANG
KYAAAK!
YAA!!
CLANG
WOOO...
KRRR....
ARGH...
UHHH....

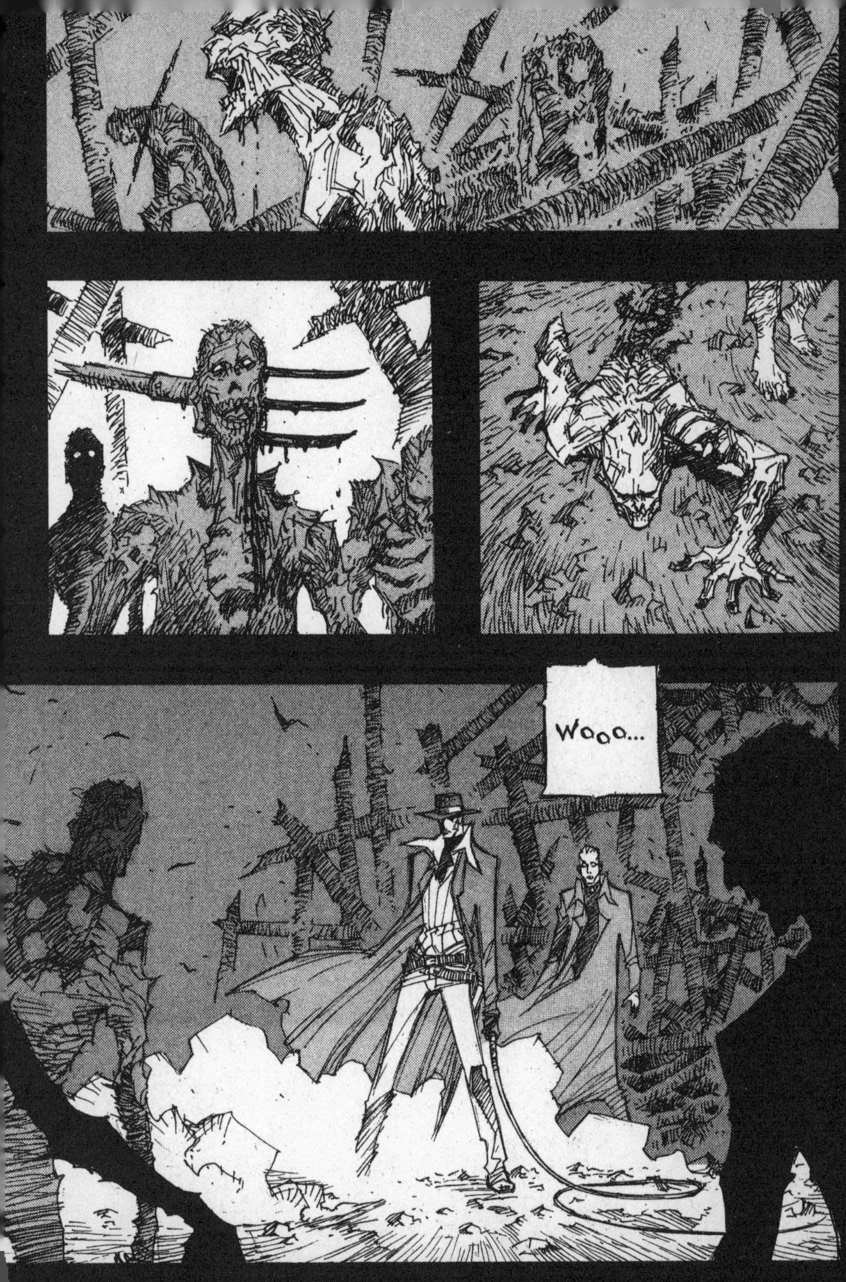
Wooo...

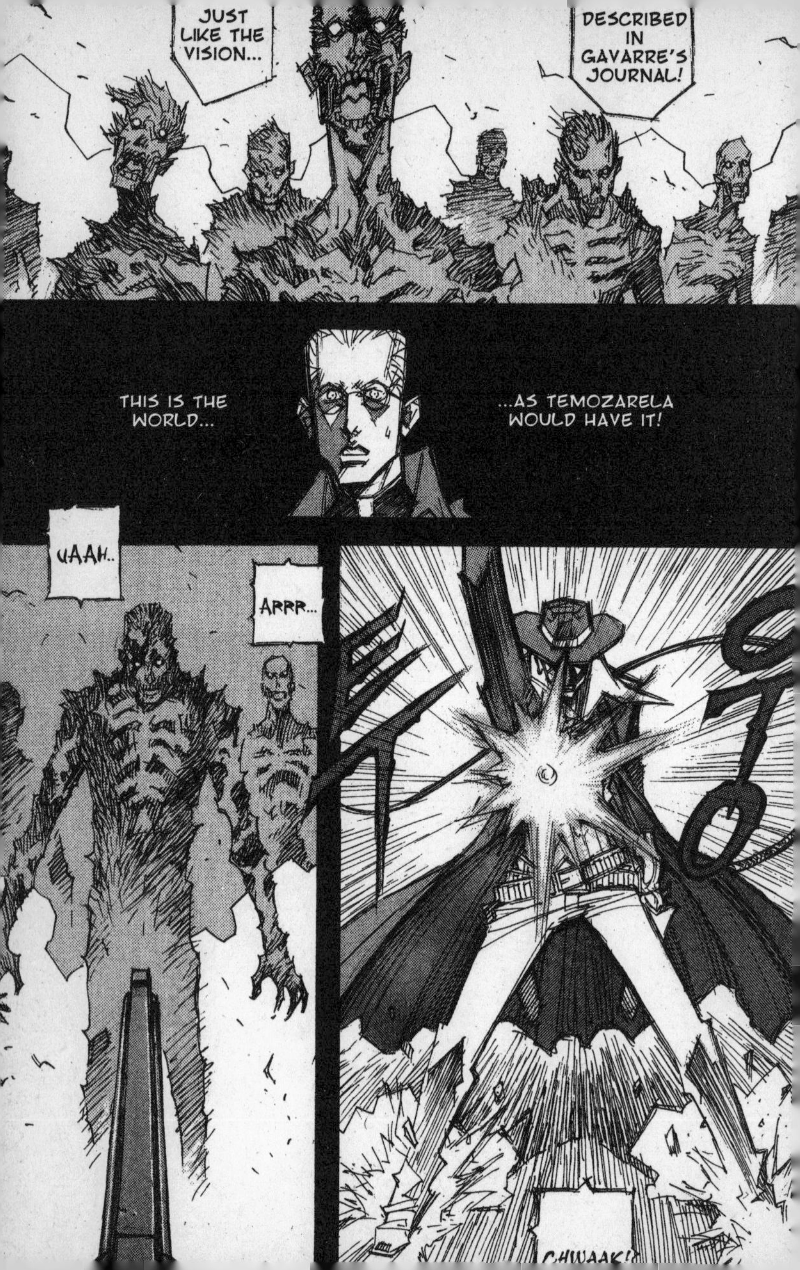
JUST LIKE THE VISION...
DESCRIBED IN GAVARRE'S JOURNAL!
THIS IS THE WORLD...
...AS TEMOZARELA WOULD HAVE IT!
UAAH..
ARRR...
CHWAAK!

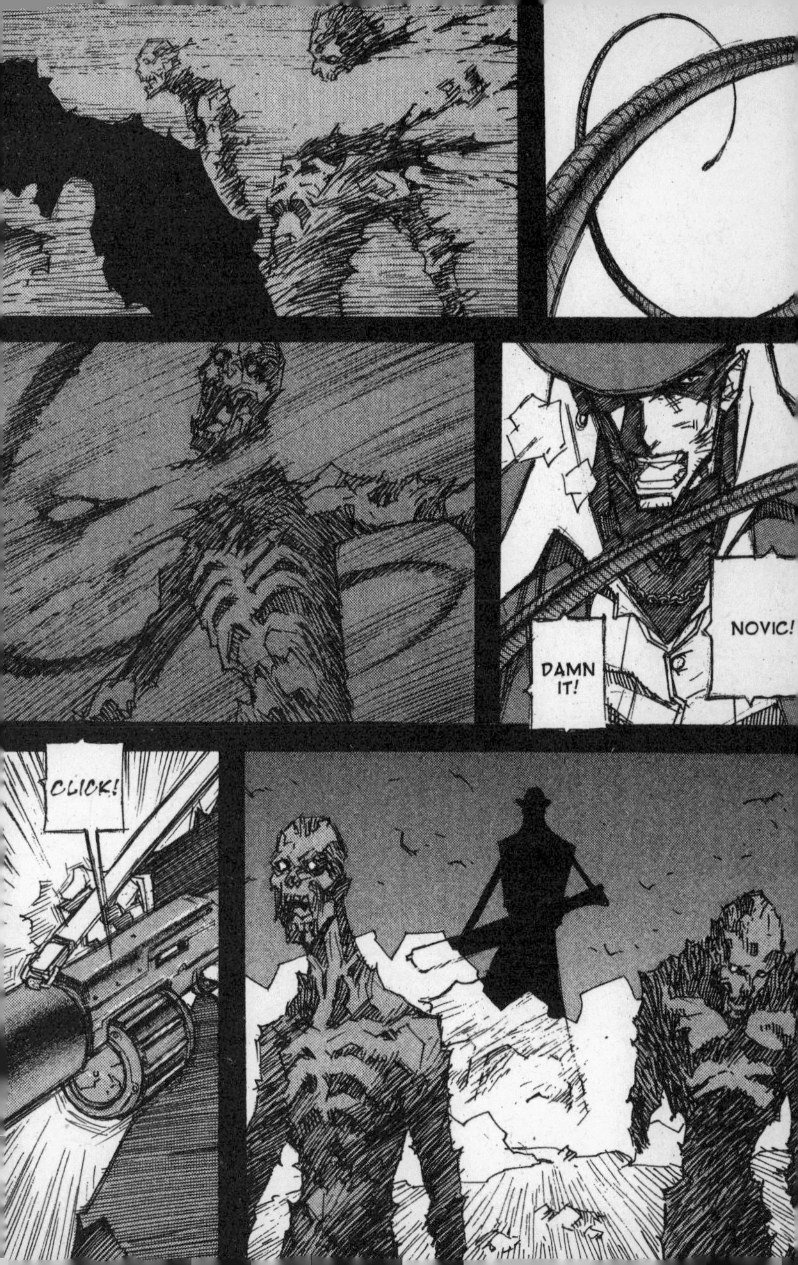
NOVIC!
DAMN IT!
CLICK!

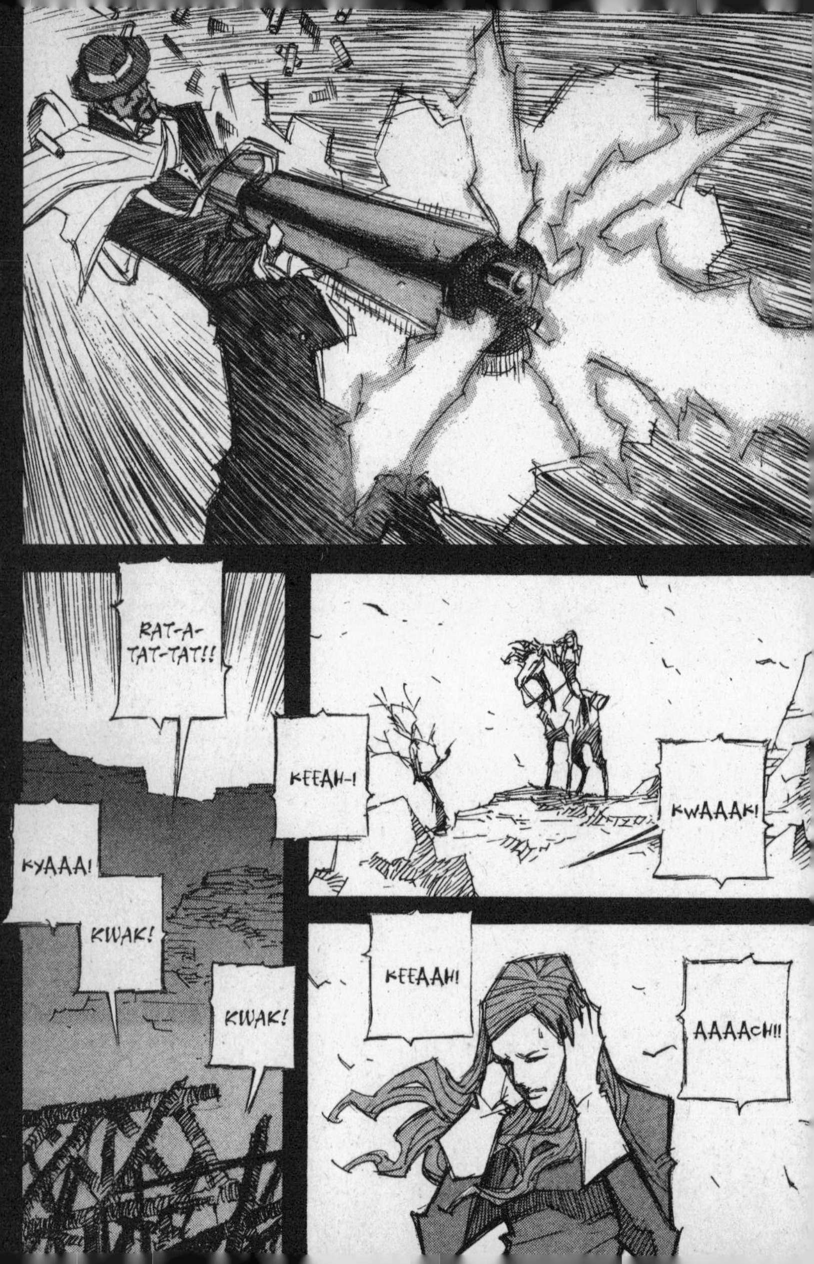
KWAAAK!
KEEAAH!
AAAACH!!
KEEAH-!
RAT-A-TAT-TAT!!
KYAAA!
KWAK!
KWAK!

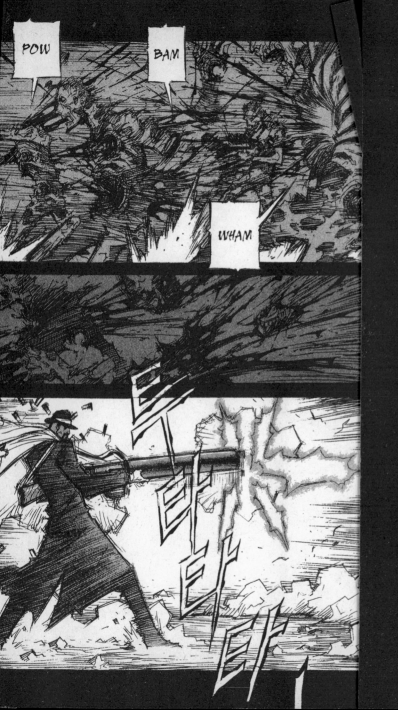

POW

BAM

WHAM

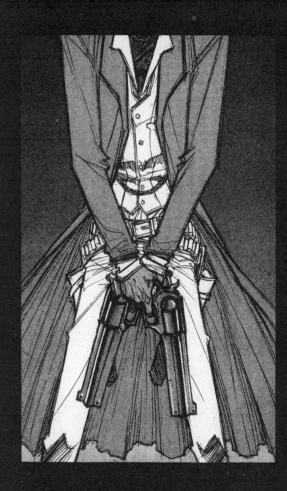

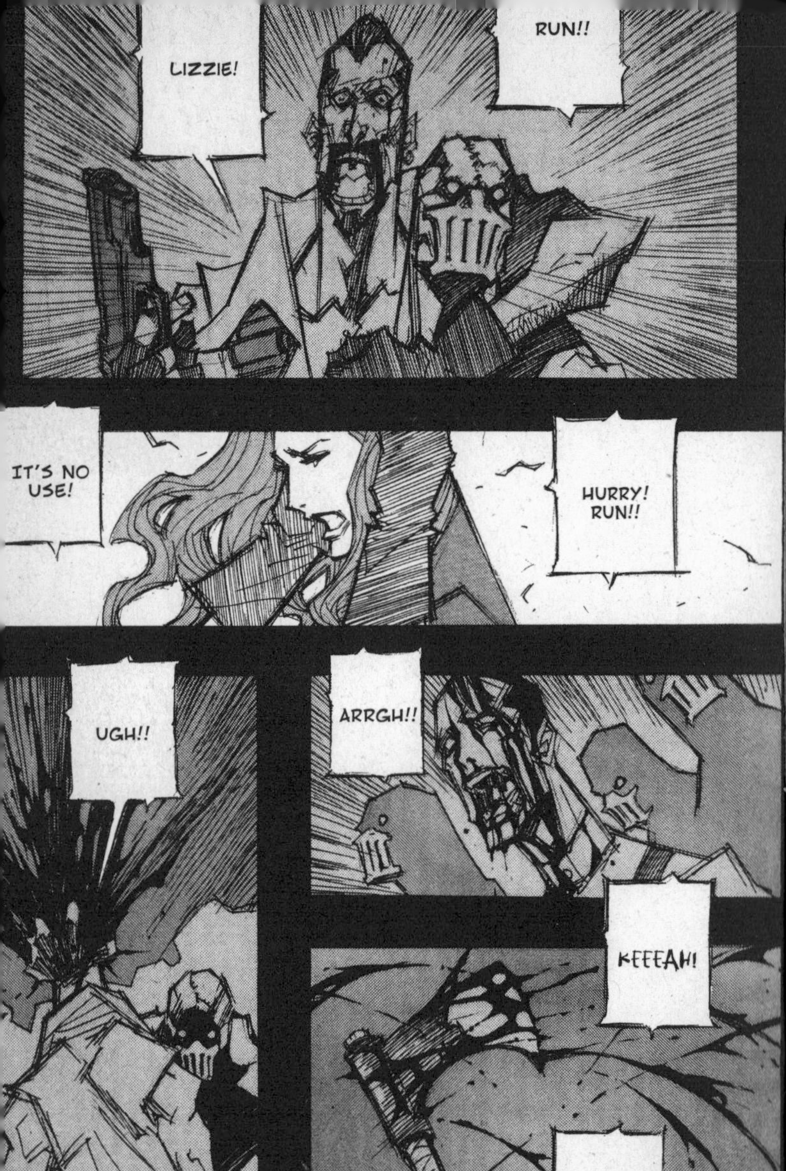
LIZZIE!
RUN!!
IT'S NO USE!
HURRY! RUN!!
UGH!!
ARRGH!!
KEEEAH!
AAAGH!

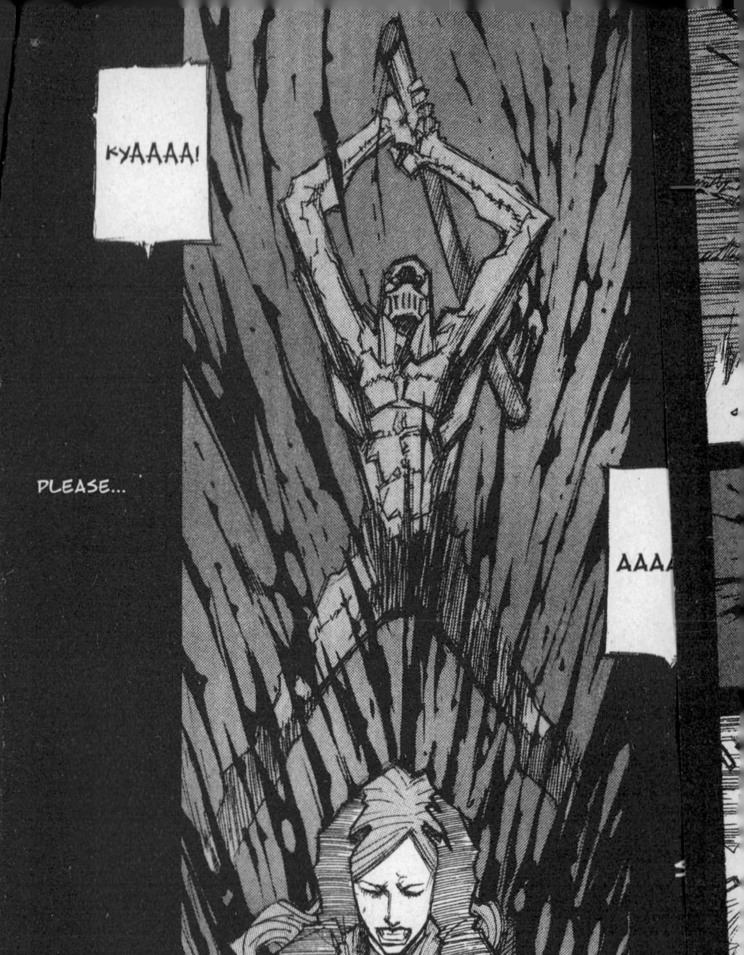
KYAAAA!
PLEASE...
AAAA
ST

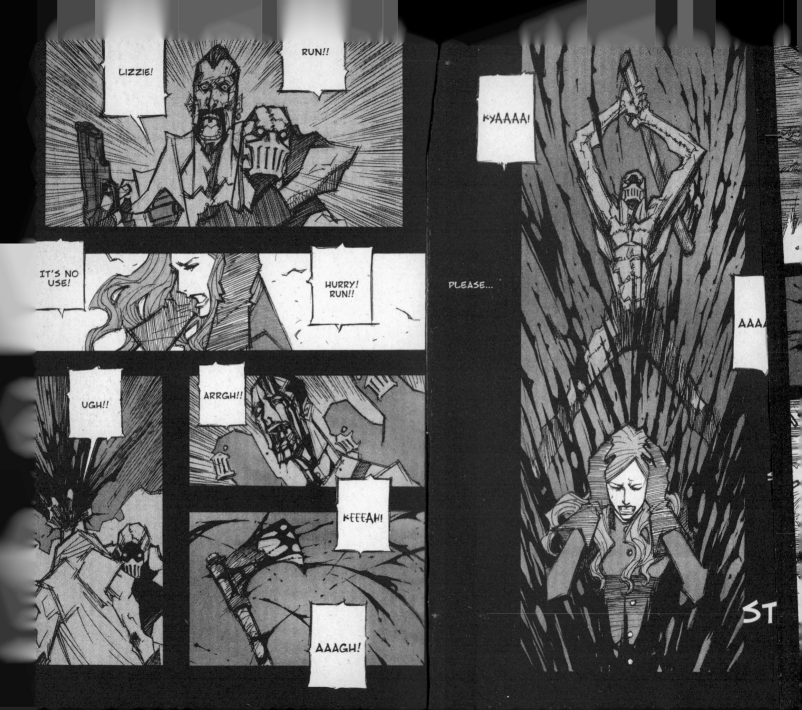

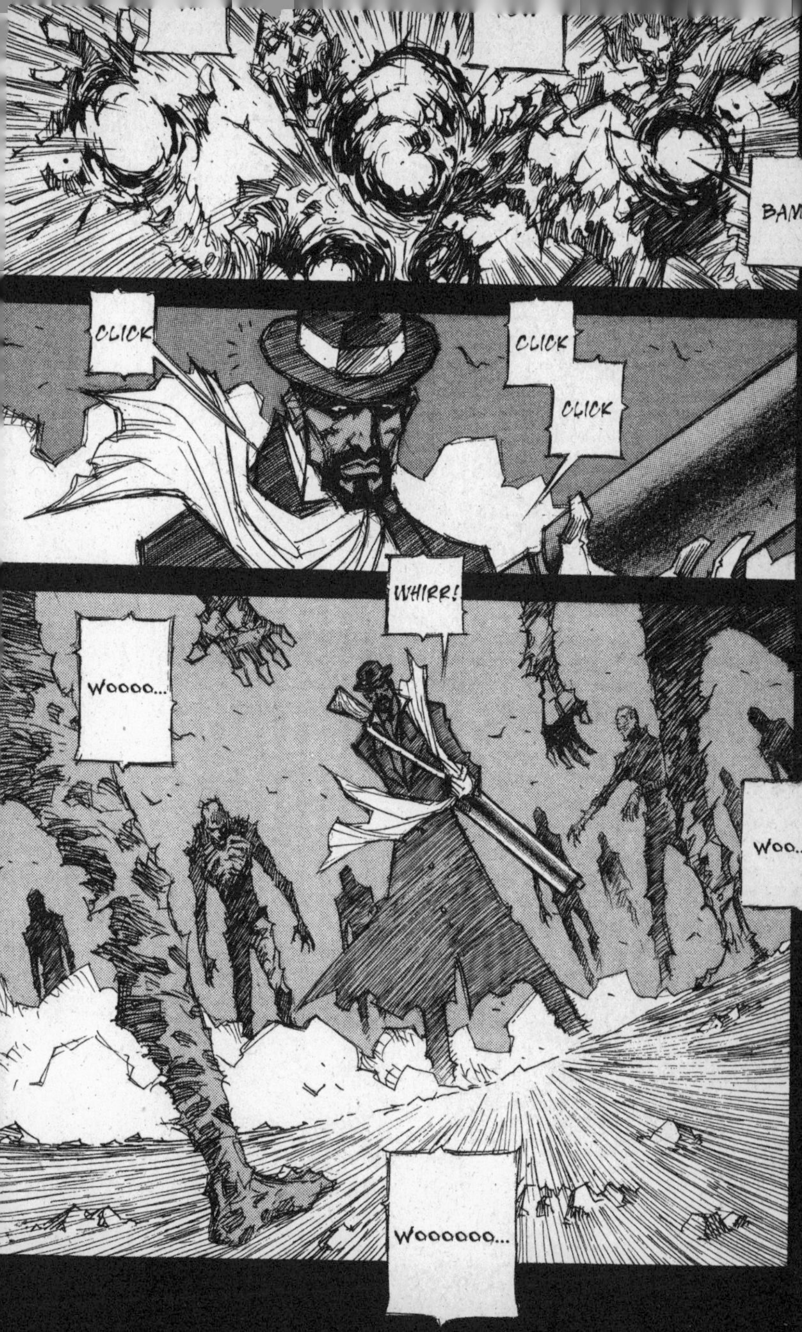
BAM
CLICK
CLICK
CLICK
WHIRR!
Woo..
Woooo...
Wooooo...

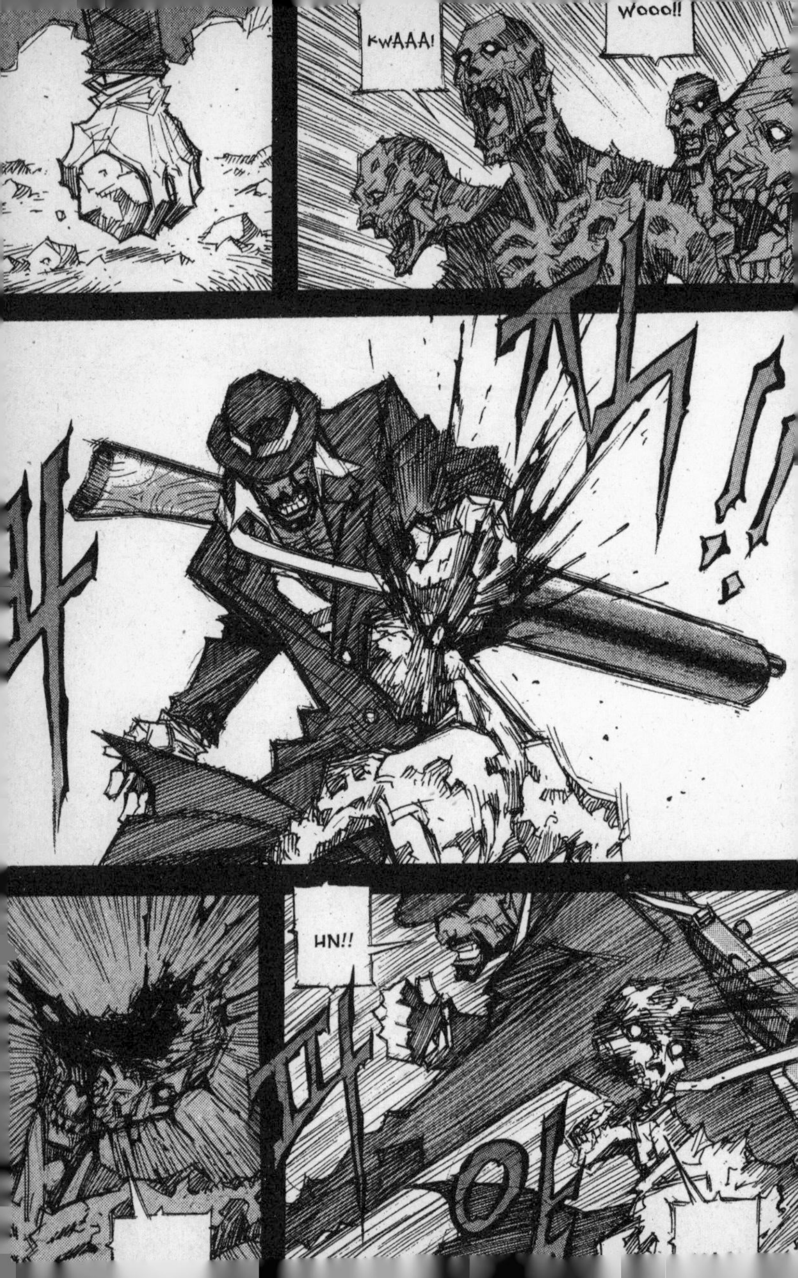
Wooo!!
KWAAA!
HN!!

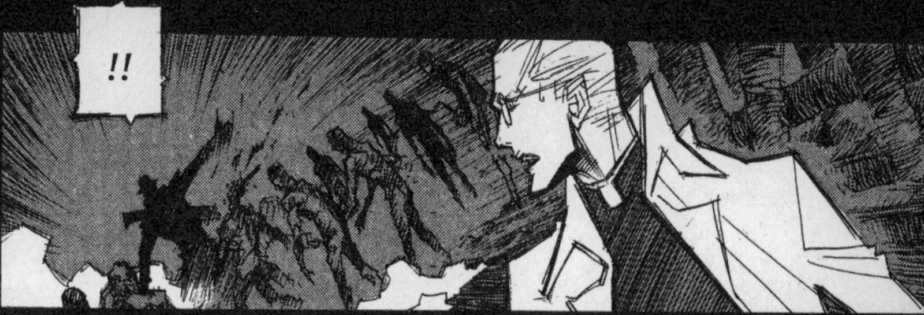
!!
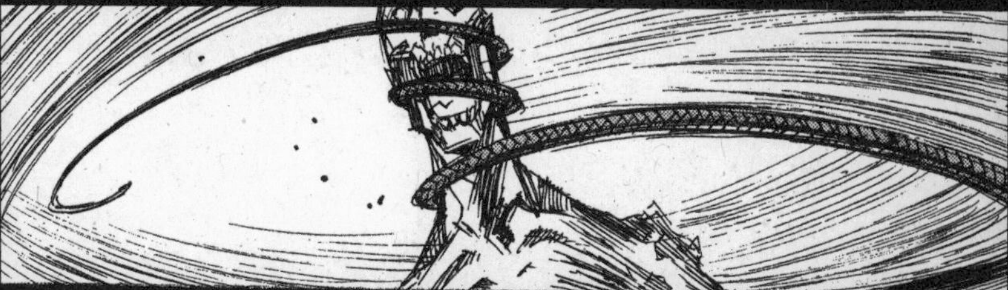
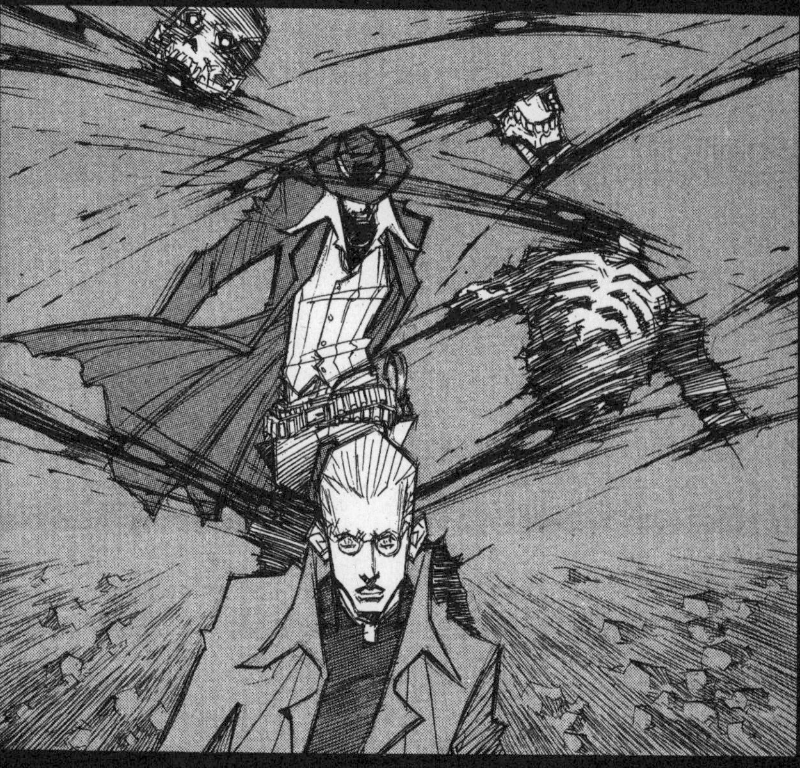

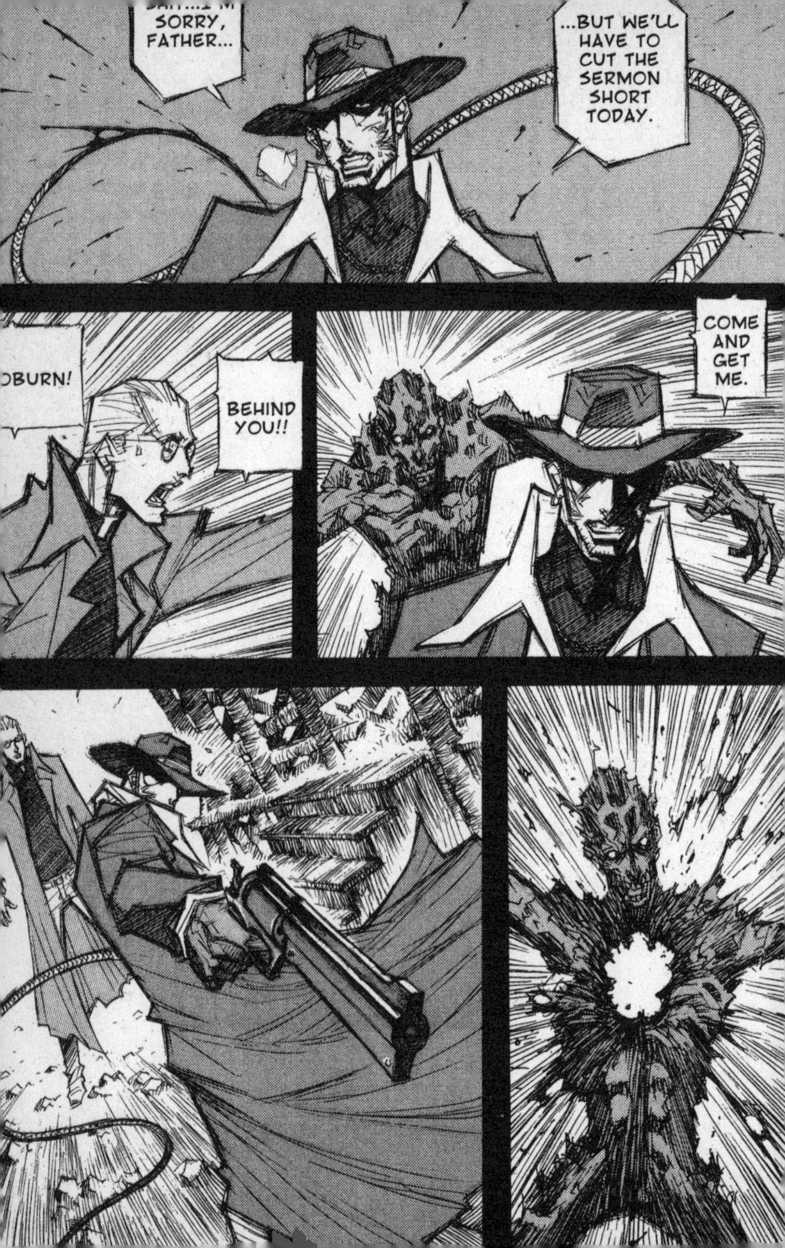
SORRY, FATHER...
...BUT WE'LL HAVE TO CUT THE SERMON SHORT TODAY.
OBURN!
BEHIND YOU!!
COME AND GET ME.

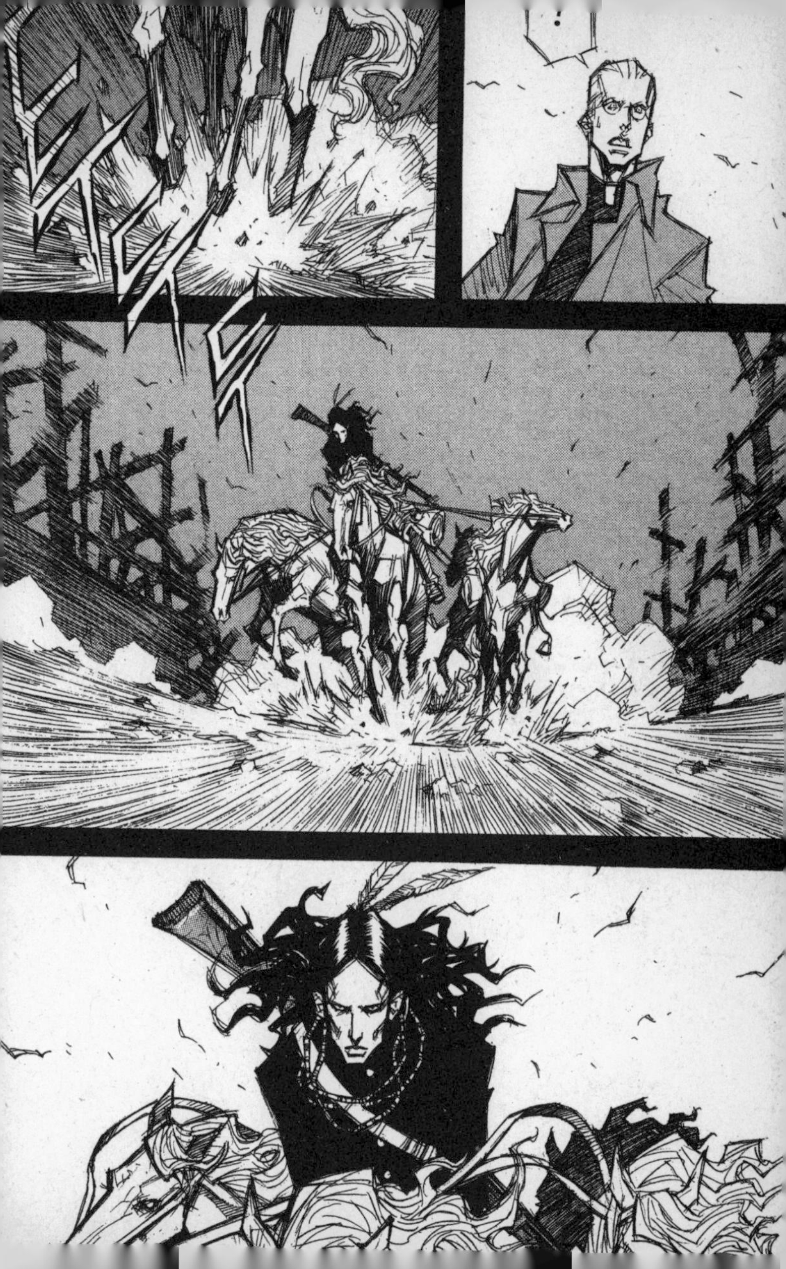

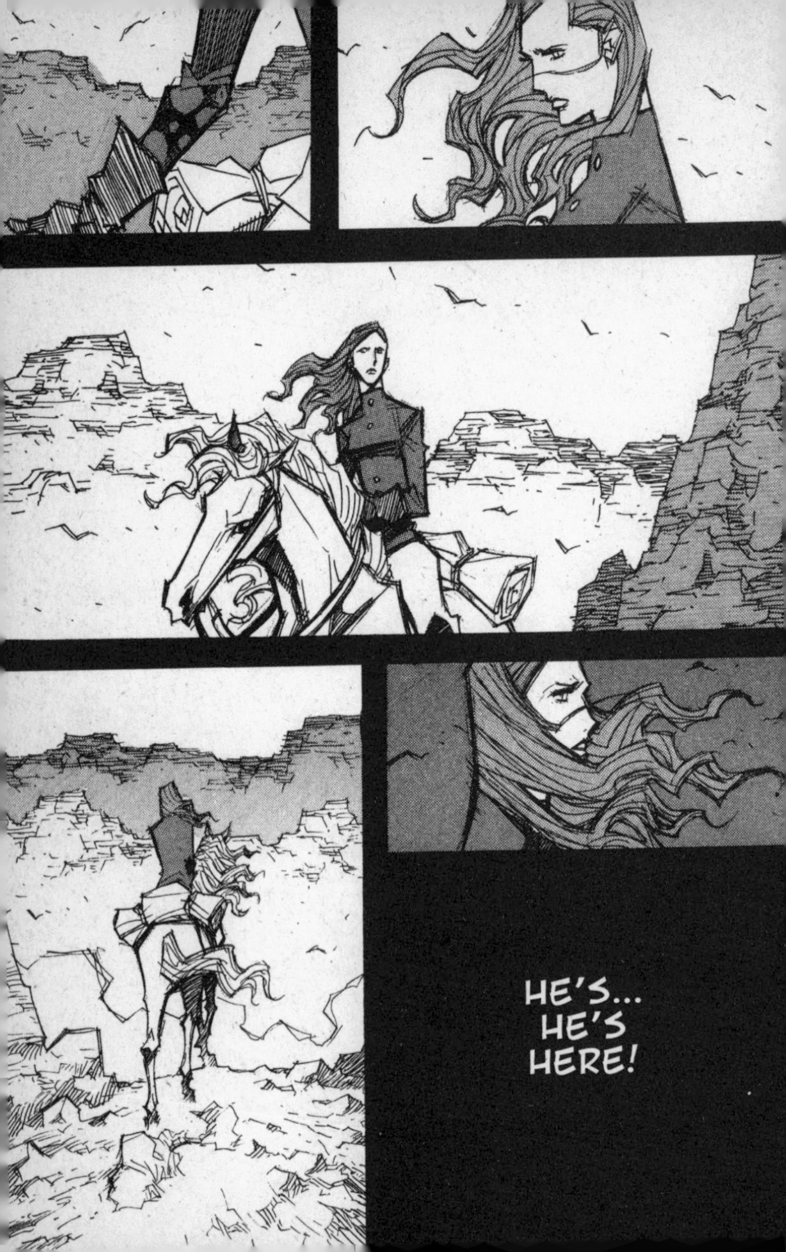
HE'S...
HE'S
HERE!

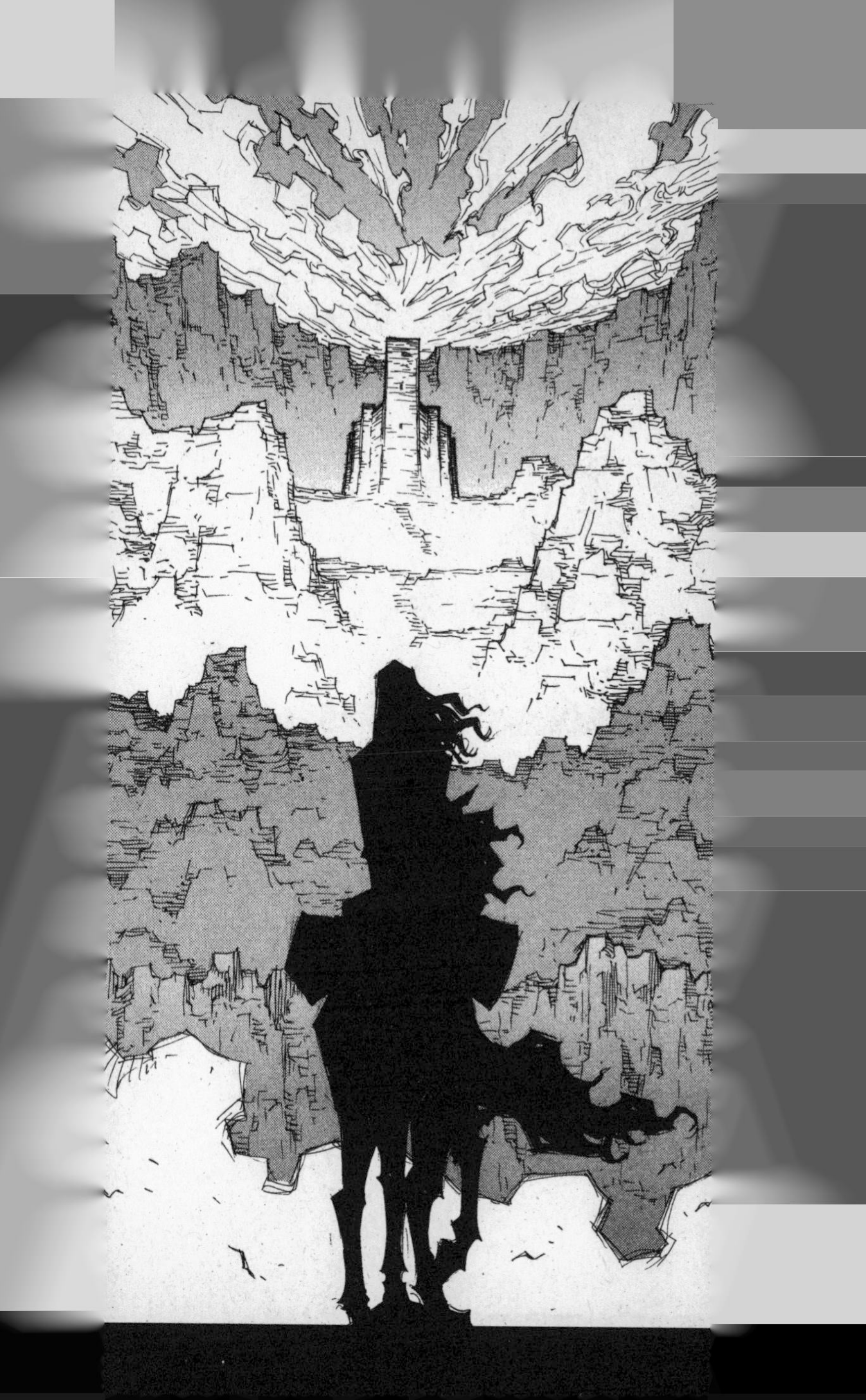

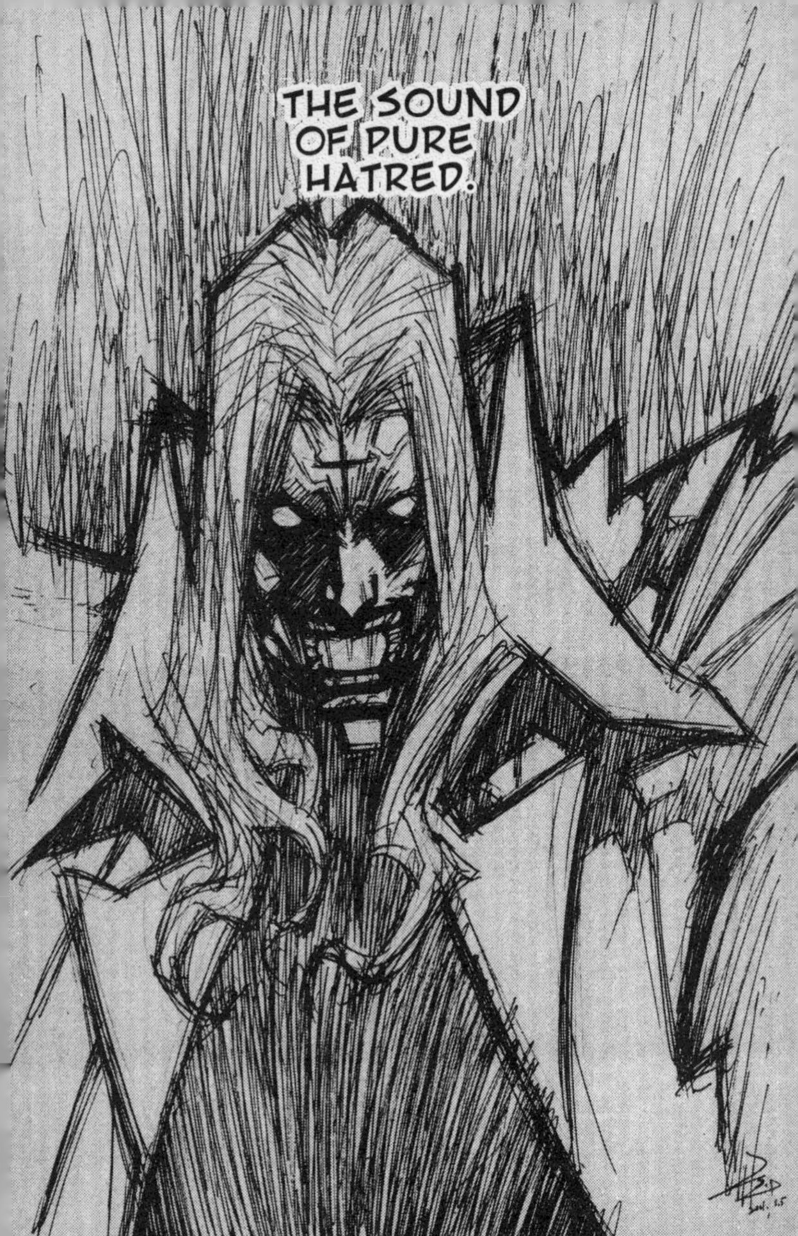
THE SOUND OF PURE HATRED.

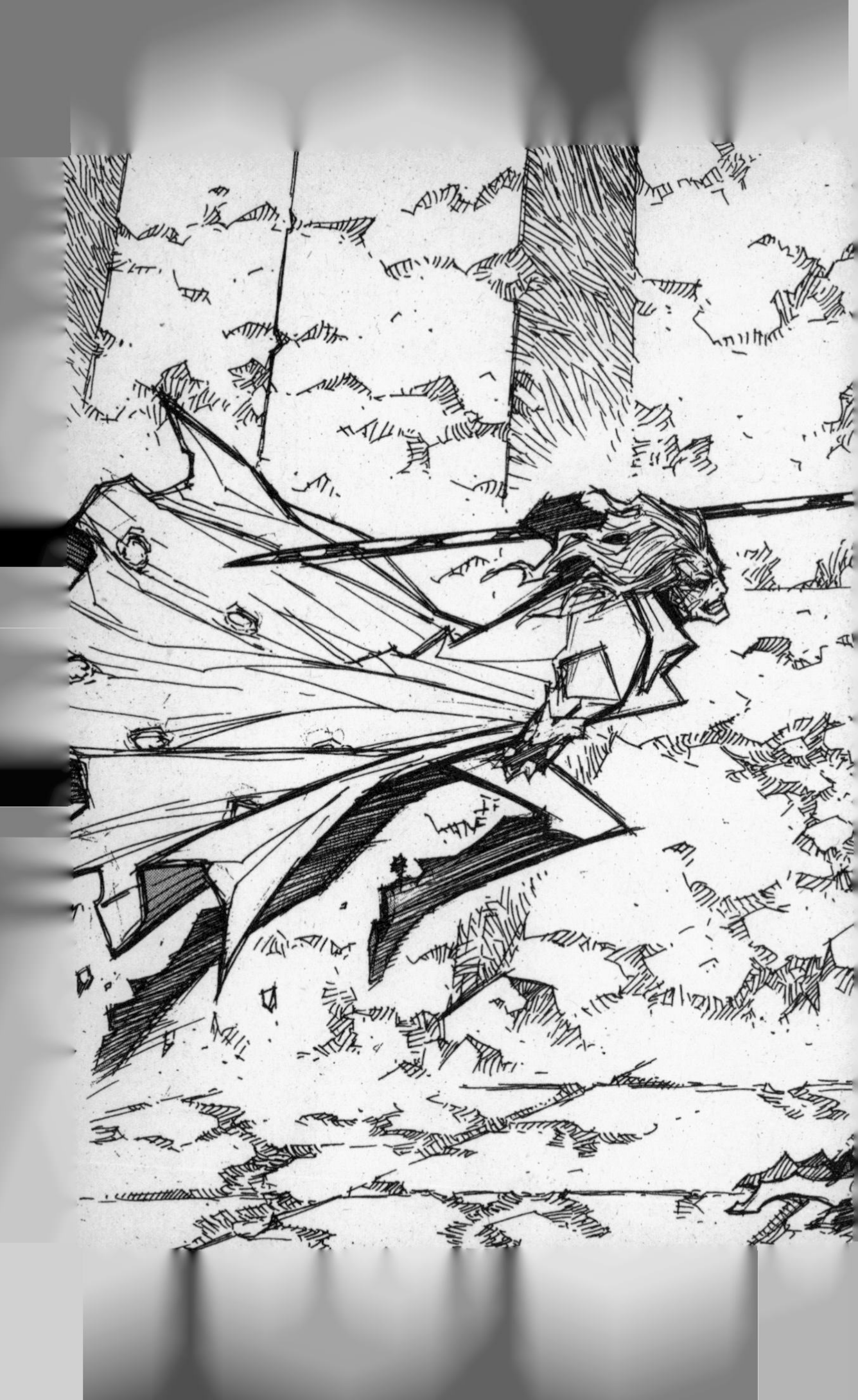

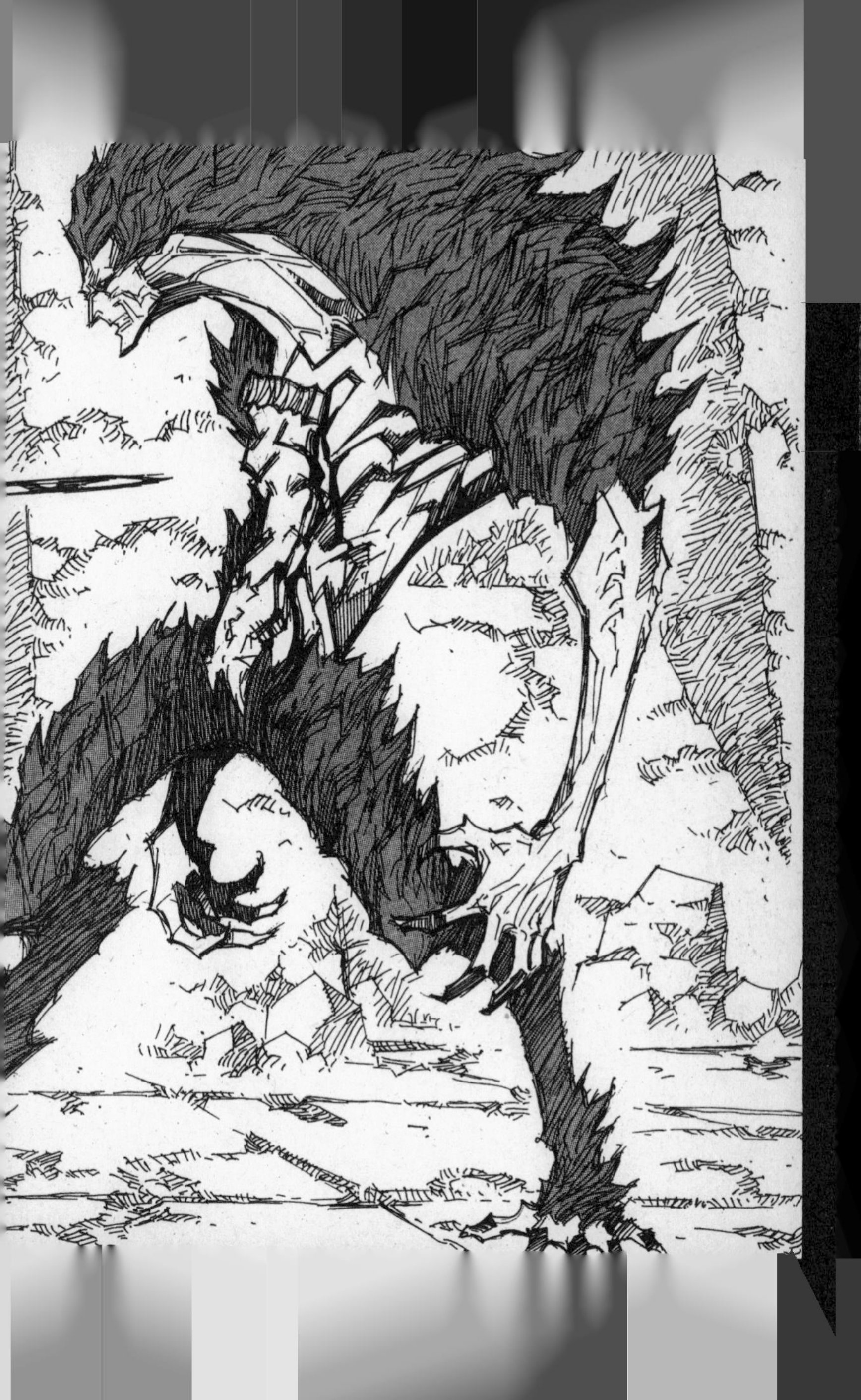

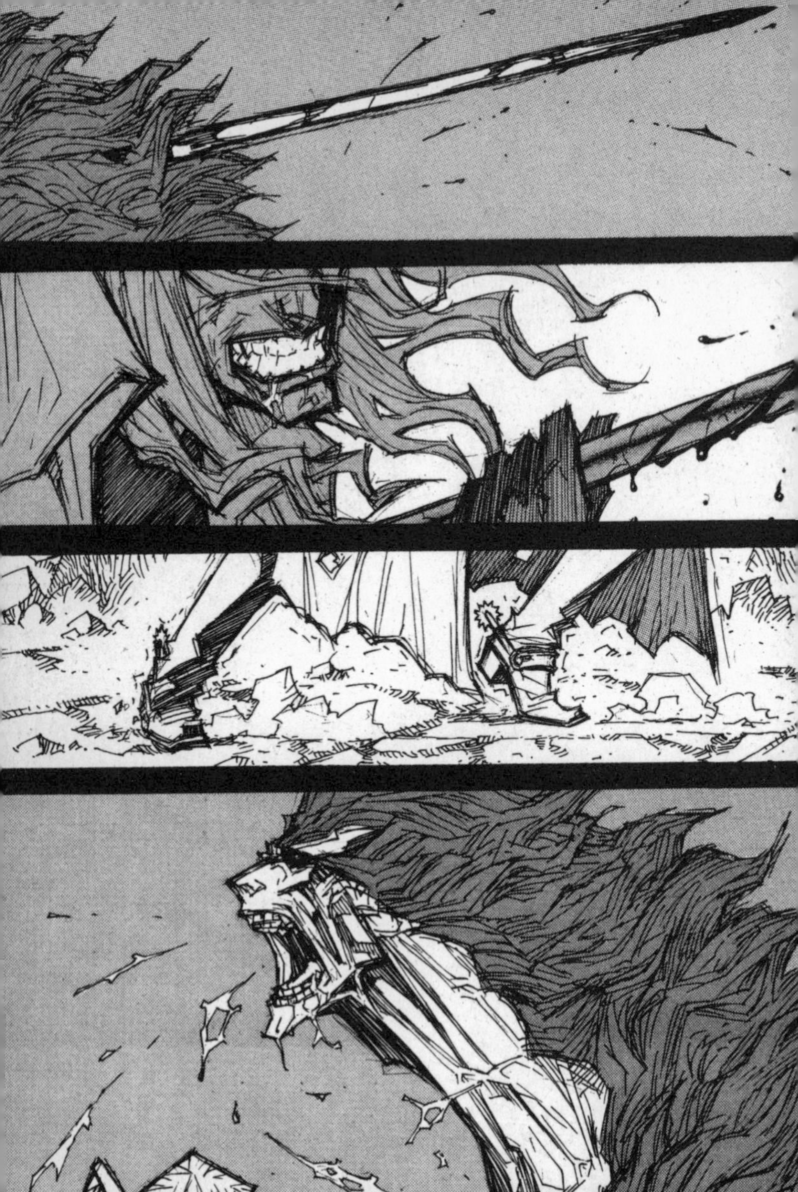

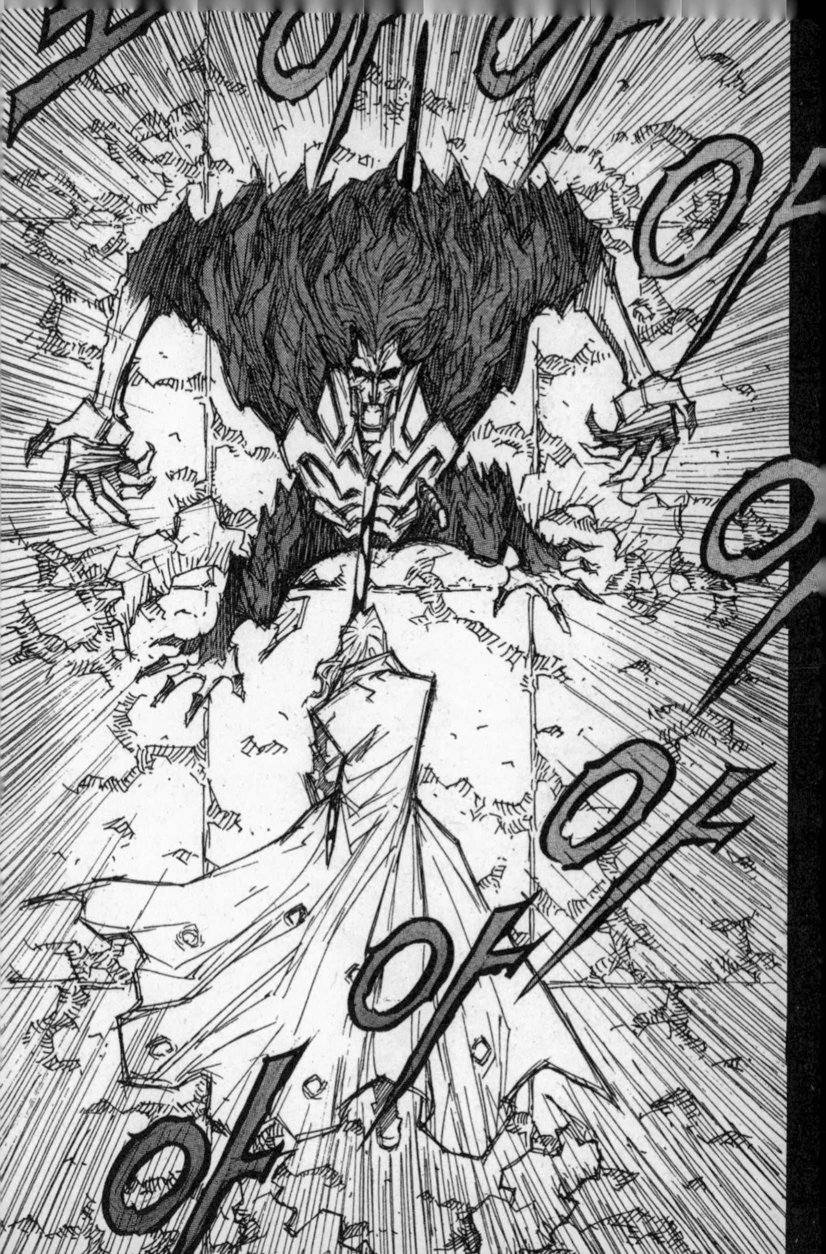

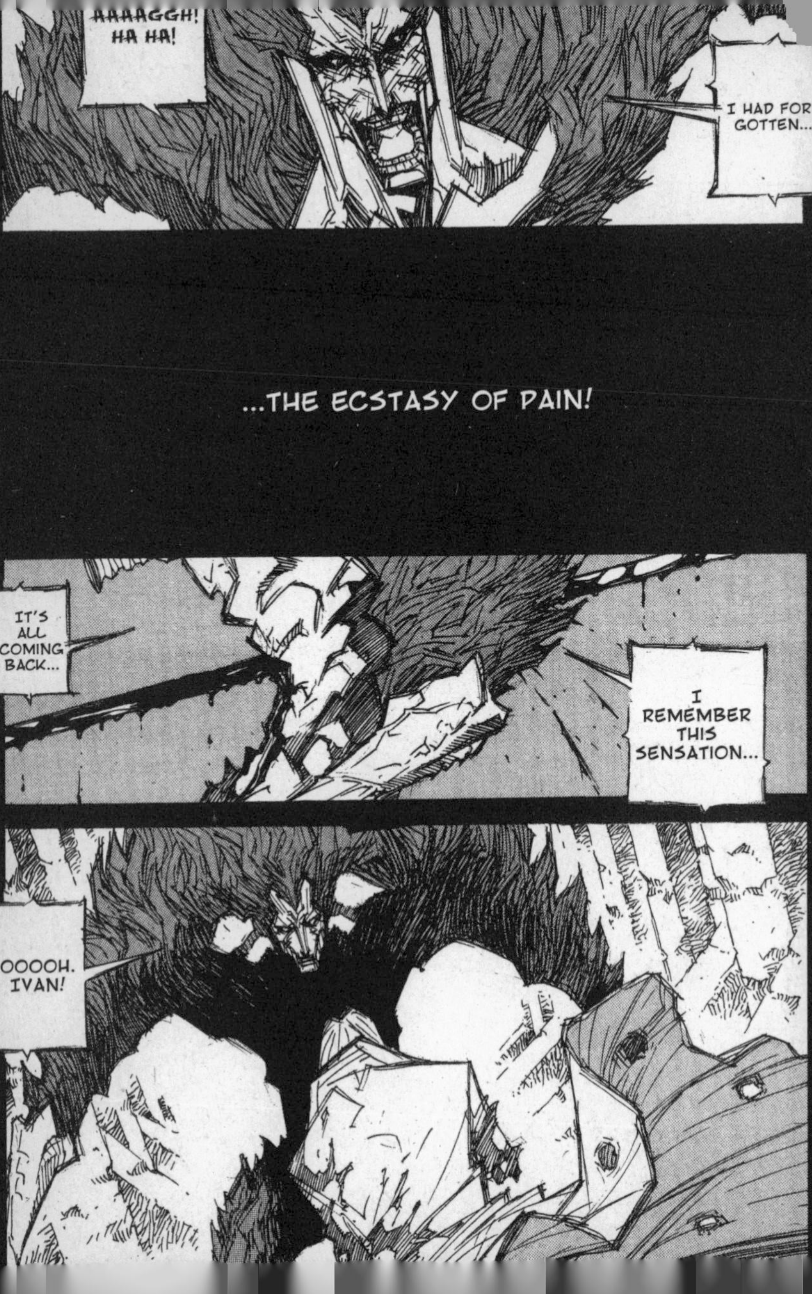
AAAAGGH! HA HA!
I HAD FOR GOTTEN...
...THE ECSTASY OF PAIN!
I REMEMBER THIS SENSATION...
IT'S ALL COMING BACK...
OOOOH. IVAN!

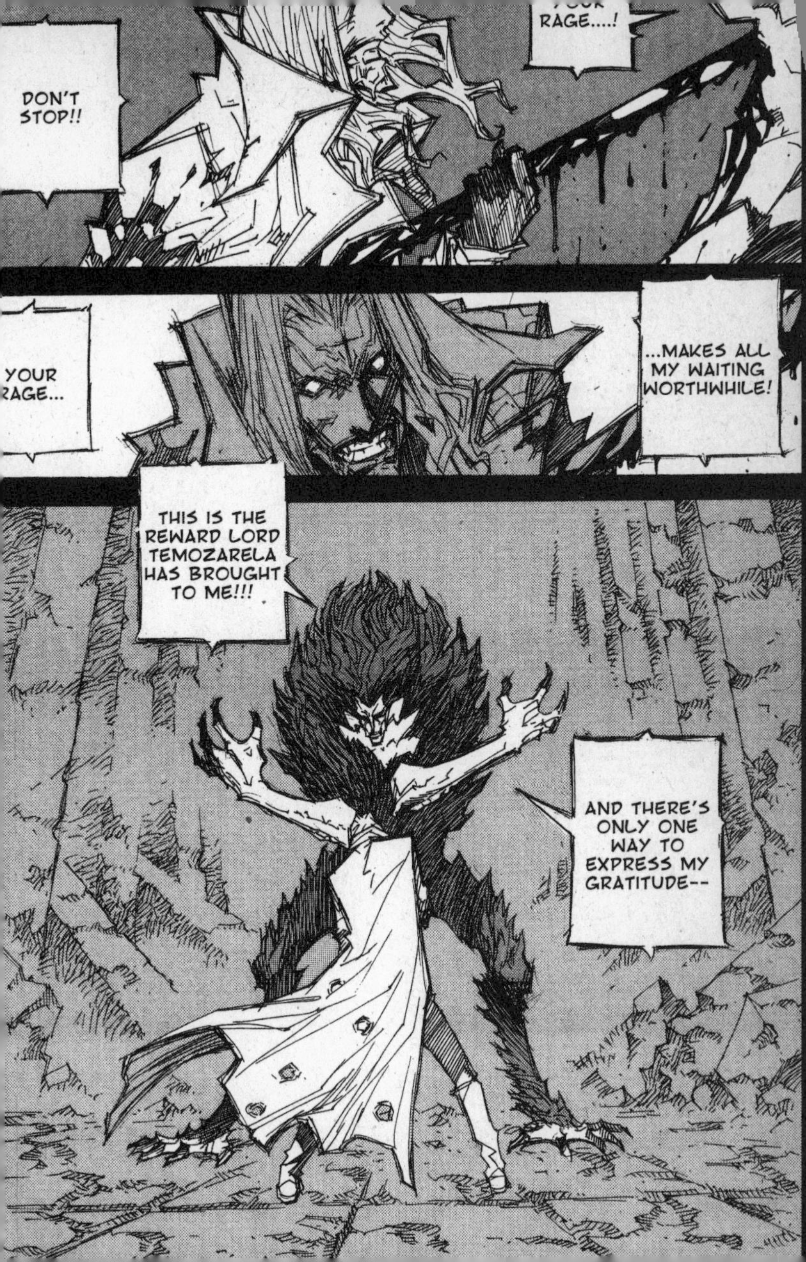
DON'T STOP!!
RAGE....!
YOUR RAGE...
...MAKES ALL MY WAITING WORTHWHILE!
THIS IS THE REWARD LORD TEMOZARELA HAS BROUGHT TO ME!!!
AND THERE'S ONLY ONE WAY TO EXPRESS MY GRATITUDE--

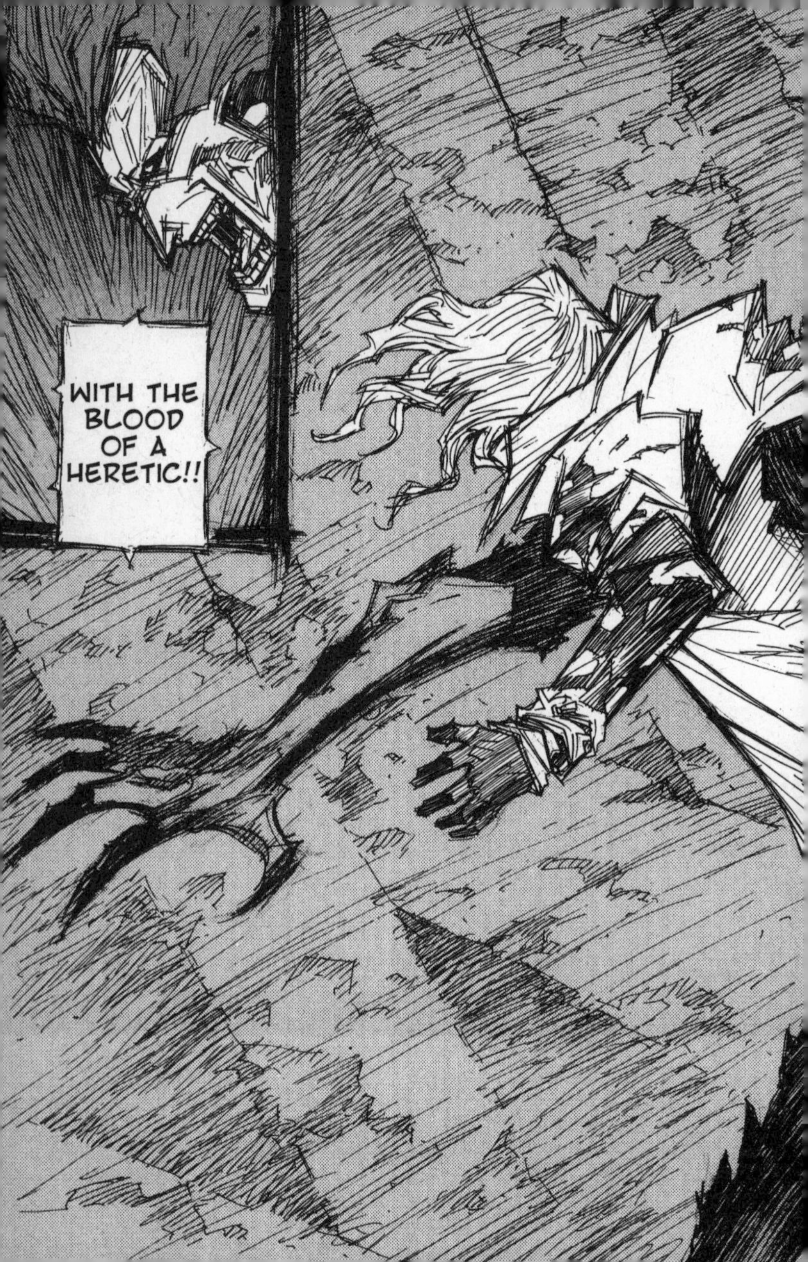
WITH THE BLOOD OF A HERETIC!!

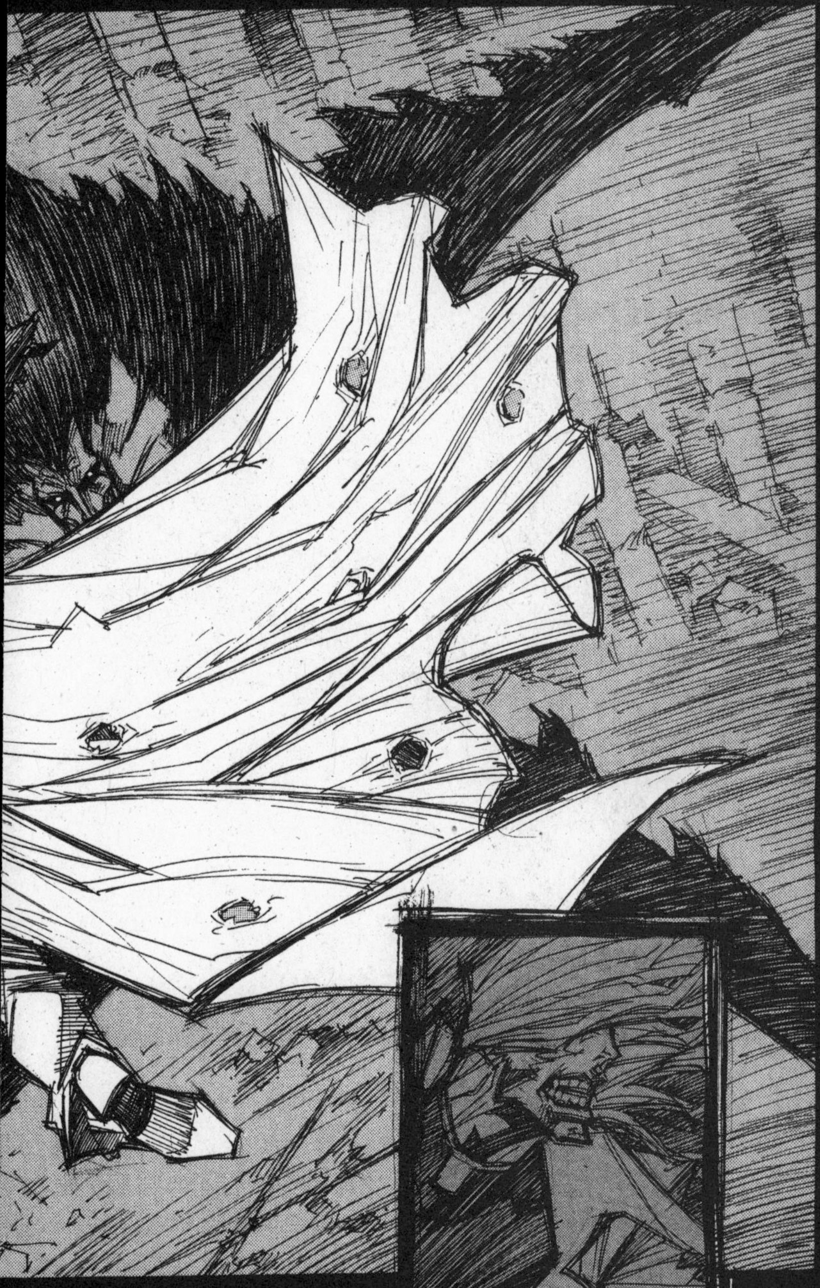

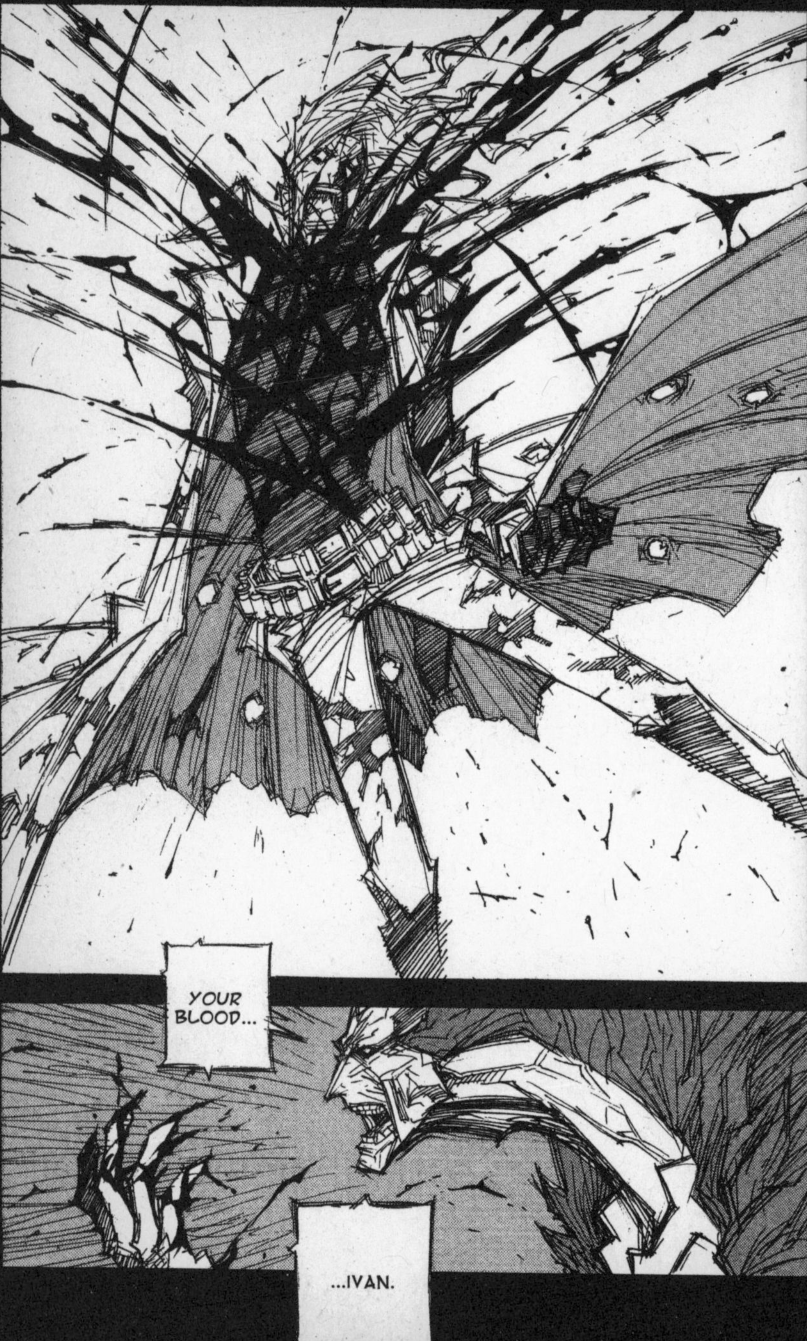
YOUR BLOOD...
...IVAN.

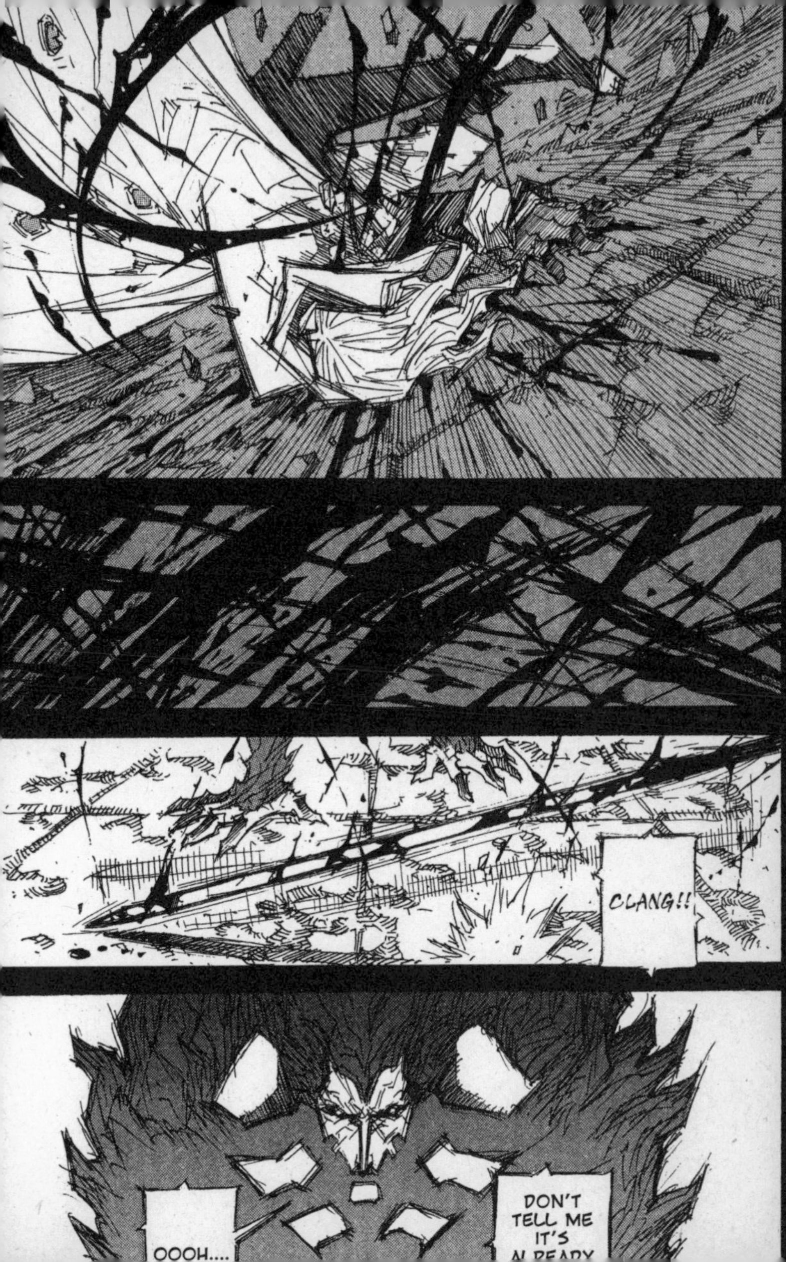
CLANG!!
DON'T TELL ME IT'S
OOOH....

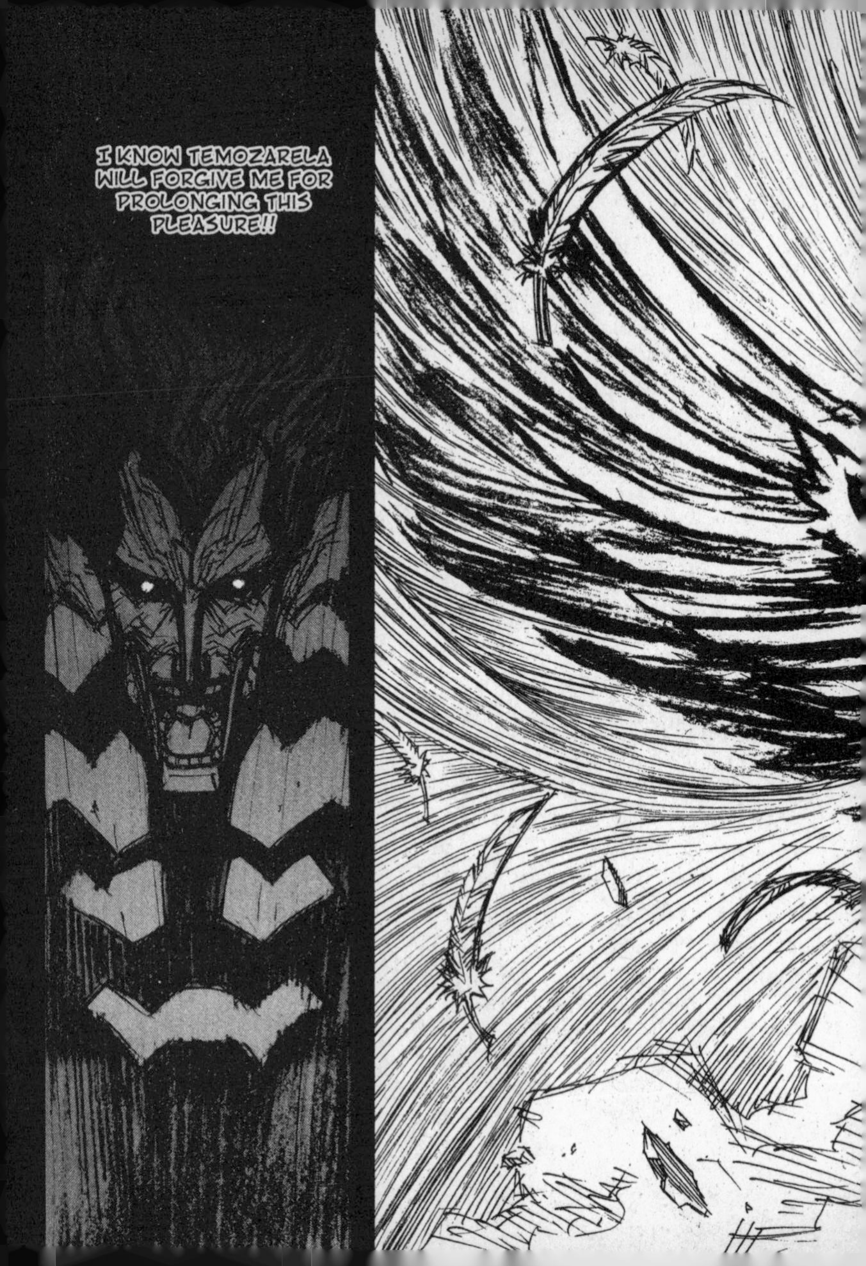
I KNOW TEMOZARELA WILL FORGIVE ME FOR PROLONGING THIS PLEASURE!!

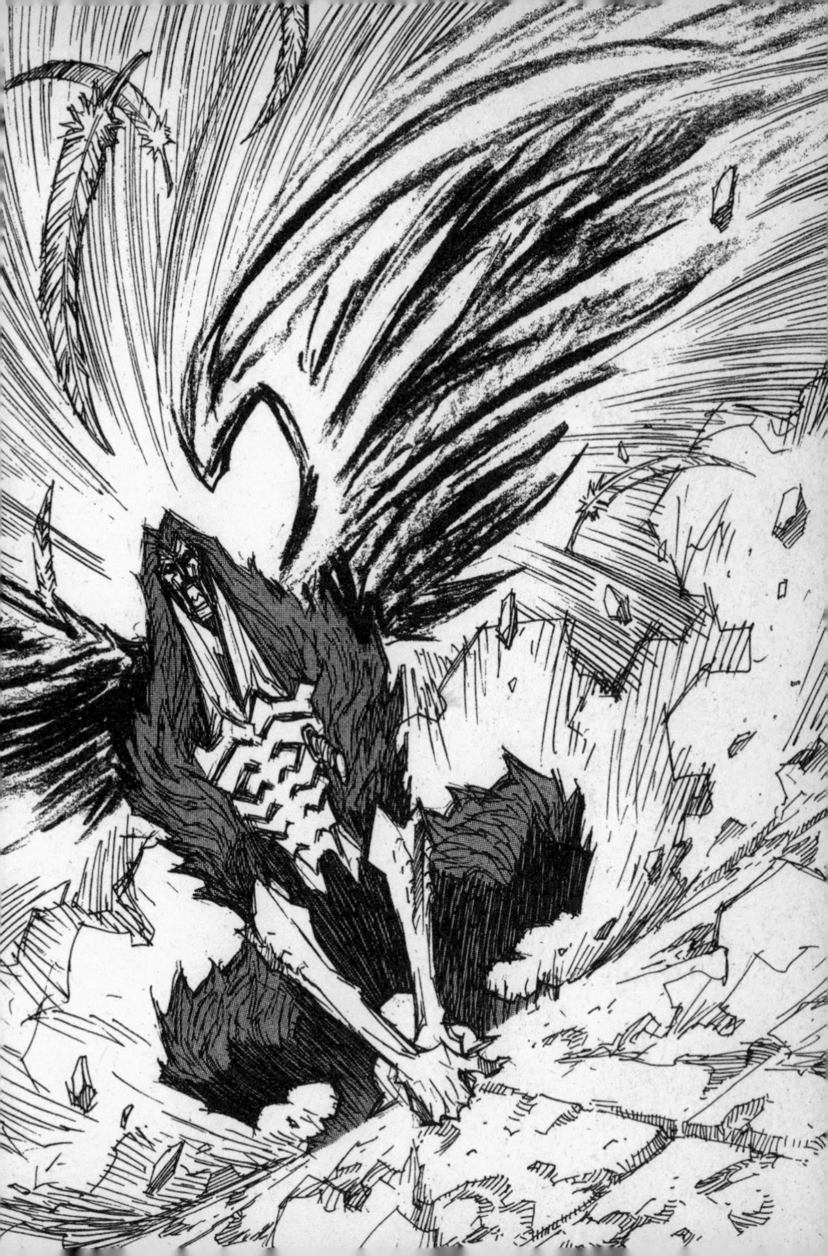

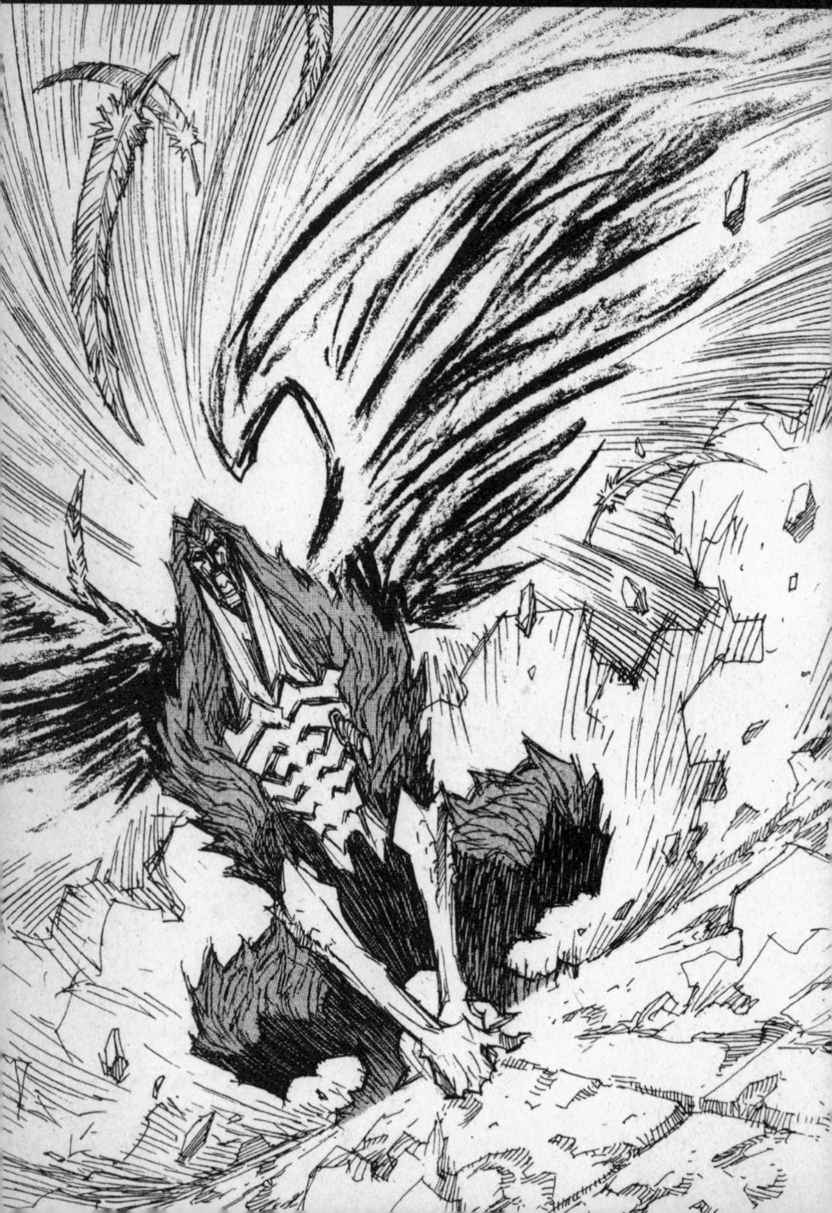

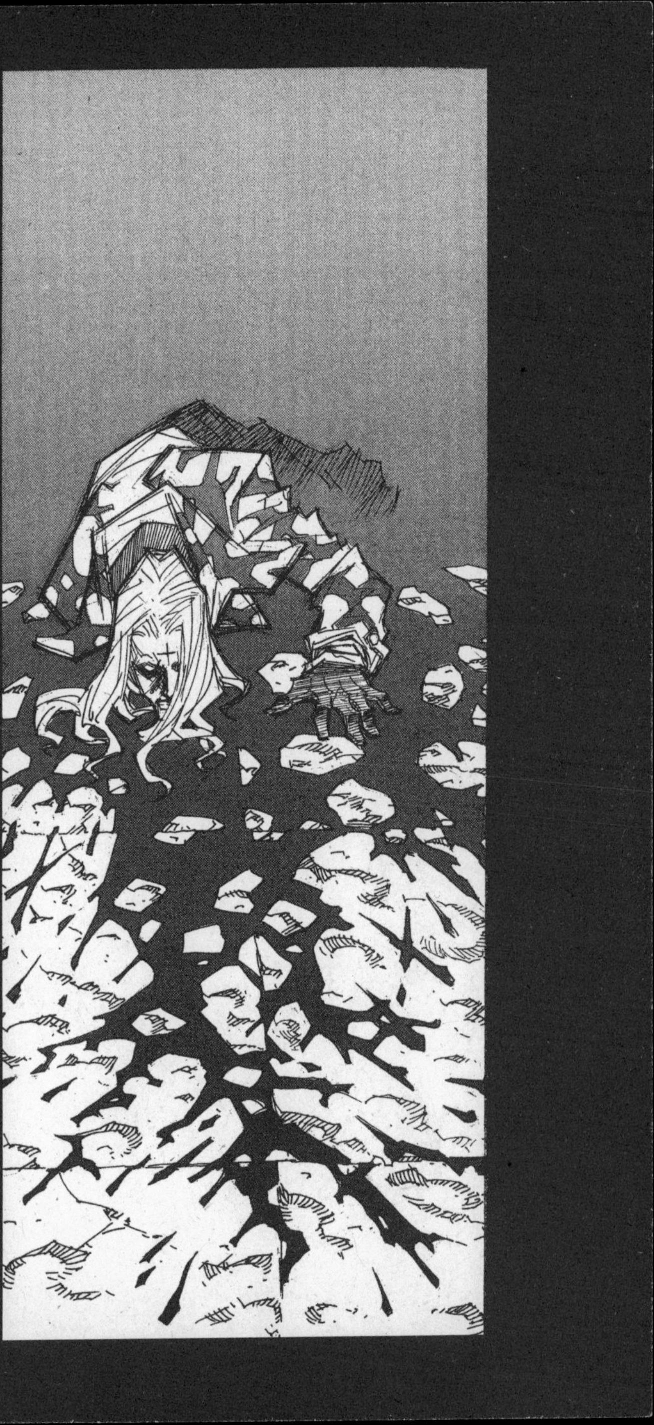

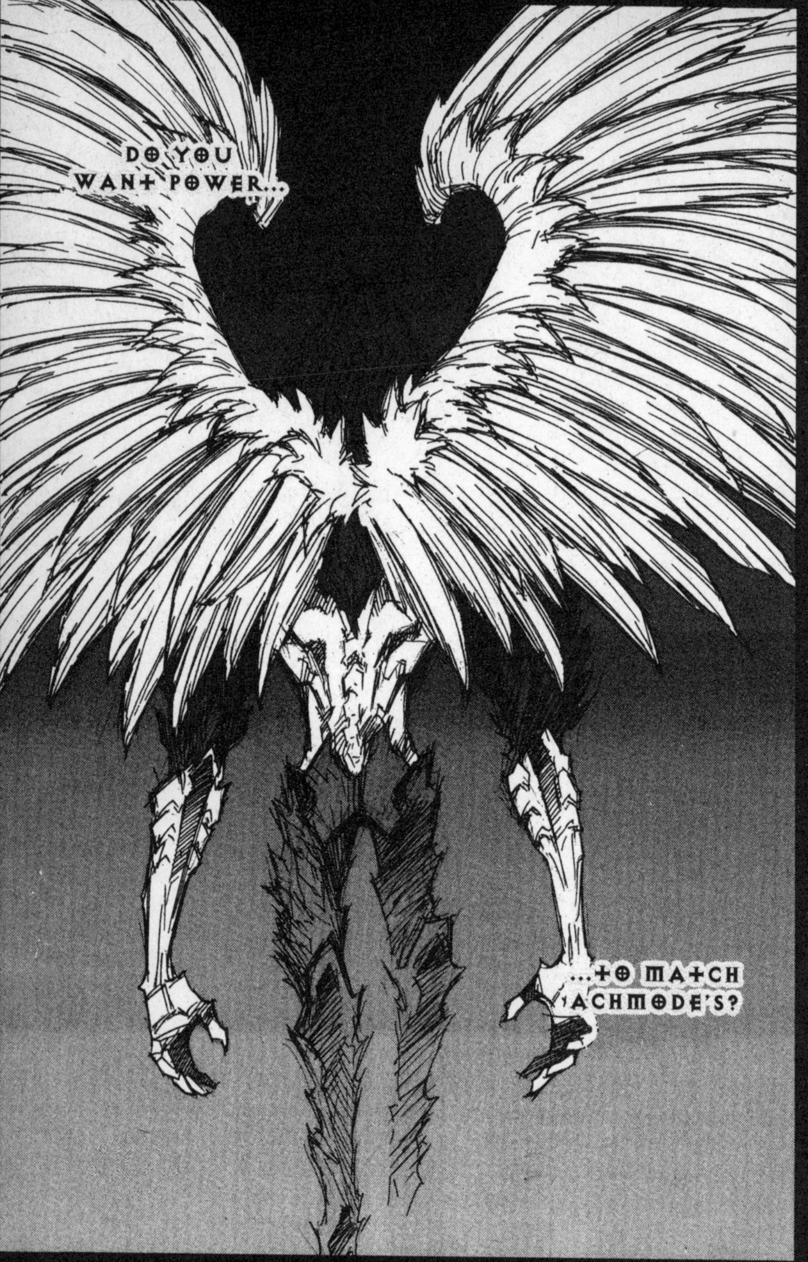
DO YOU WANT POWER...
...TO MATCH ACHMODE'S?

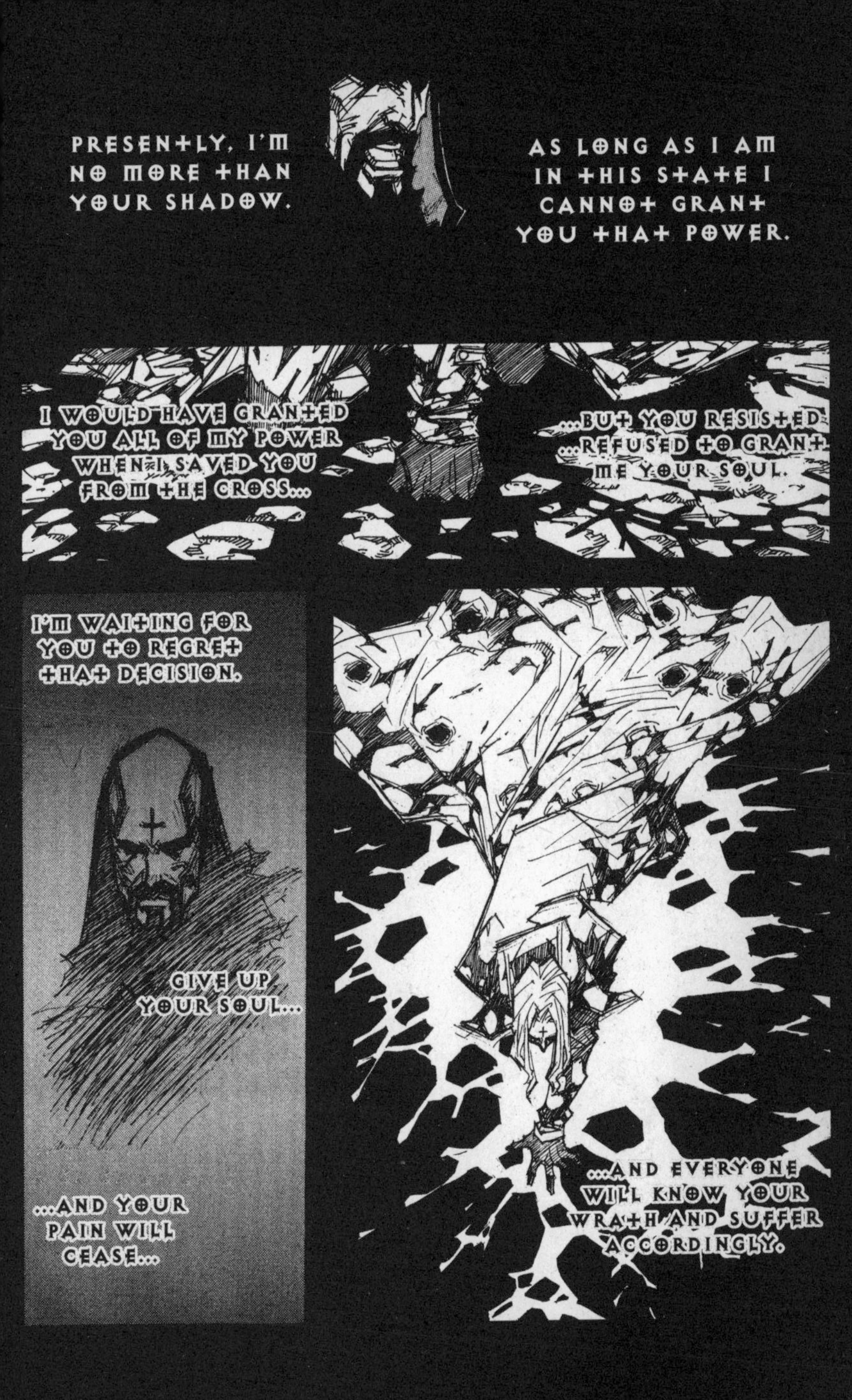
PRESENTLY, I'M NO MORE THAN YOUR SHADOW.
AS LONG AS I AM IN THIS STATE I CANNOT GRANT YOU THAT POWER.
I WOULD HAVE GRANTED YOU ALL OF MY POWER WHEN I SAVED YOU FROM THE CROSS...
...BUT YOU RESISTED ...REFUSED TO GRANT ME YOUR SOUL.
I'M WAITING FOR YOU TO REGRET THAT DECISION.
GIVE UP YOUR SOUL...
...AND YOUR PAIN WILL CEASE...
...AND EVERYONE WILL KNOW YOUR WRATH AND SUFFER ACCORDINGLY.

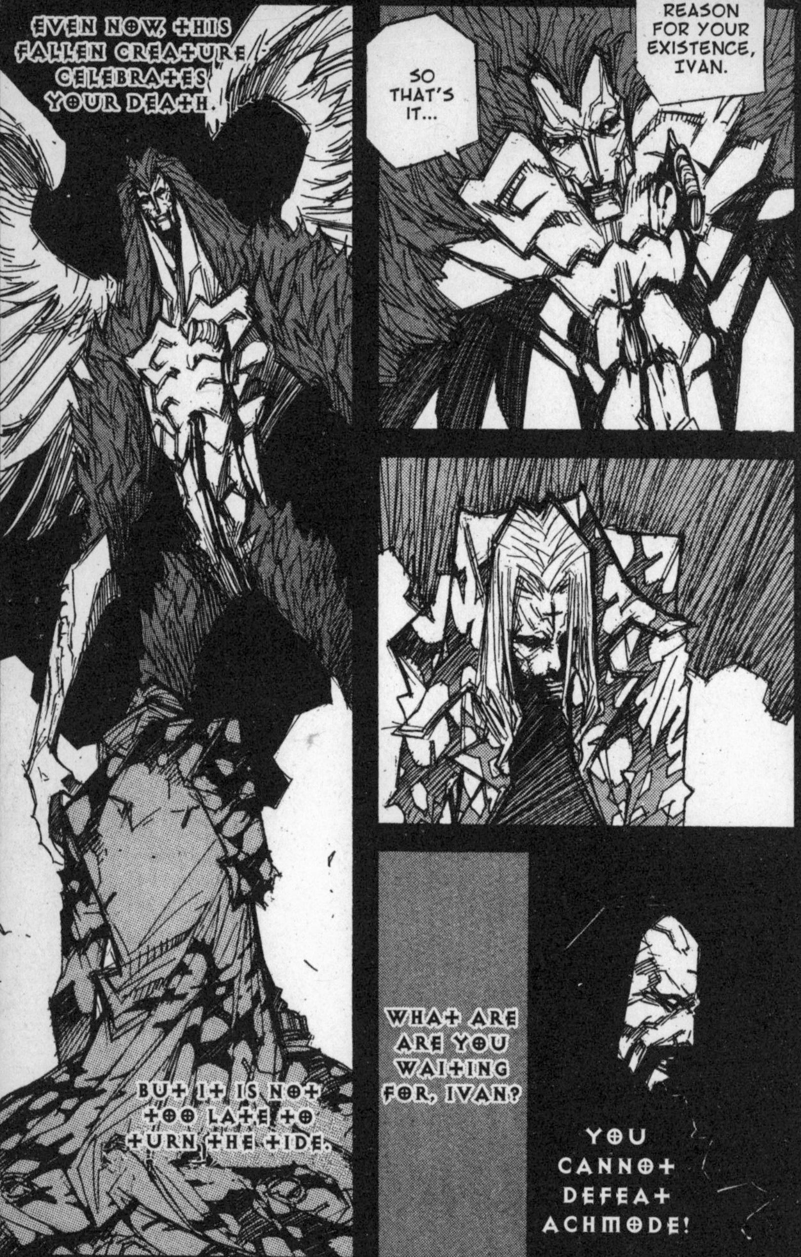
EVEN NOW, THIS FALLEN CREATURE CELEBRATES YOUR DEATH.
BUT IT IS NOT TOO LATE TO TURN THE TIDE.
SO THAT'S IT...
THAT'S THE REASON FOR YOUR EXISTENCE, IVAN.
WHAT ARE ARE YOU WAITING FOR, IVAN?
YOU CANNOT DEFEAT ACHMODE!

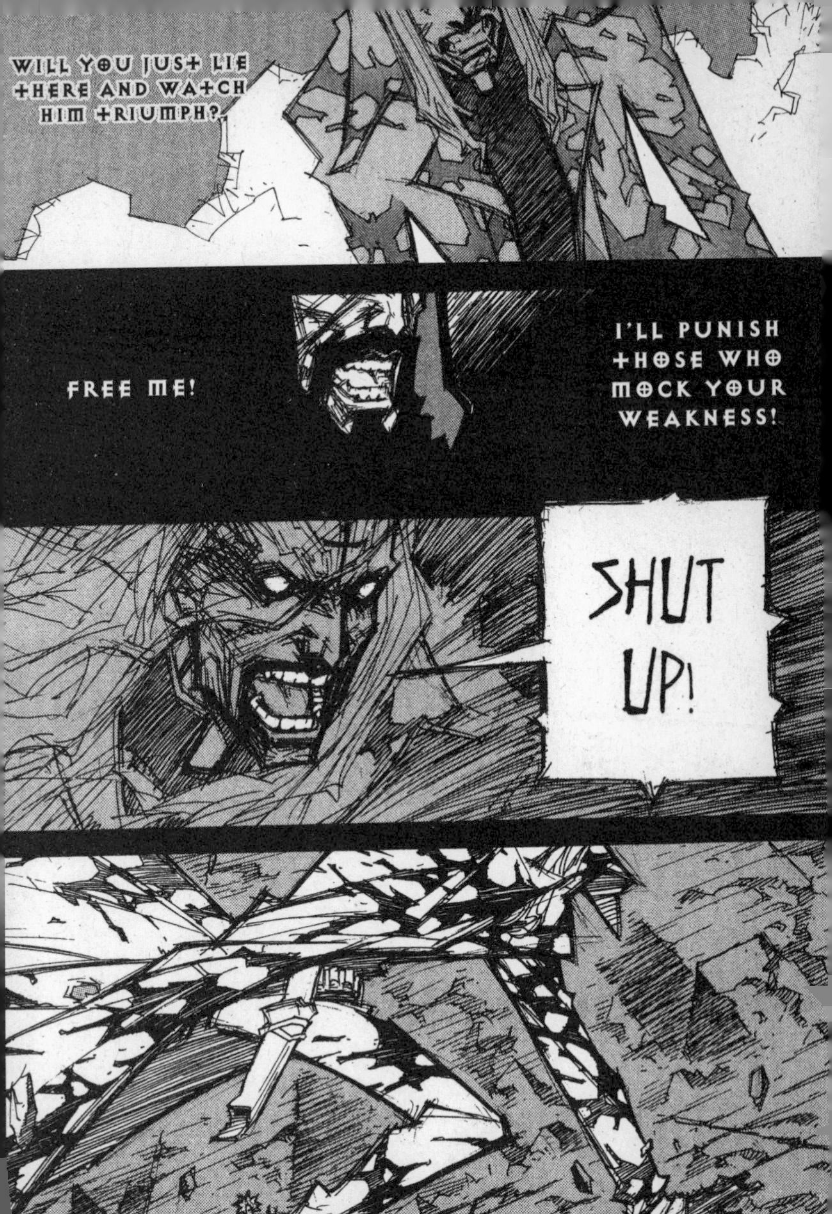
WILL YOU JUST LIE THERE AND WATCH HIM TRIUMPH?
I'LL PUNISH THOSE WHO MOCK YOUR WEAKNESS!
FREE ME!
SHUT UP!

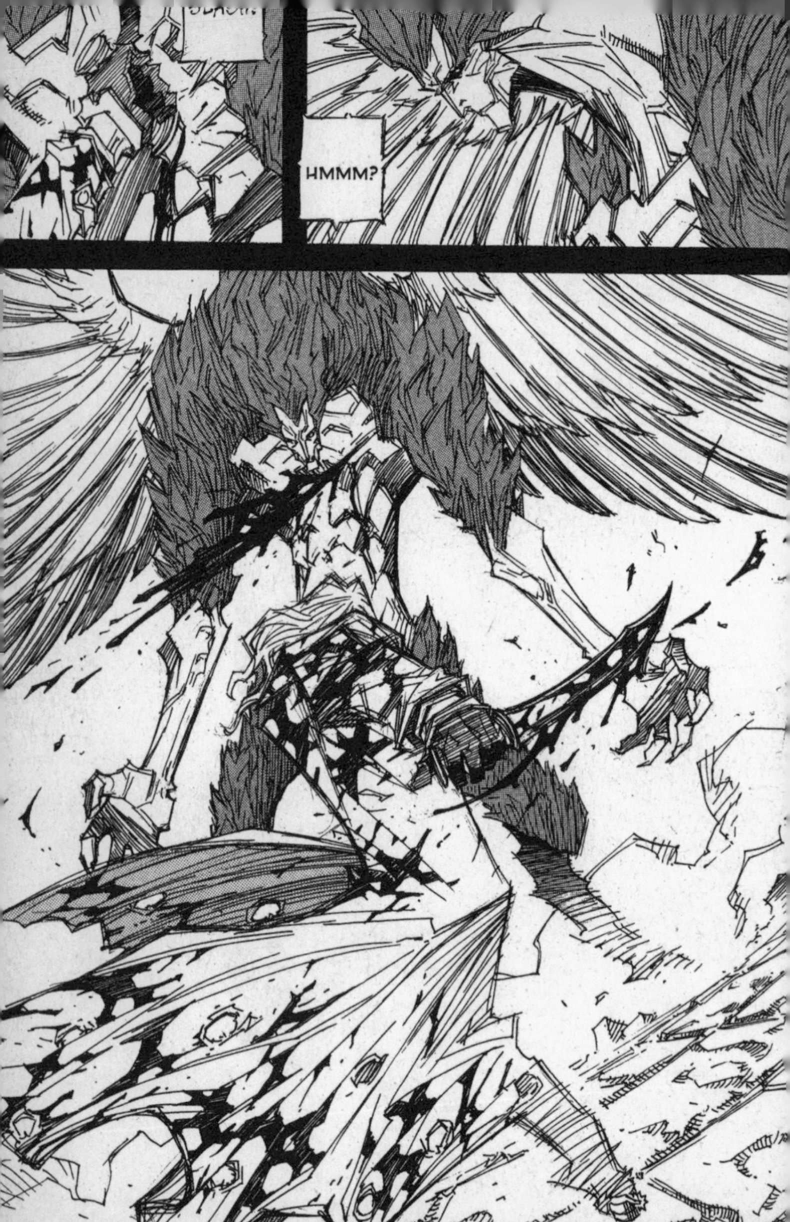
HMMM?

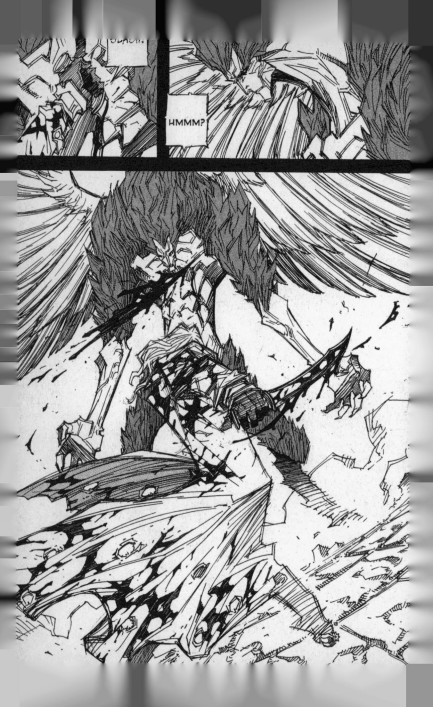

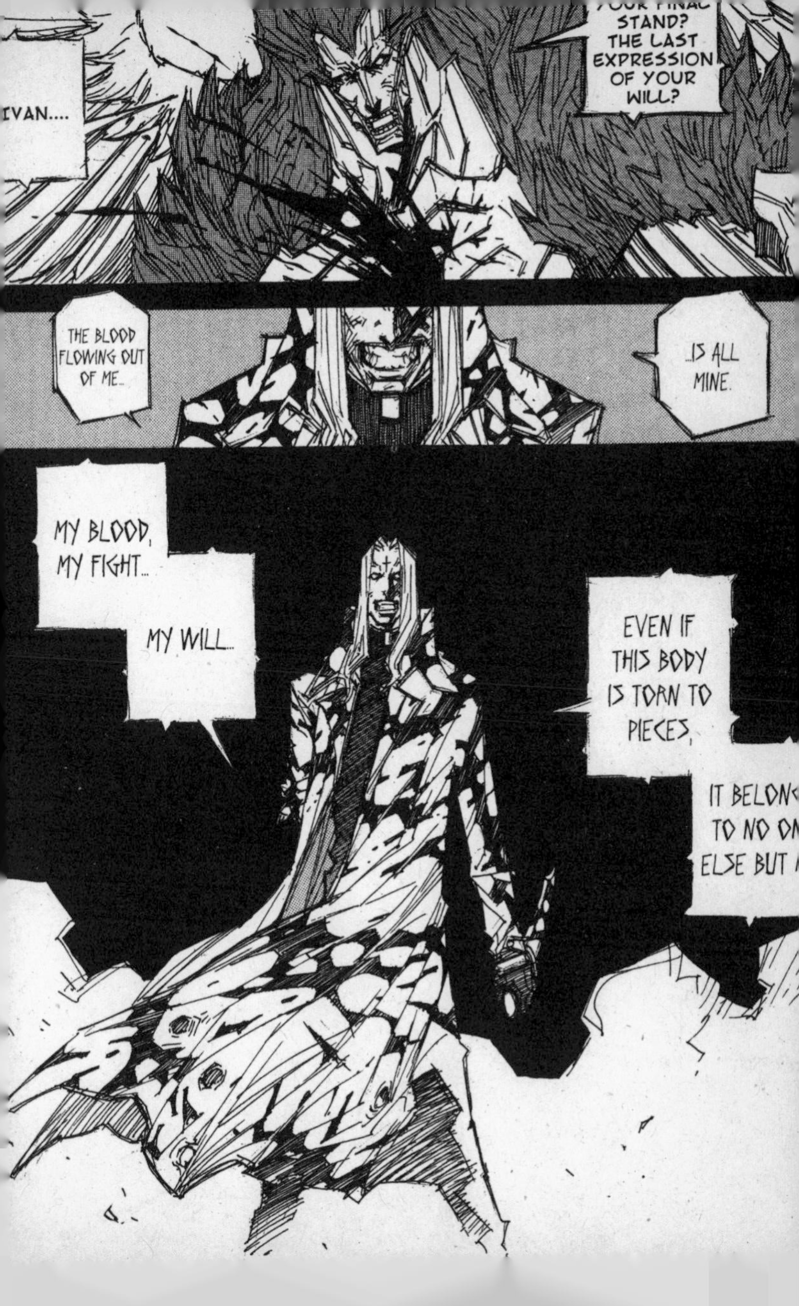
IVAN....
STAND? THE LAST EXPRESSION OF YOUR WILL?
THE BLOOD FLOWING OUT OF ME...
...IS ALL MINE.
MY BLOOD, MY FIGHT...
MY WILL...
EVEN IF THIS BODY IS TORN TO PIECES,
IT BELON TO NO ON ELSE BUT

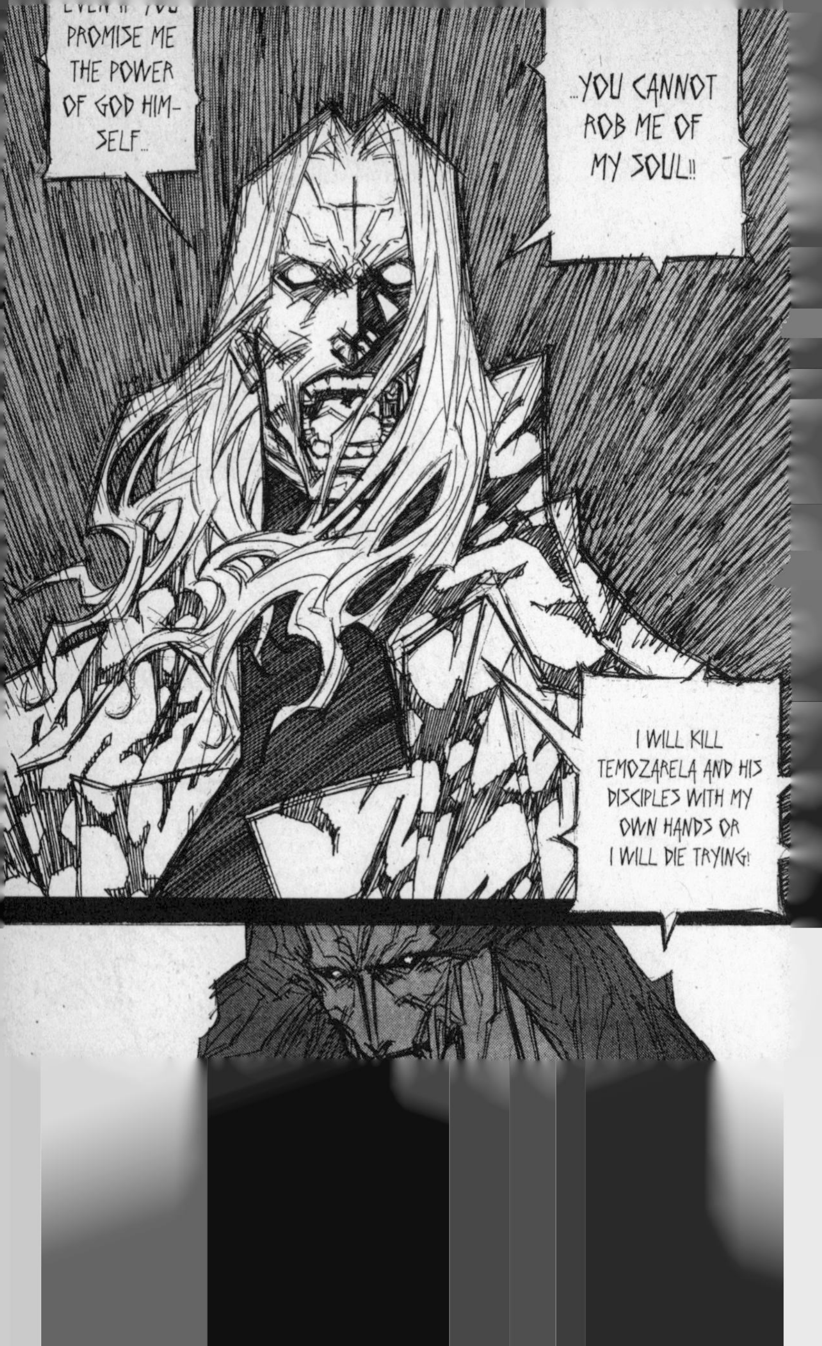
PROMISE ME THE POWER OF GOD HIM-SELF...
...YOU CANNOT ROB ME OF MY SOUL!!
I WILL KILL TEMOZARELA AND HIS DISCIPLES WITH MY OWN HANDS OR I WILL DIE TRYING!

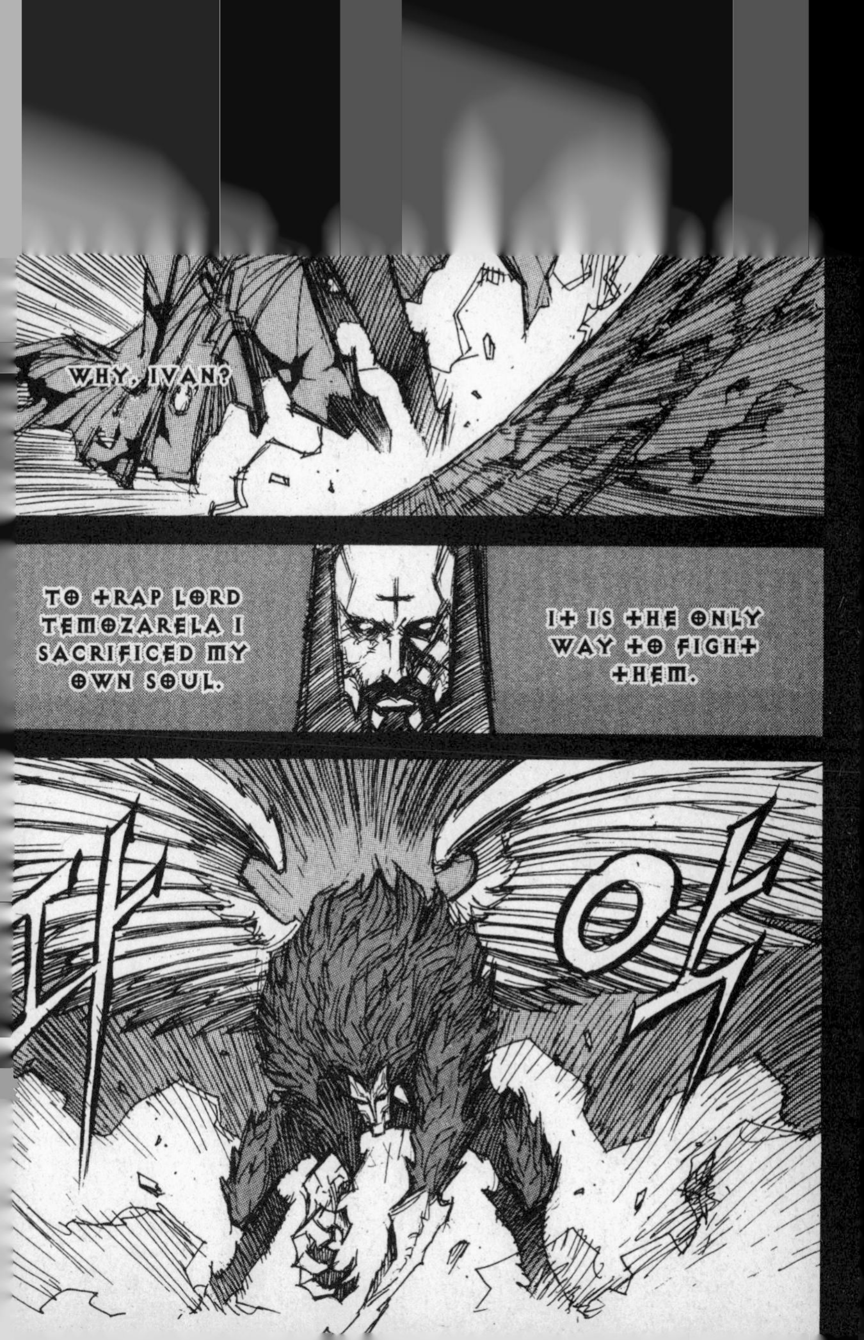
WHY, IVAN?
TO TRAP LORD TEMOZARELA I SACRIFICED MY OWN SOUL.
IT IS THE ONLY WAY TO FIGHT THEM.

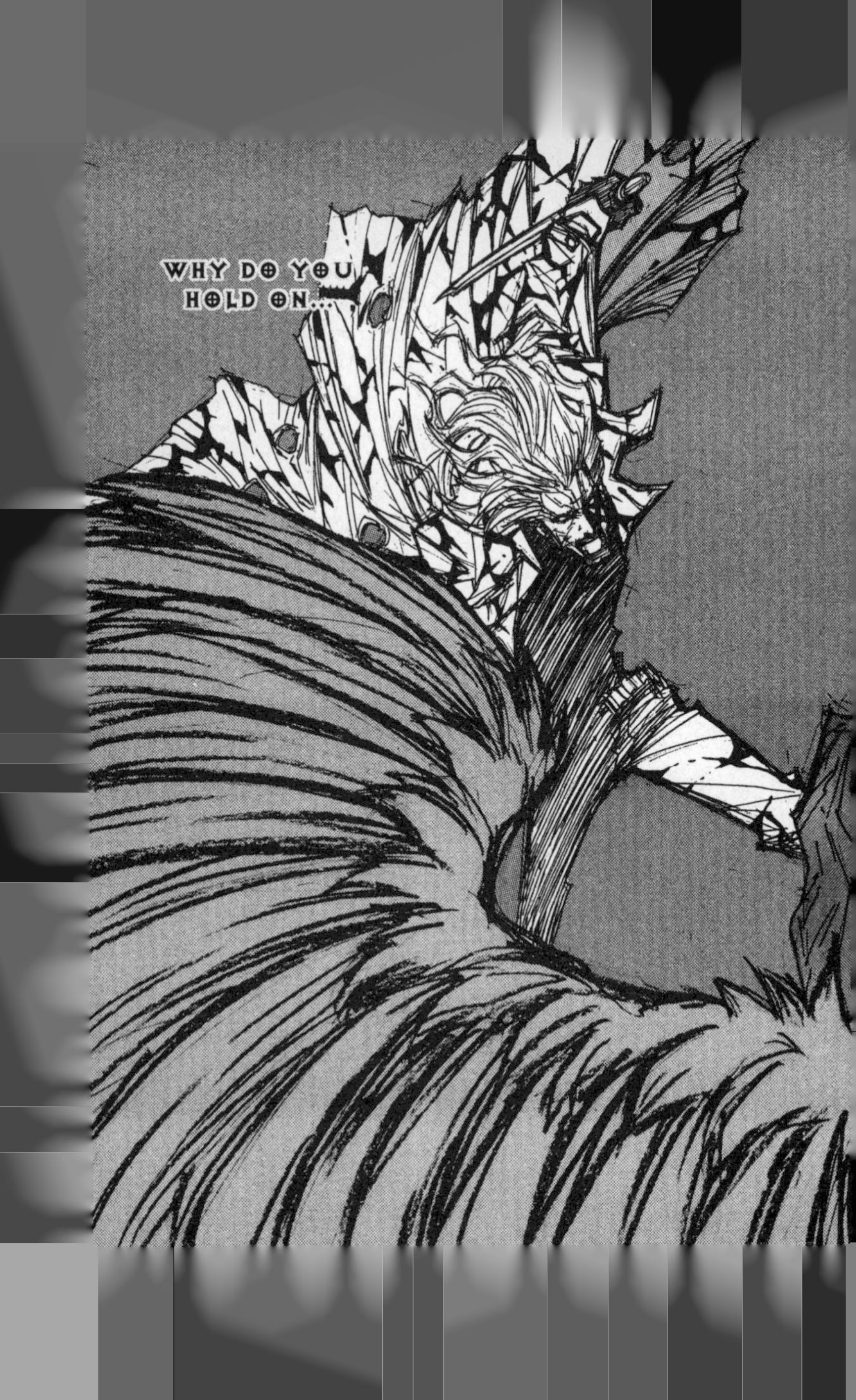
WHY DO YOU HOLD ON...

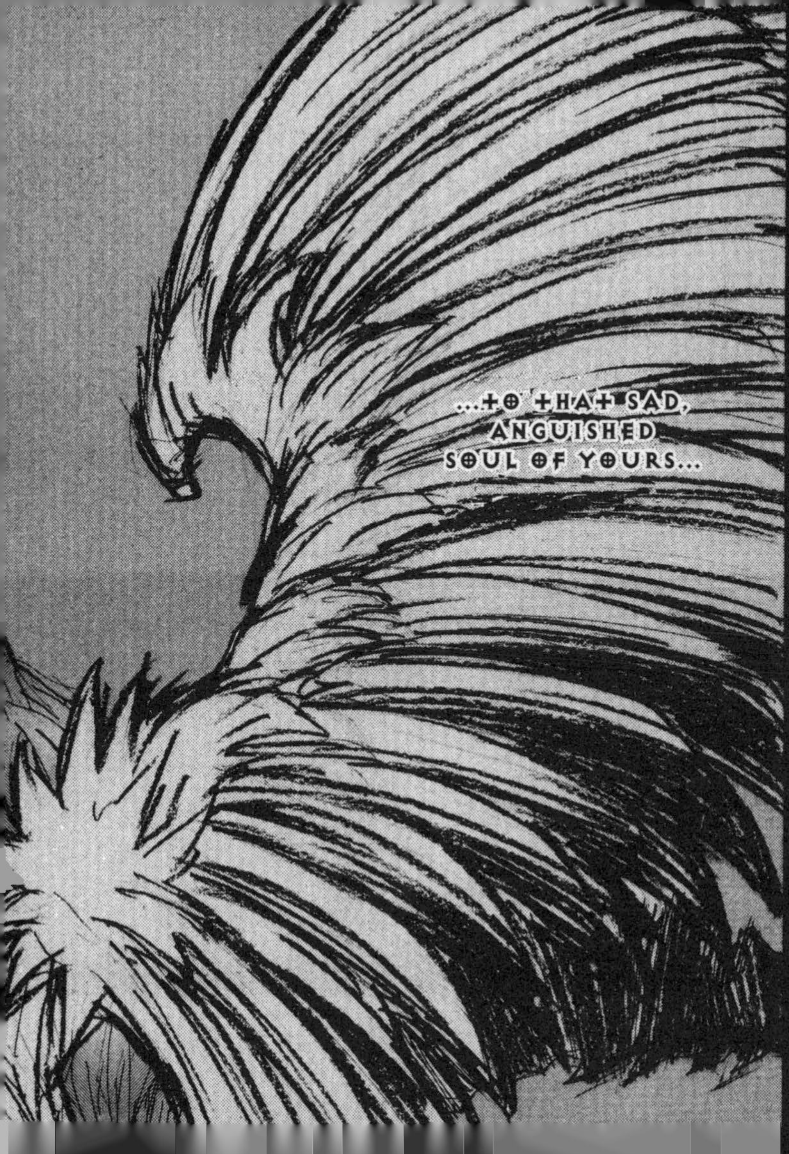
...TO THAT SAD, ANGUISHED SOUL OF YOURS...

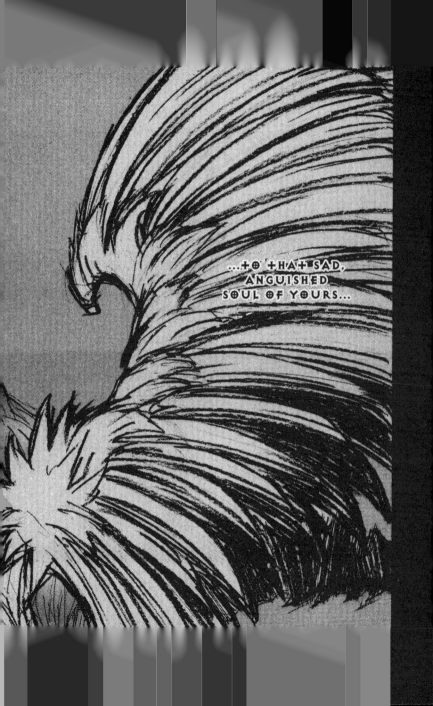

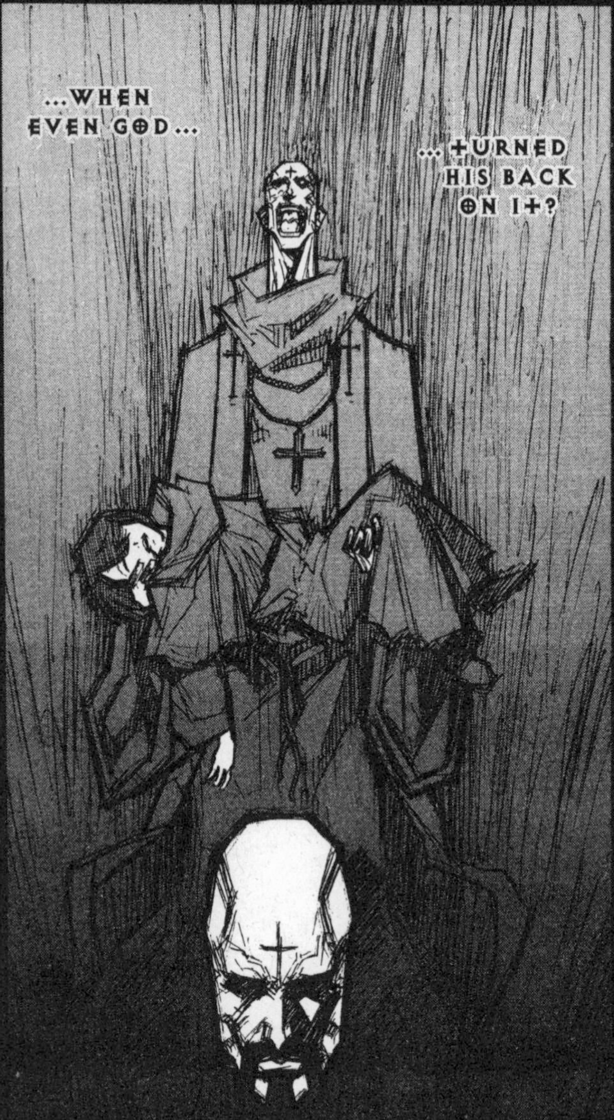
...WHEN EVEN GOD...
...TURNED HIS BACK ON IT?

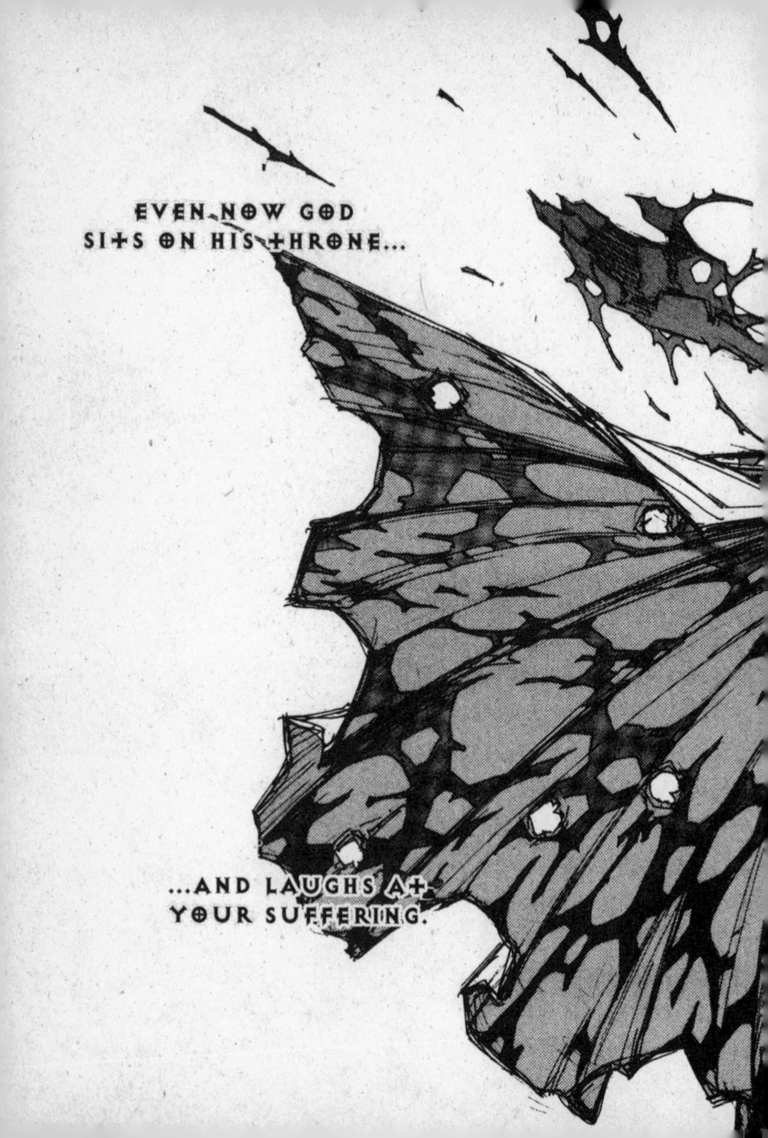
EVEN NOW GOD SITS ON HIS THRONE...
...AND LAUGHS AT YOUR SUFFERING.

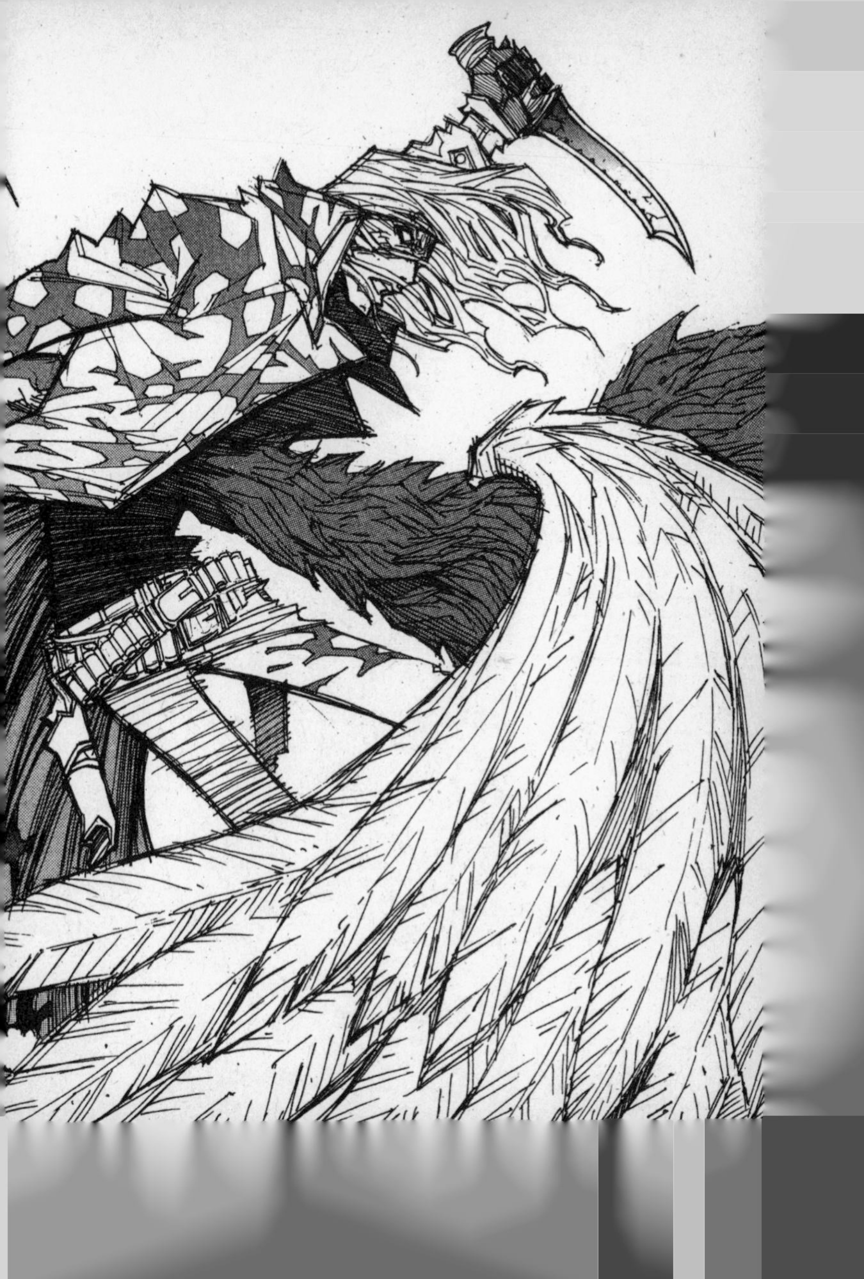

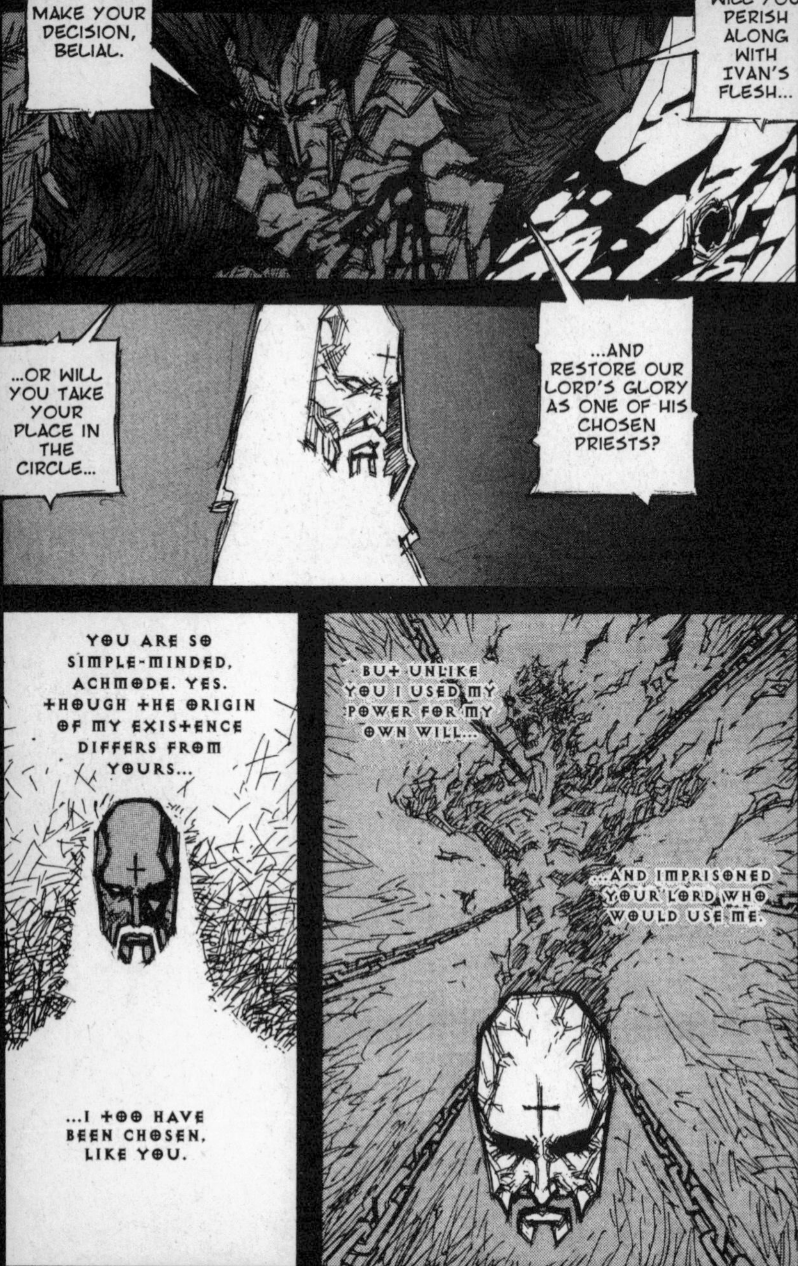
MAKE YOUR DECISION, BELIAL.
WILL YOU PERISH ALONG WITH IVAN'S FLESH...
...OR WILL YOU TAKE YOUR PLACE IN THE CIRCLE...
...AND RESTORE OUR LORD'S GLORY AS ONE OF HIS CHOSEN PRIESTS?
YOU ARE SO SIMPLE-MINDED, ACHMODE. YES. THOUGH THE ORIGIN OF MY EXISTENCE DIFFERS FROM YOURS...
...I TOO HAVE BEEN CHOSEN, LIKE YOU.
BUT UNLIKE YOU I USED MY POWER FOR MY OWN WILL...
...AND IMPRISONED YOUR LORD WHO WOULD USE ME.

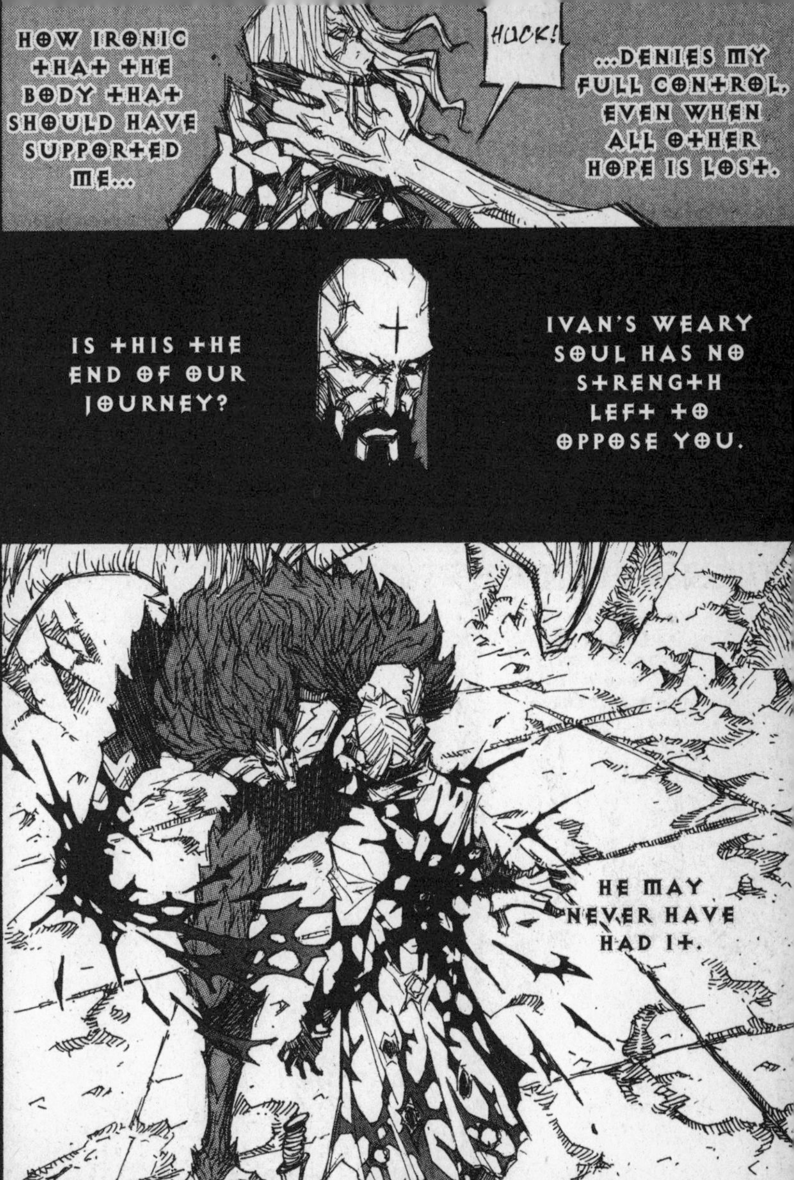
HOW IRONIC THAT THE BODY THAT SHOULD HAVE SUPPORTED ME...
HUCK!
...DENIES MY FULL CONTROL, EVEN WHEN ALL OTHER HOPE IS LOST.
IS THIS THE END OF OUR JOURNEY?
IVAN'S WEARY SOUL HAS NO STRENGTH LEFT TO OPPOSE YOU.
HE MAY NEVER HAVE HAD IT.

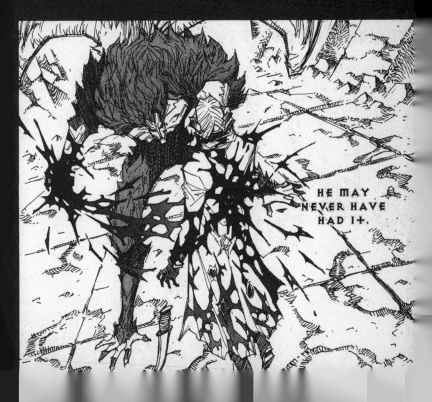

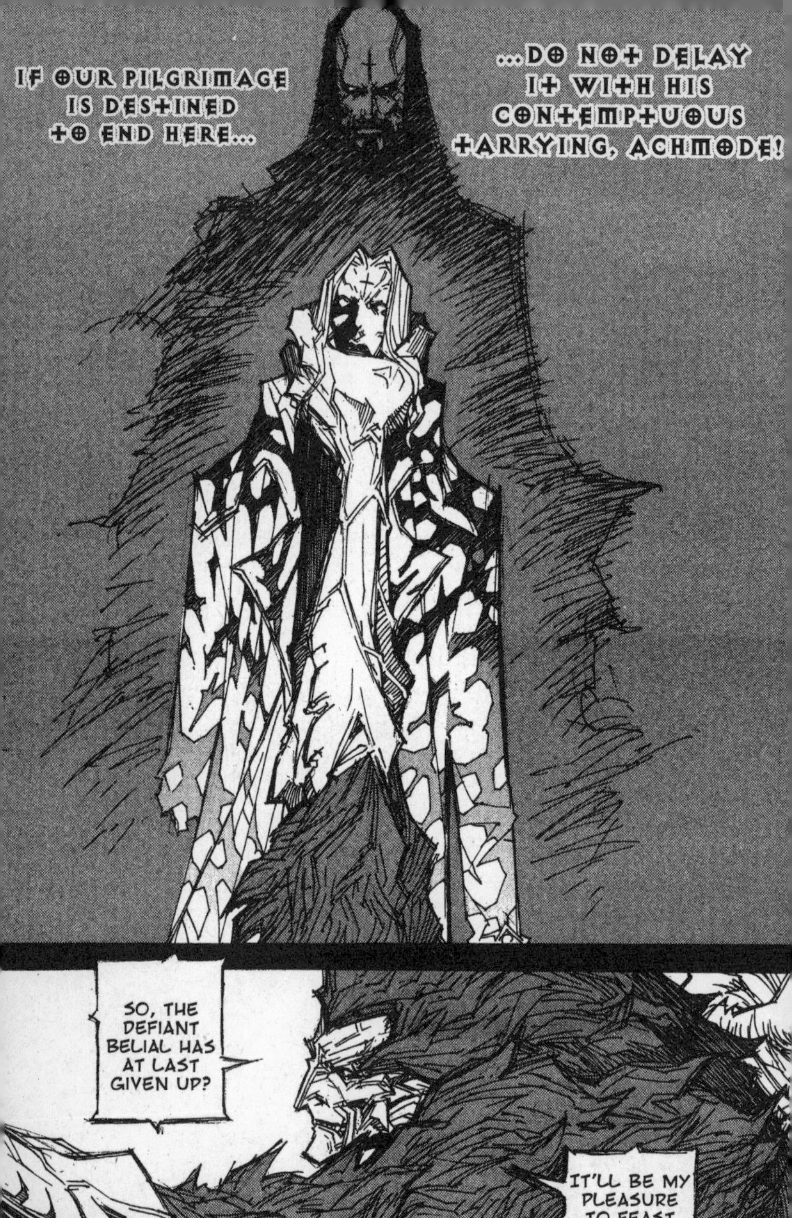
IF OUR PILGRIMAGE IS DESTINED TO END HERE...
...DO NOT DELAY IT WITH HIS CONTEMPTUOUS TARRYING, ACHMODE!
SO, THE DEFIANT BELIAL HAS AT LAST GIVEN UP?
IT'LL BE MY PLEASURE TO FEAST ON THE

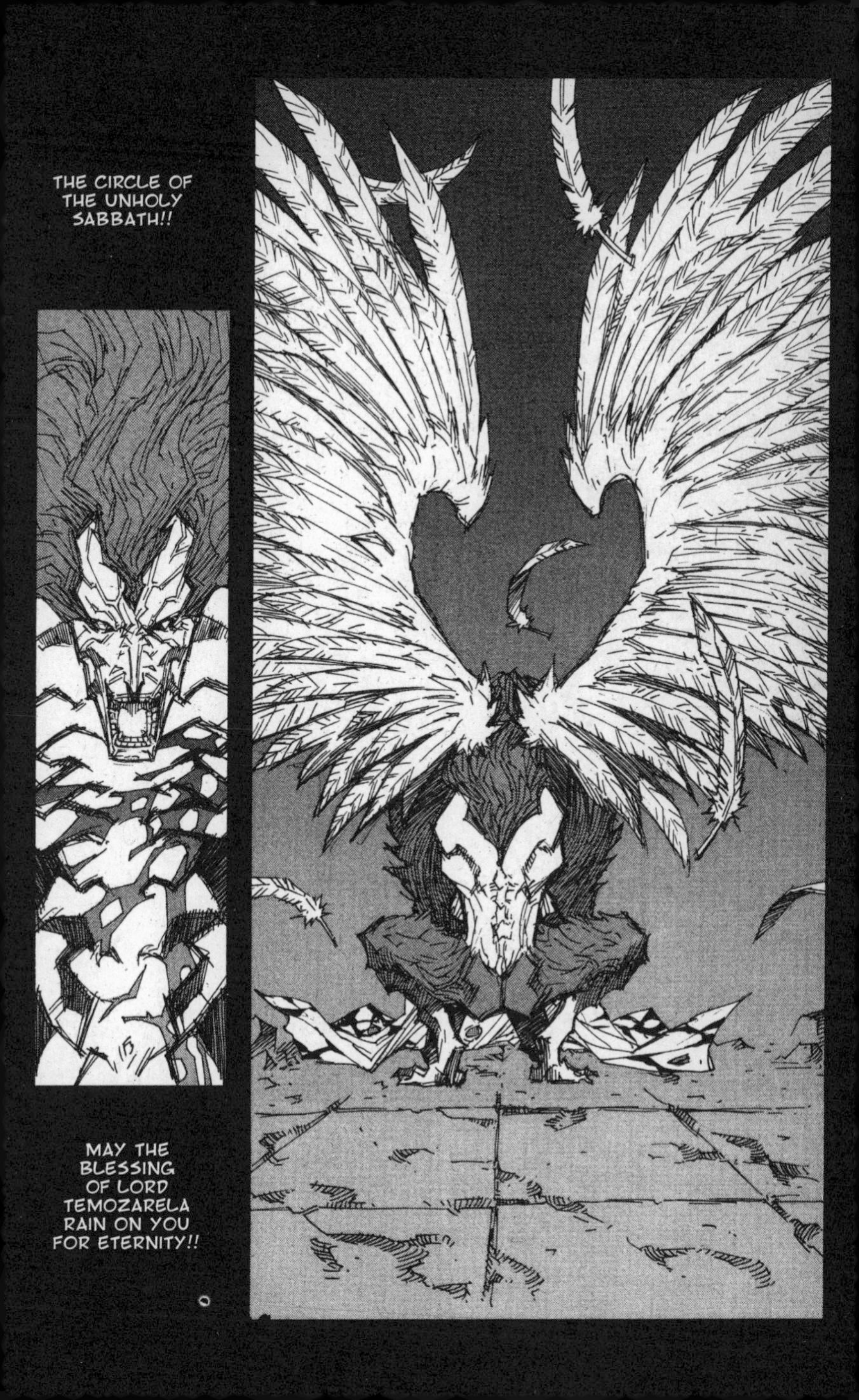
THE CIRCLE OF THE UNHOLY SABBATH!!
MAY THE BLESSING OF LORD TEMOZARELA RAIN ON YOU FOR ETERNITY!!

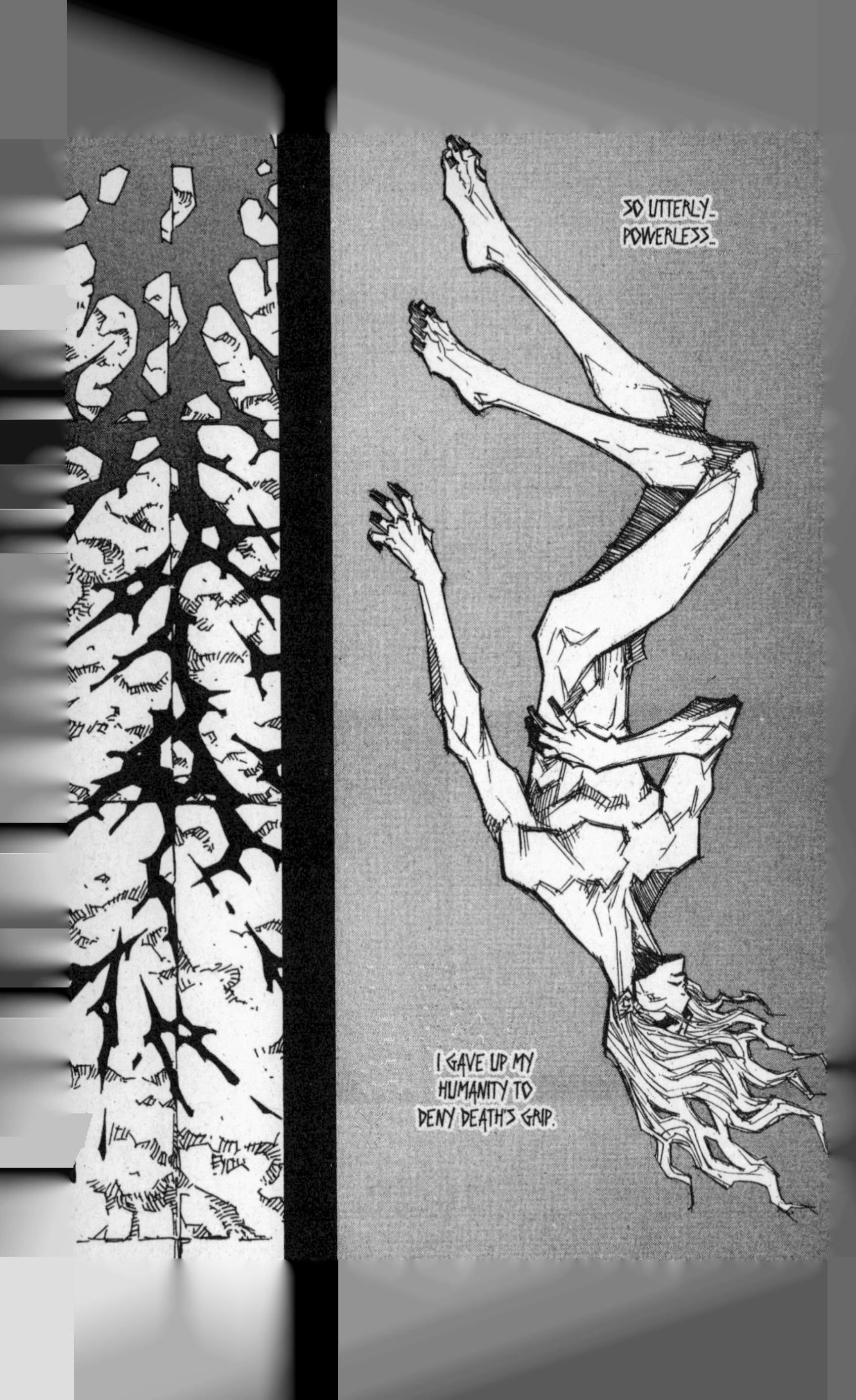
SO UTTERLY...
POWERLESS...
I GAVE UP MY HUMANITY TO DENY DEATH'S GRIP.

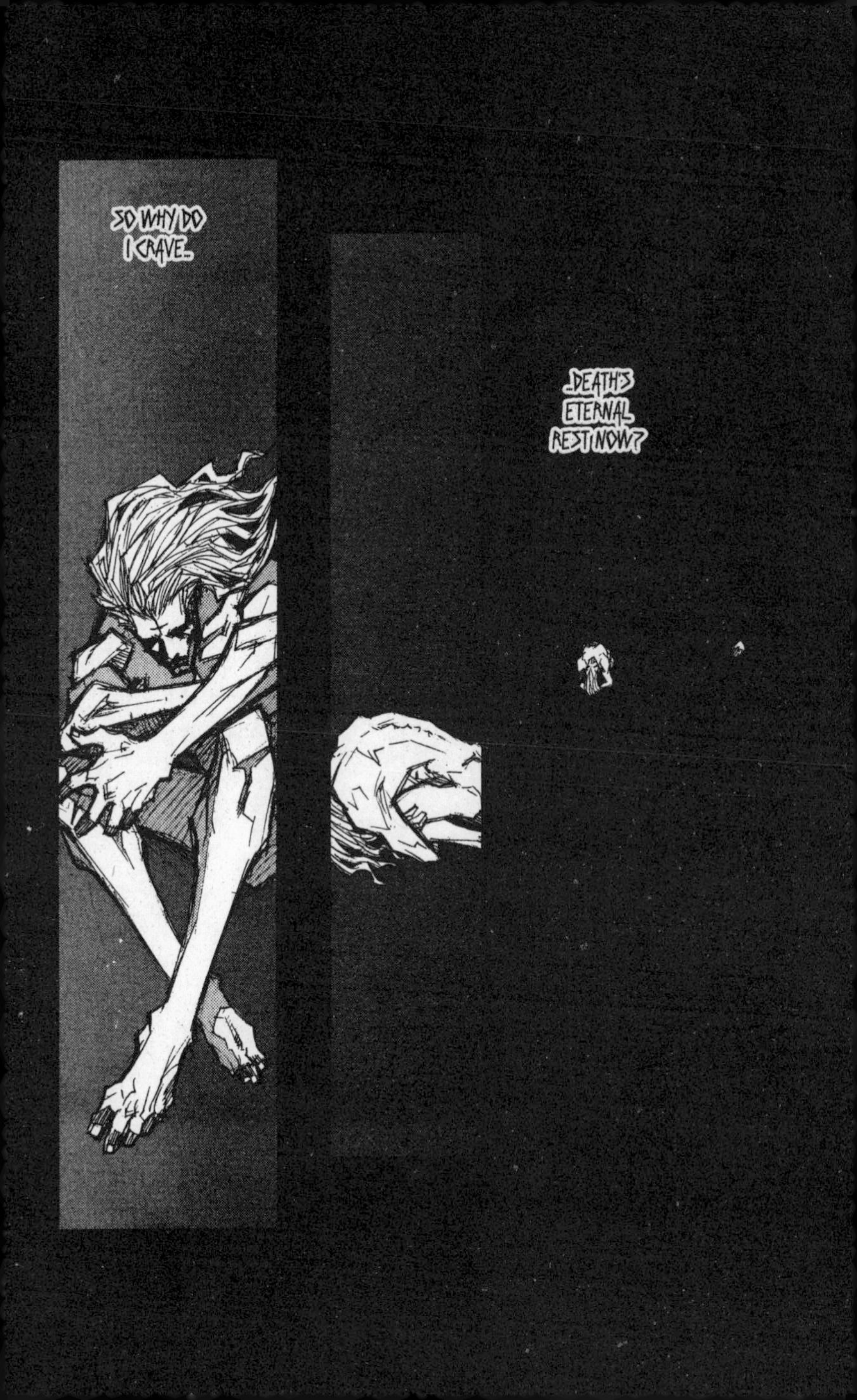
SO WHY DO I CRAVE...
...DEATH'S ETERNAL REST NOW?

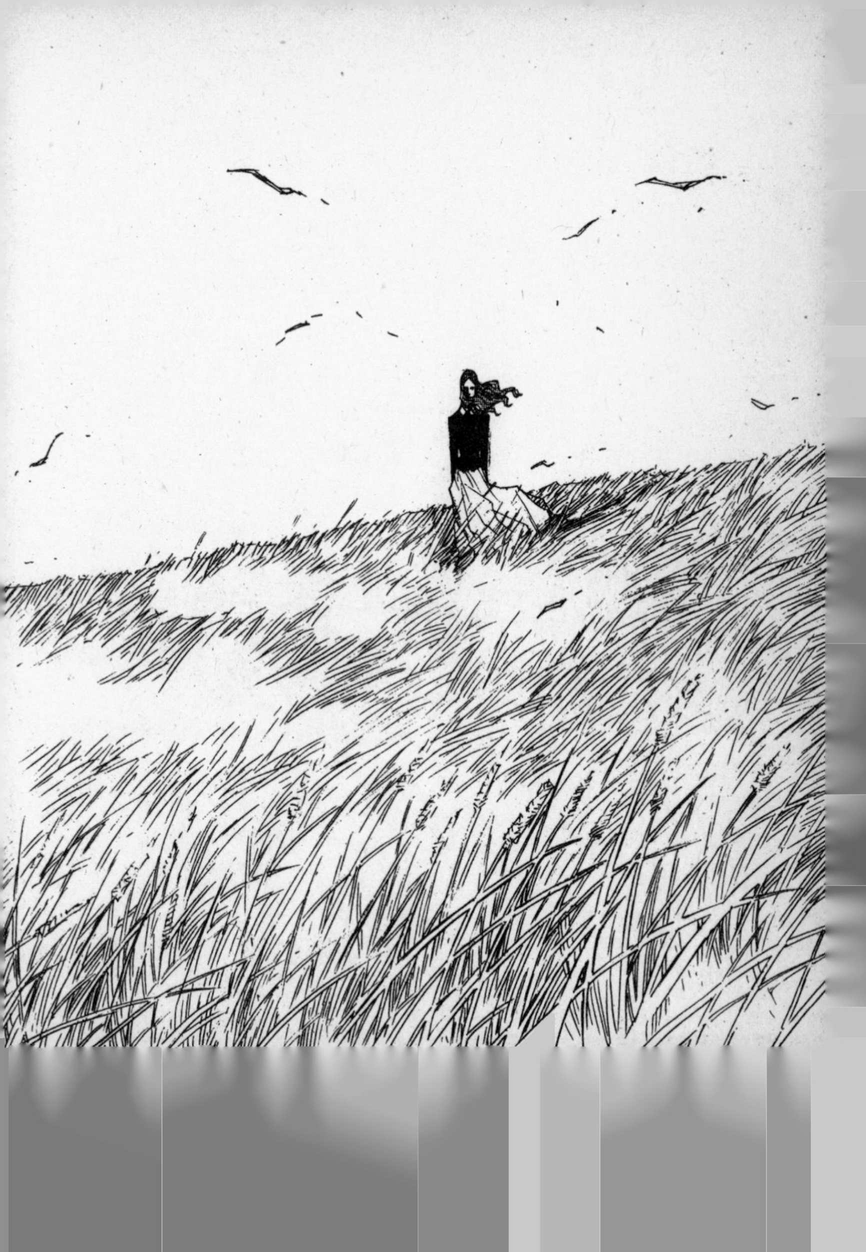

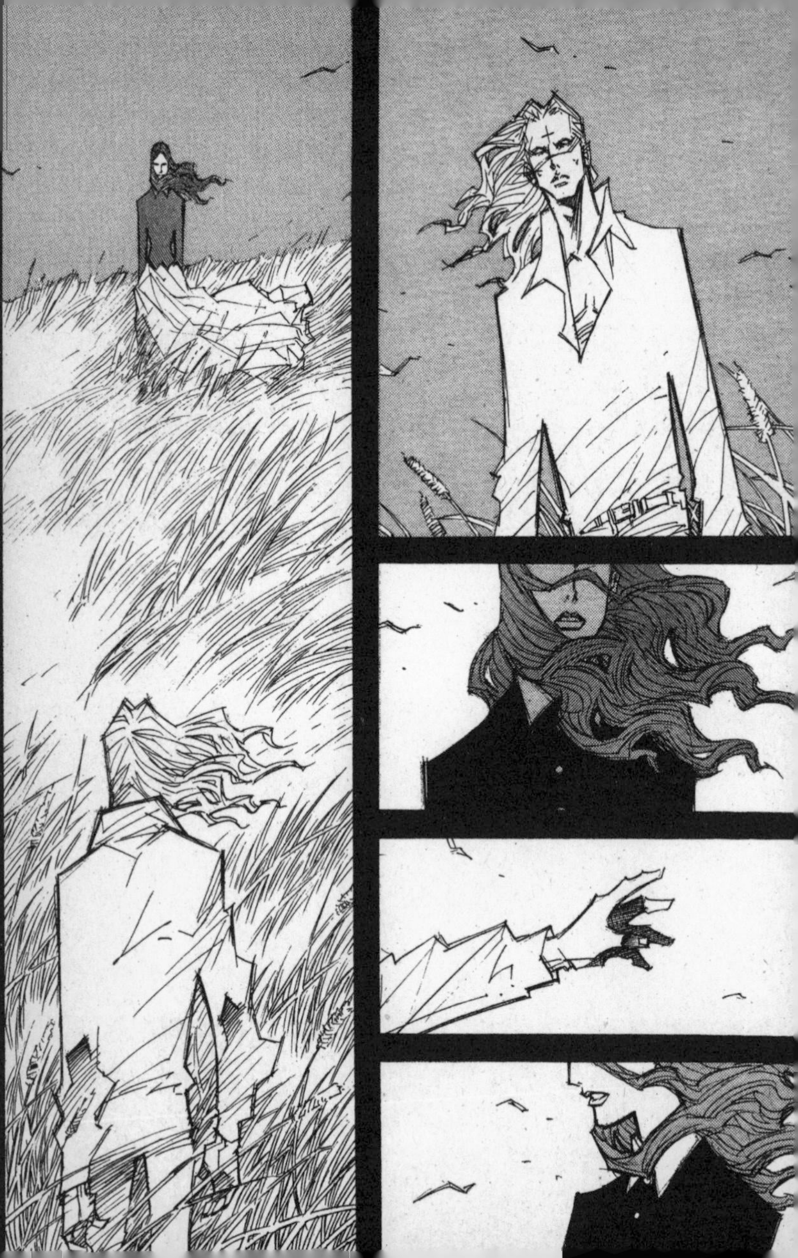

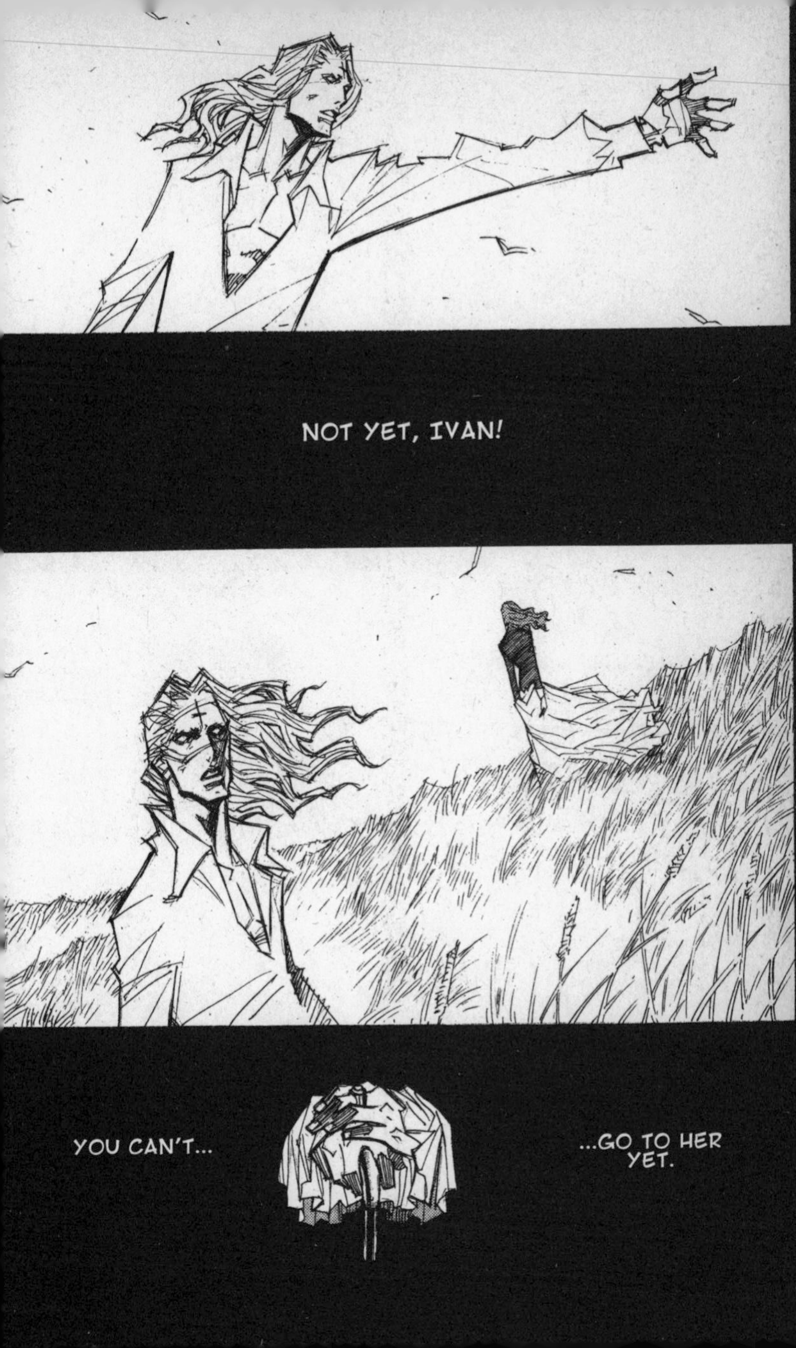
NOT YET, IVAN!
YOU CAN'T...
...GO TO HER YET.

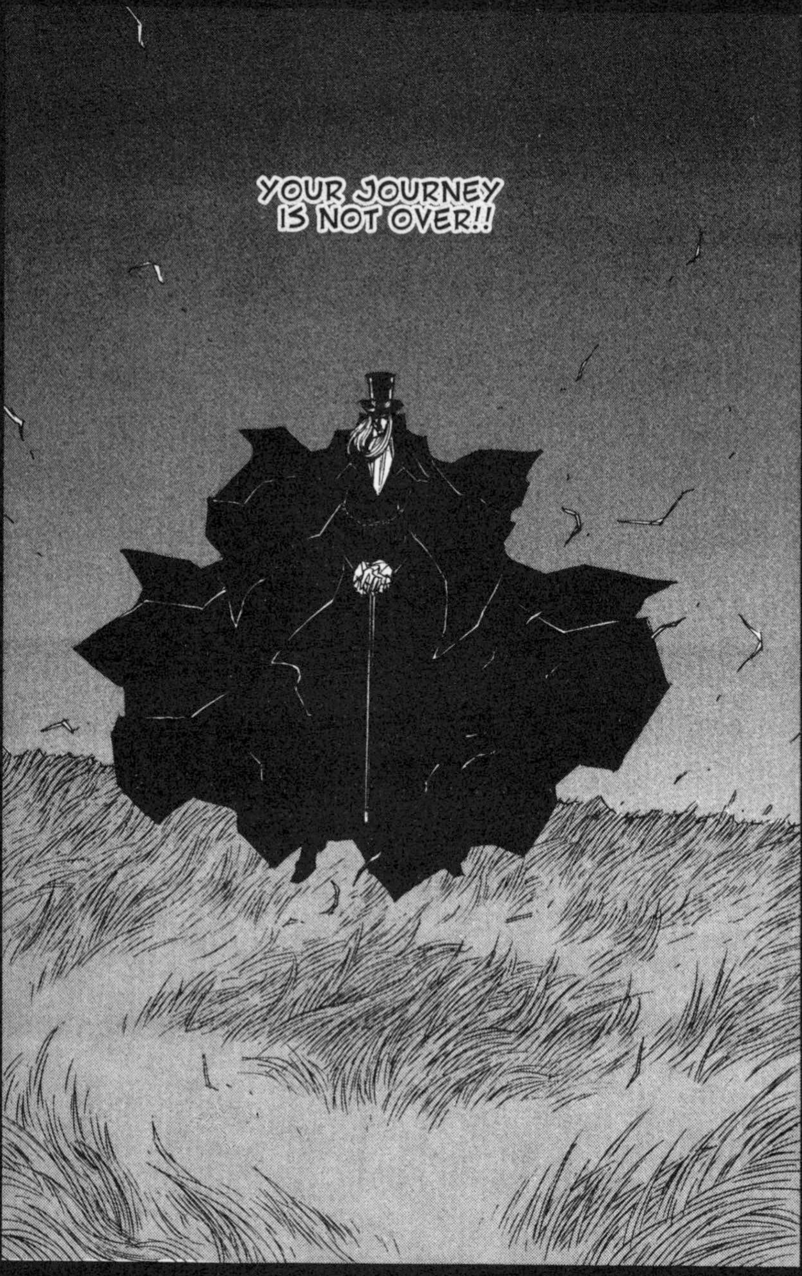
YOUR JOURNEY IS NOT OVER!!

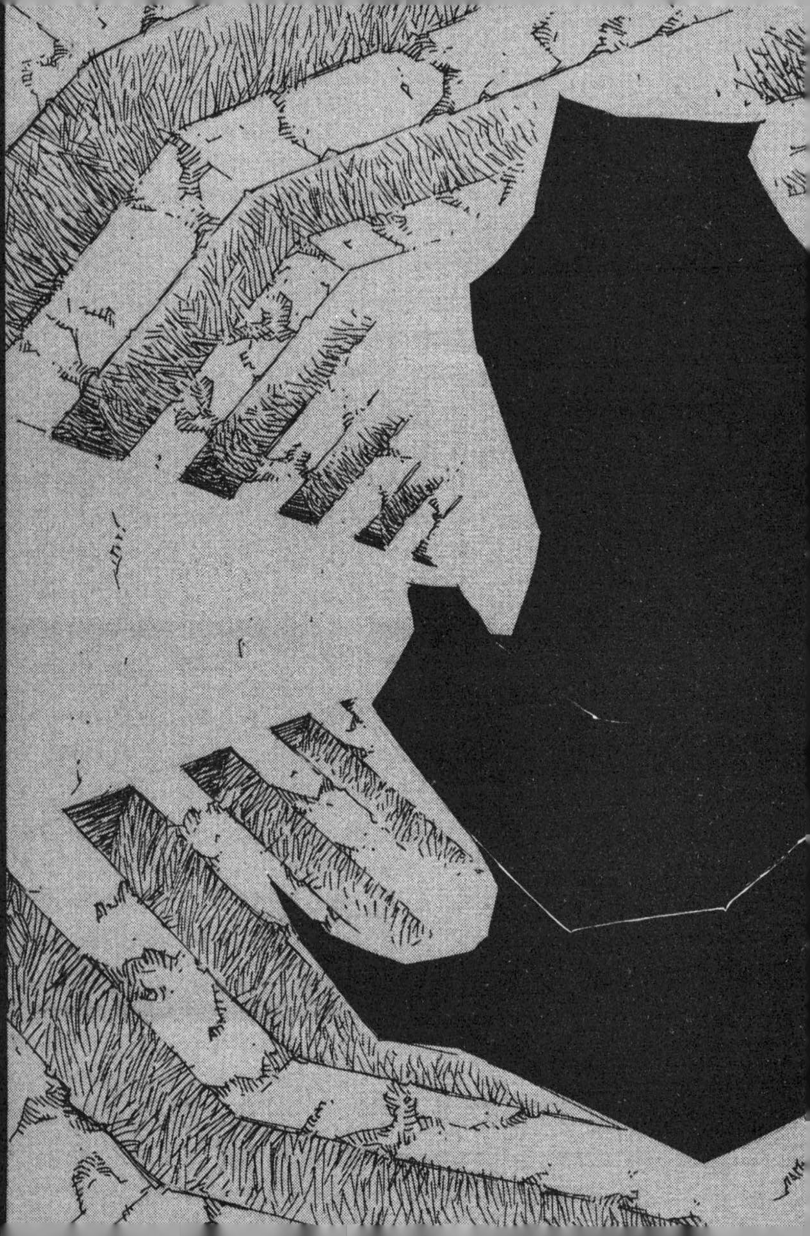

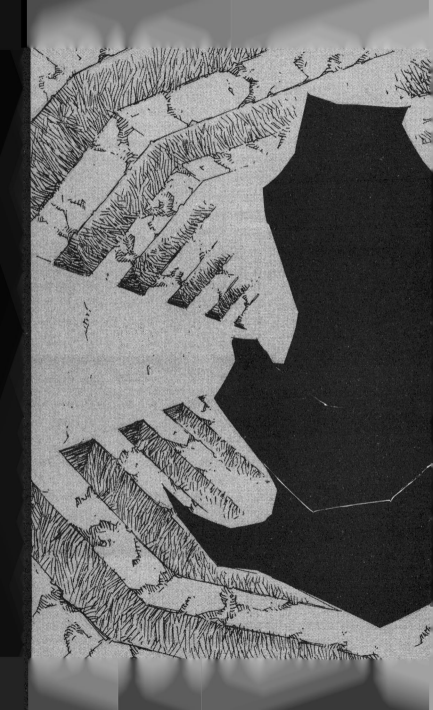

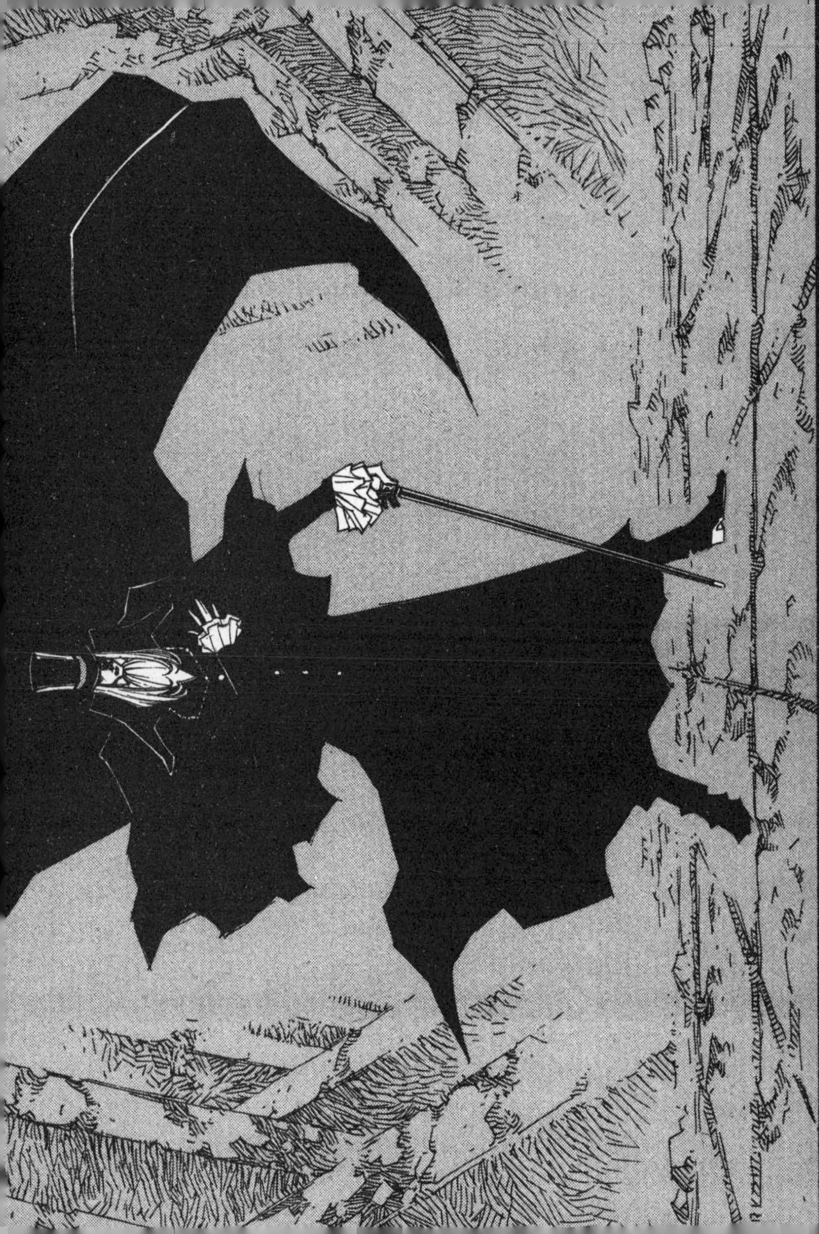

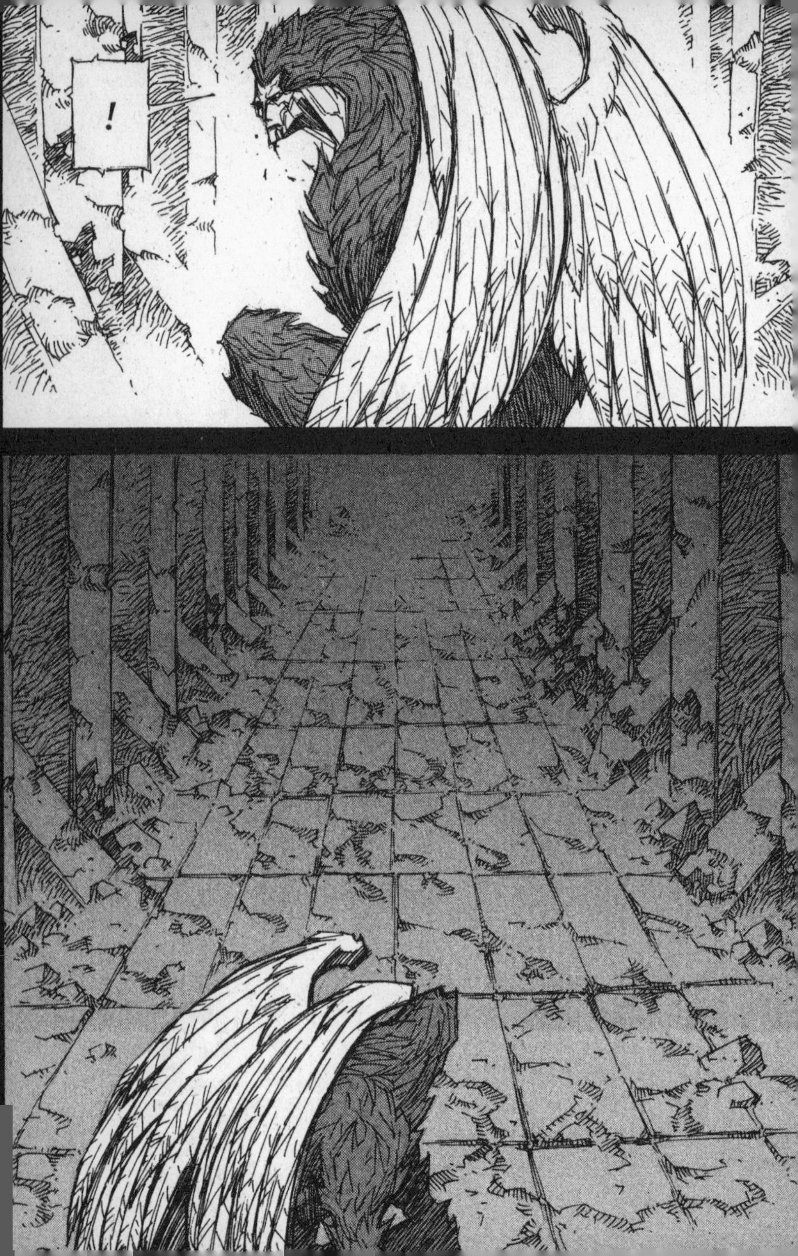
!

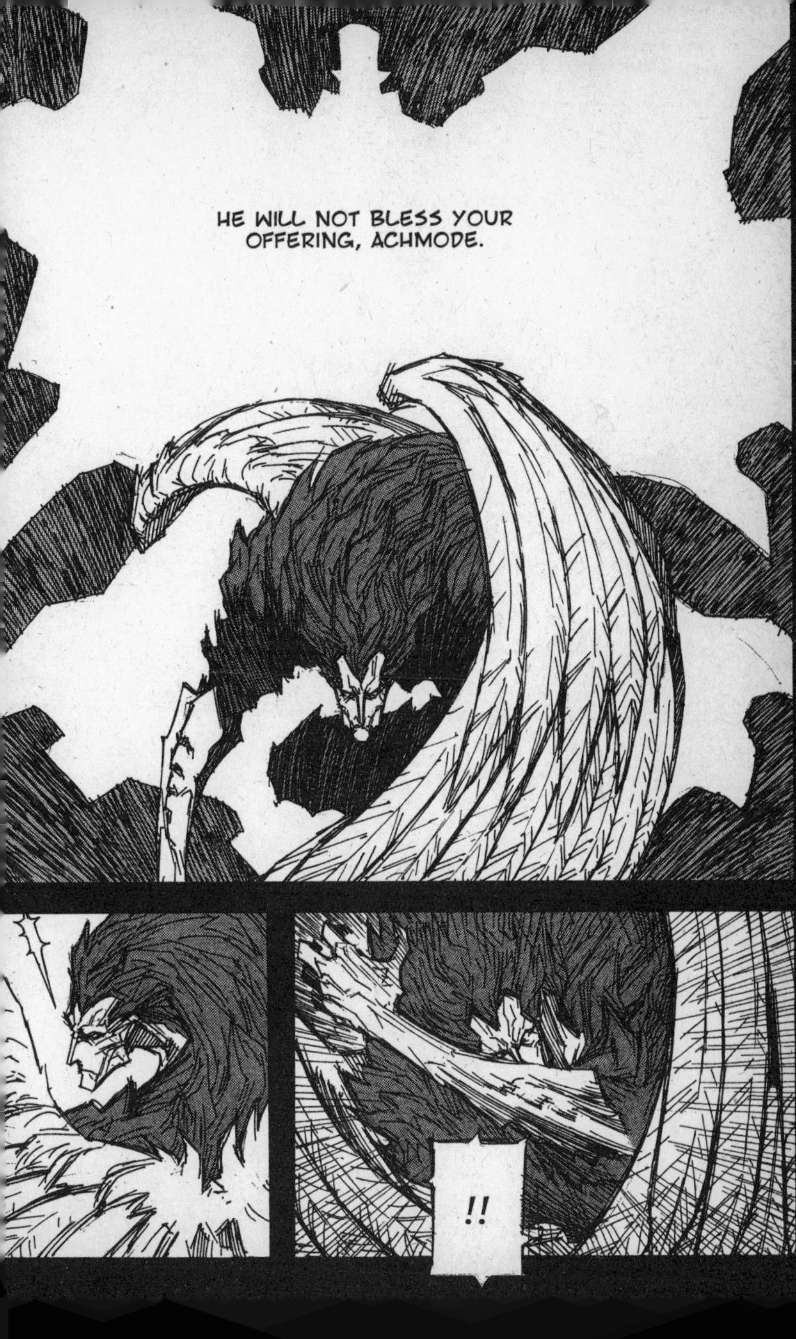
HE WILL NOT BLESS YOUR OFFERING, ACHMODE.
!!

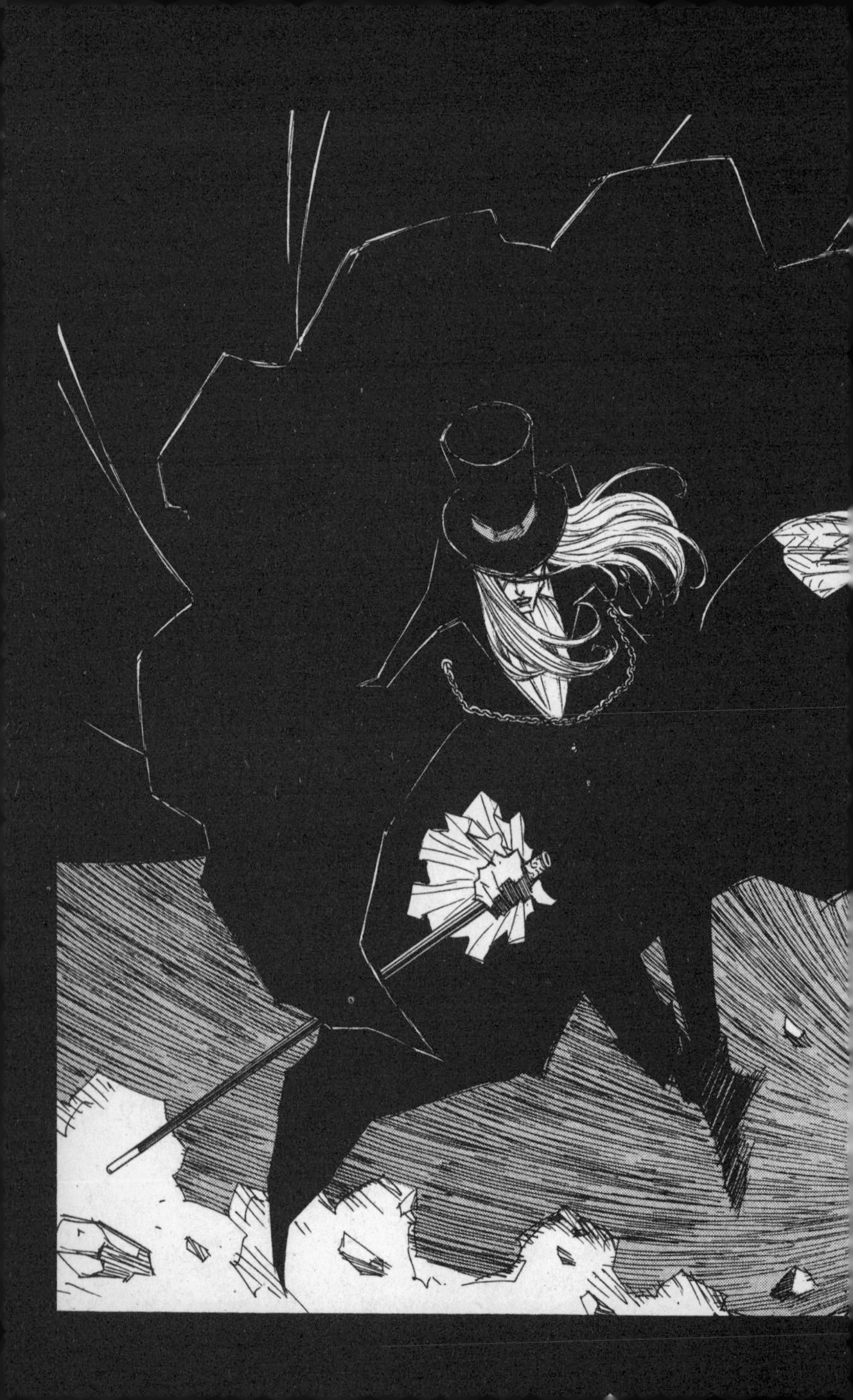

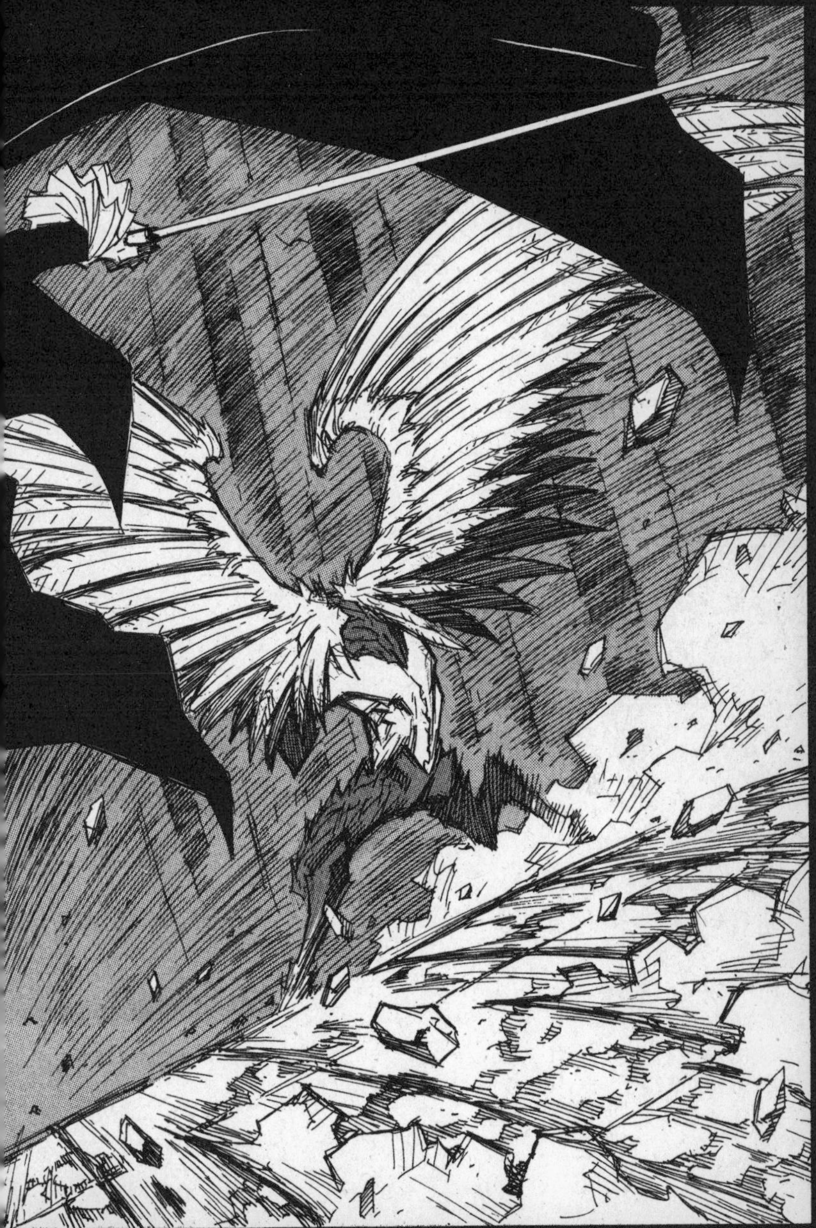

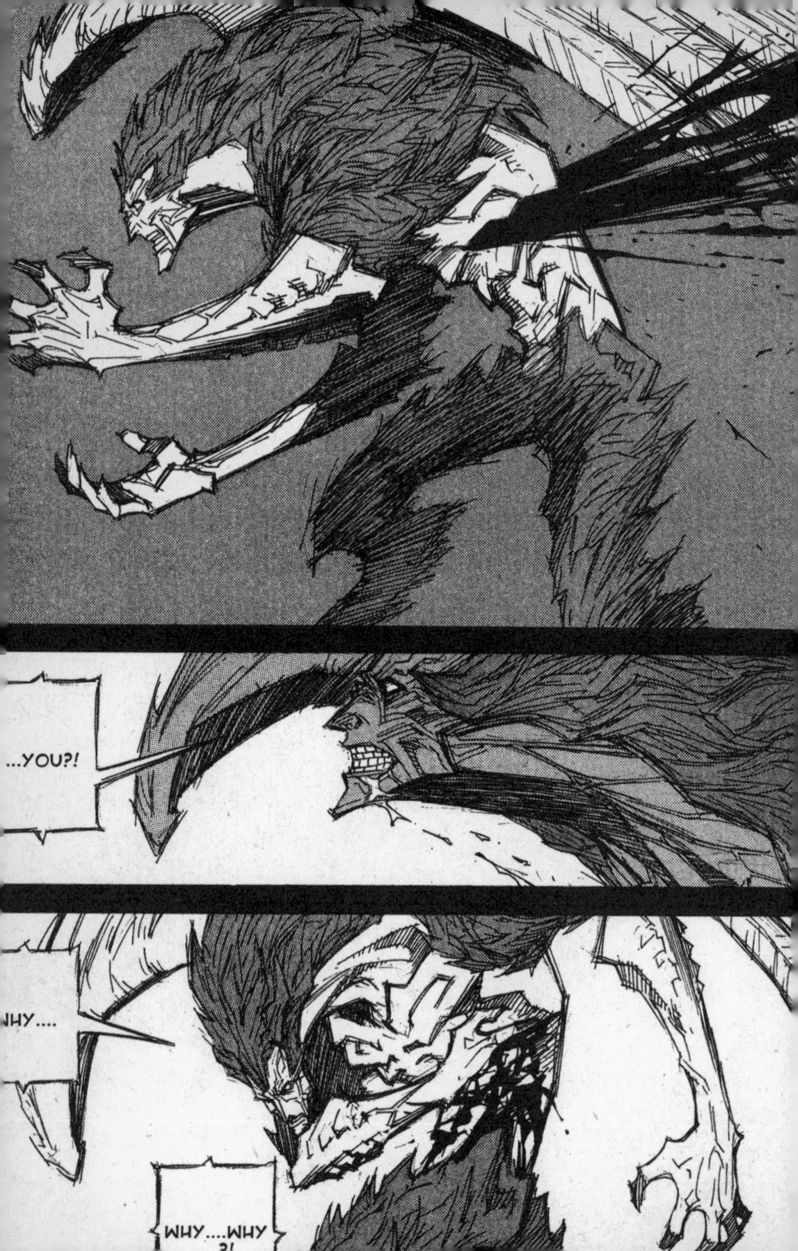
...YOU?!
HY....
WHY....WHY

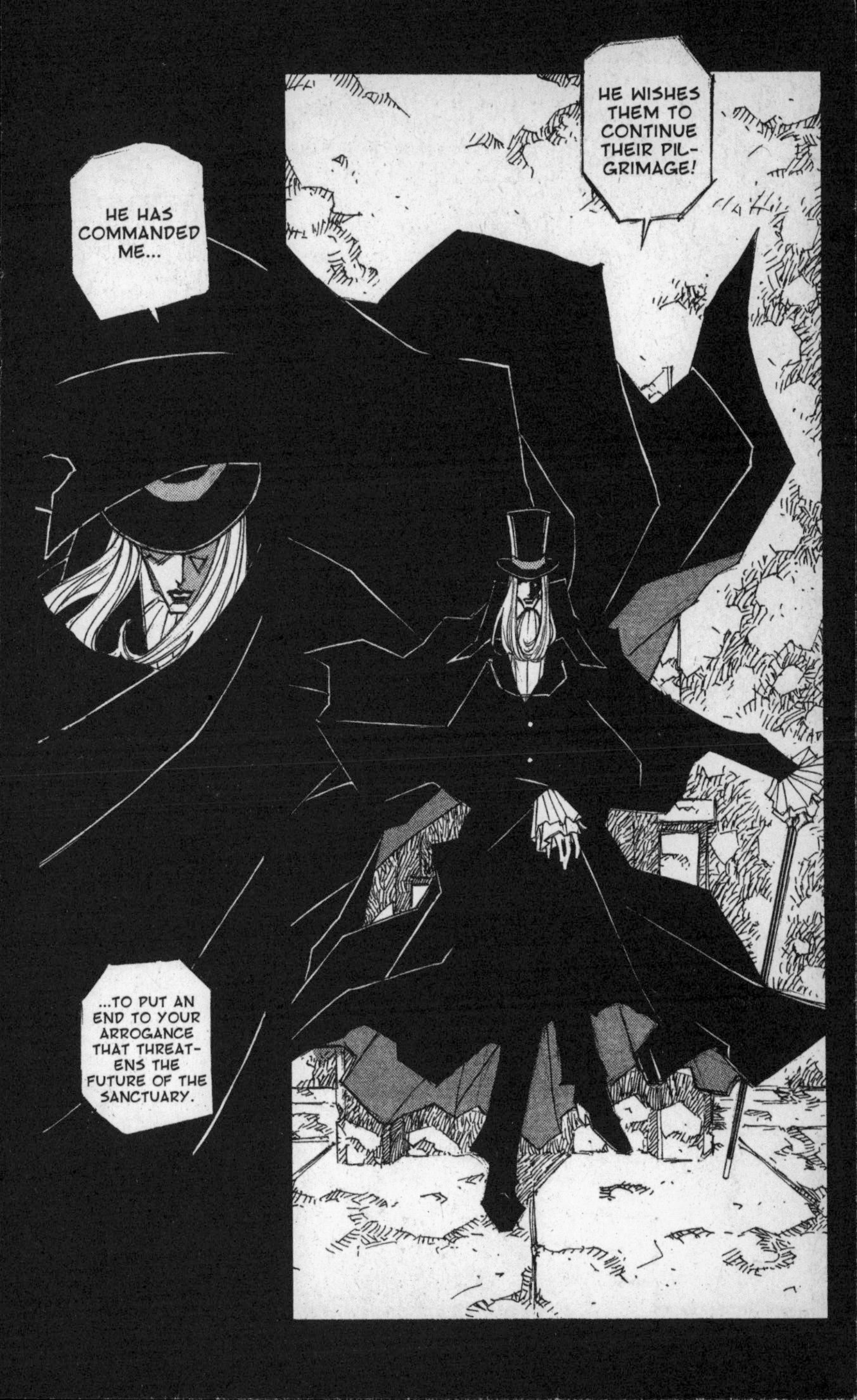
HE WISHES THEM TO CONTINUE THEIR PIL-GRIMAGE!
HE HAS COMMANDED ME...
...TO PUT AN END TO YOUR ARROGANCE THAT THREAT-ENS THE FUTURE OF THE SANCTUARY.

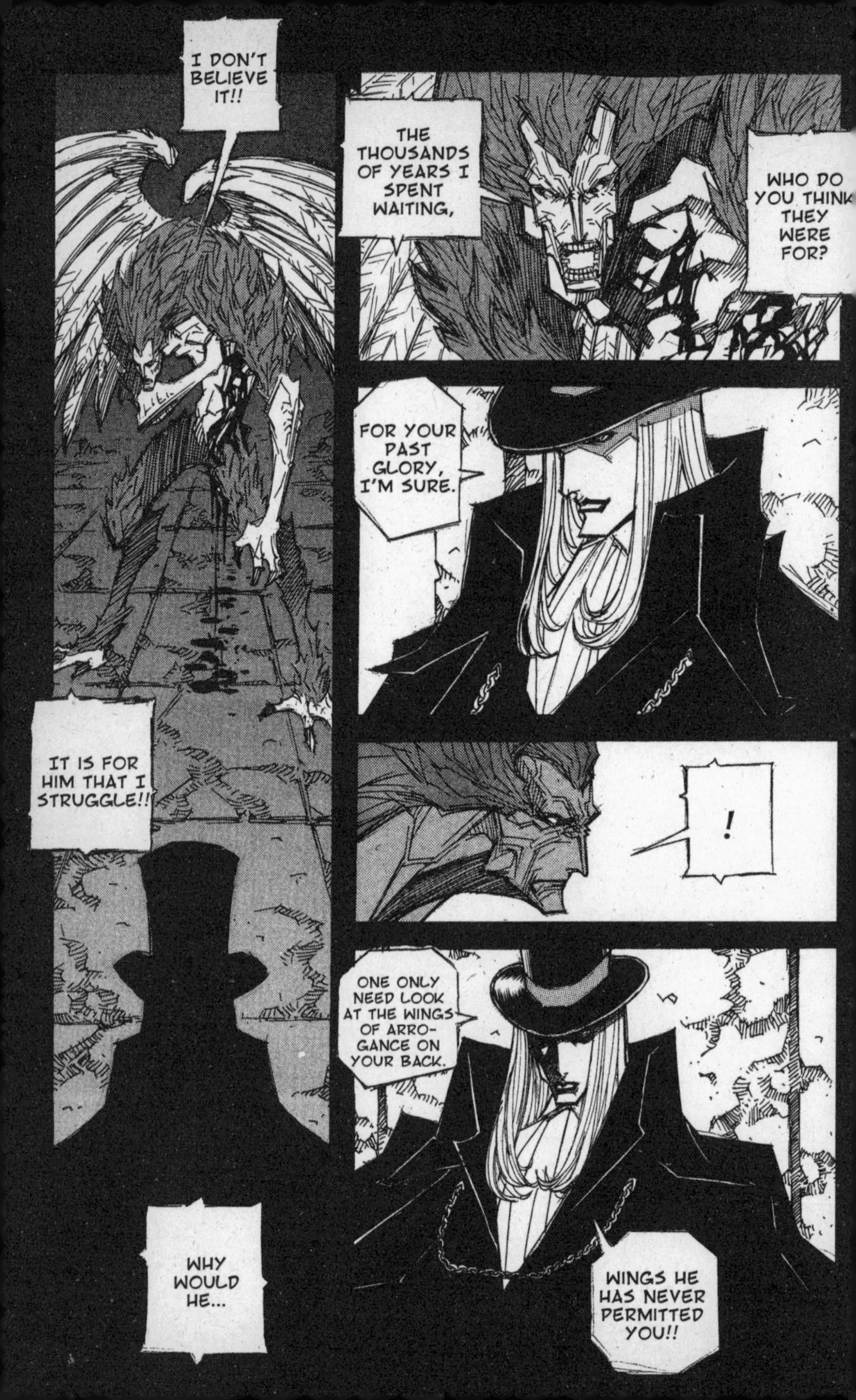
I DON'T BELIEVE IT!!
IT IS FOR HIM THAT I STRUGGLE!!
WHY WOULD HE...
THE THOUSANDS OF YEARS I SPENT WAITING,
WHO DO YOU THINK THEY WERE FOR?
FOR YOUR PAST GLORY, I'M SURE.
!
ONE ONLY NEED LOOK AT THE WINGS OF ARRO-GANCE ON YOUR BACK.
WINGS HE HAS NEVER PERMITTED YOU!!

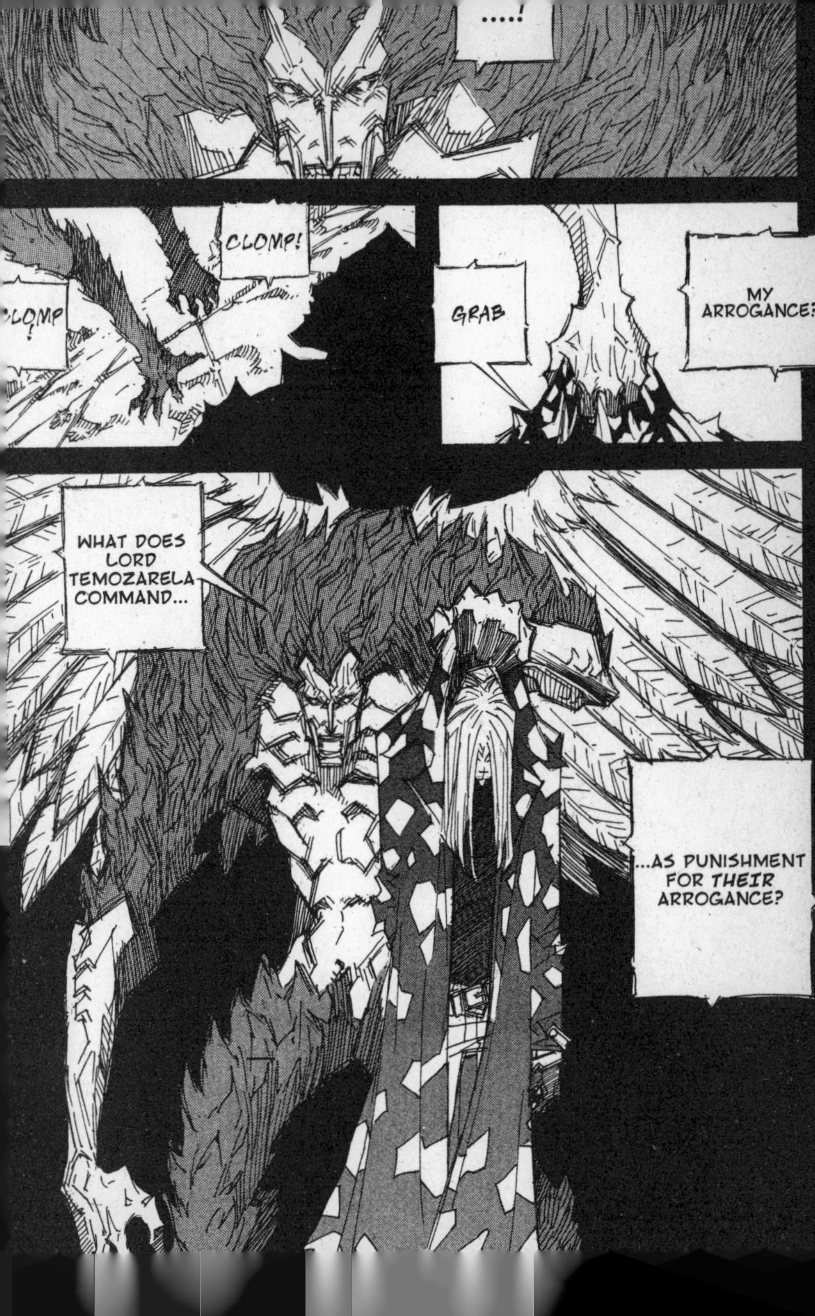
....!
MY ARROGANCE?
GRAB
CLOMP!
CLOMP
WHAT DOES LORD TEMOZARELA COMMAND...
...AS PUNISHMENT FOR THEIR ARROGANCE?

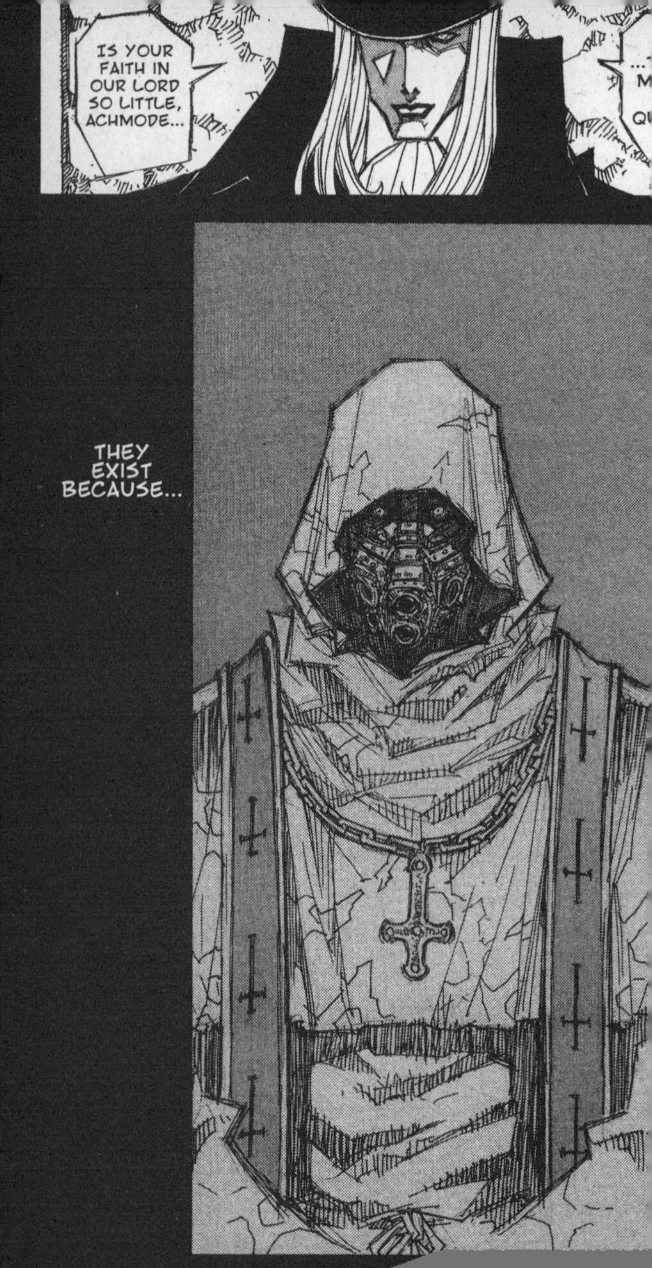
IS YOUR FAITH IN OUR LORD SO LITTLE, ACHMODE...
THEY EXIST BECAUSE...

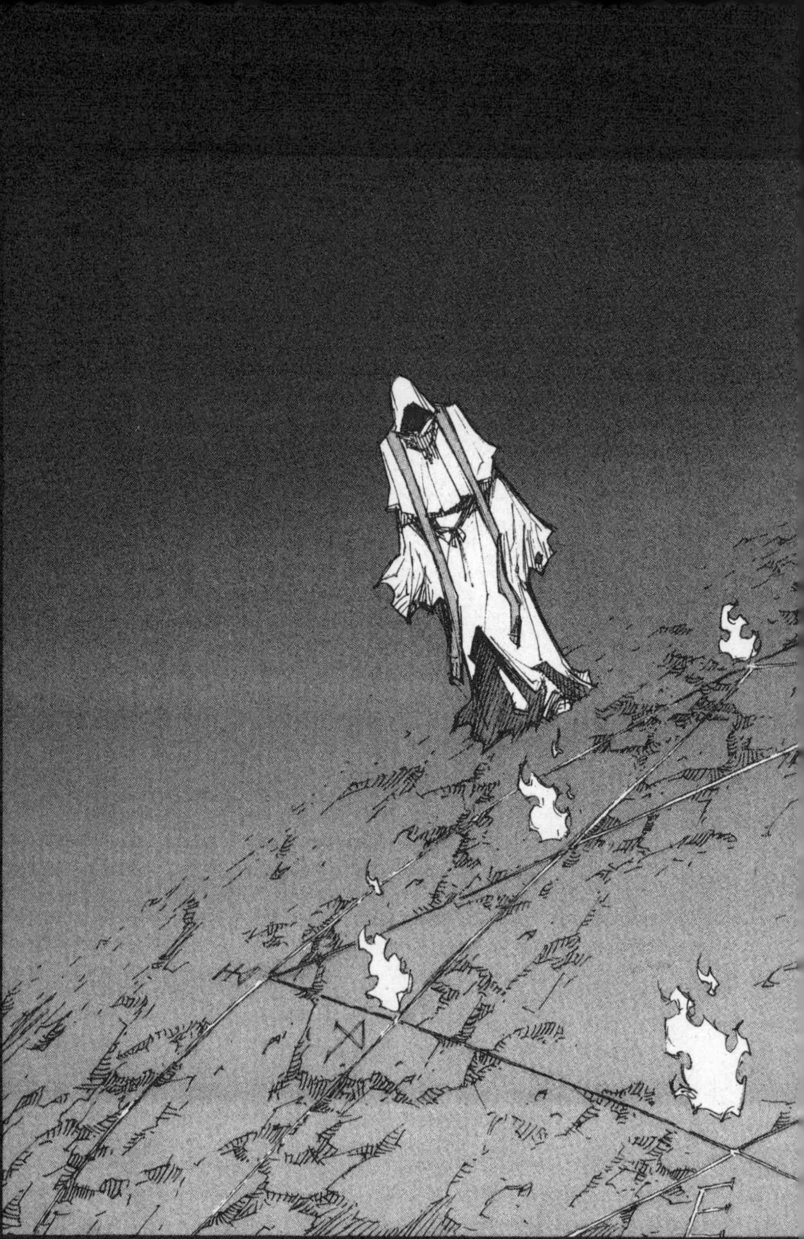

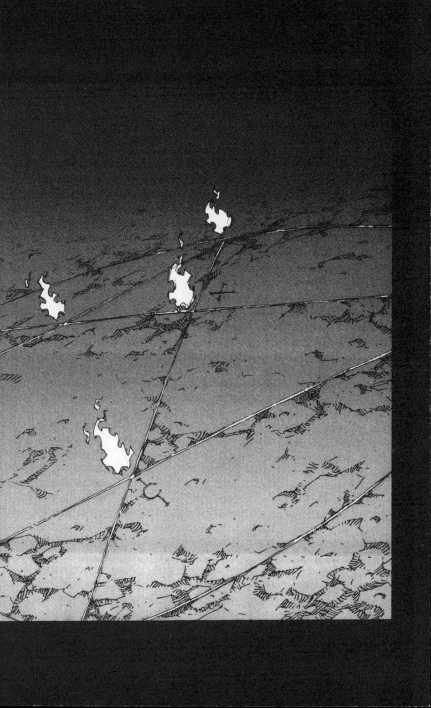

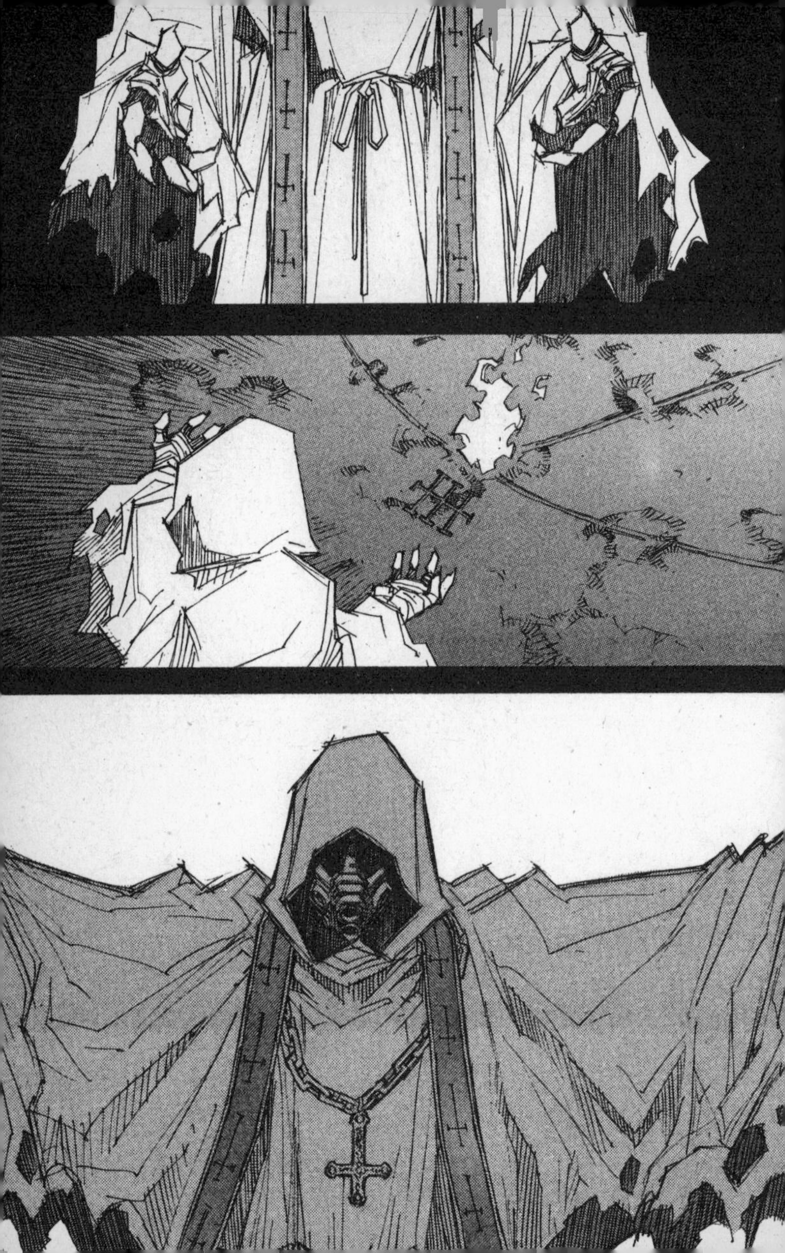

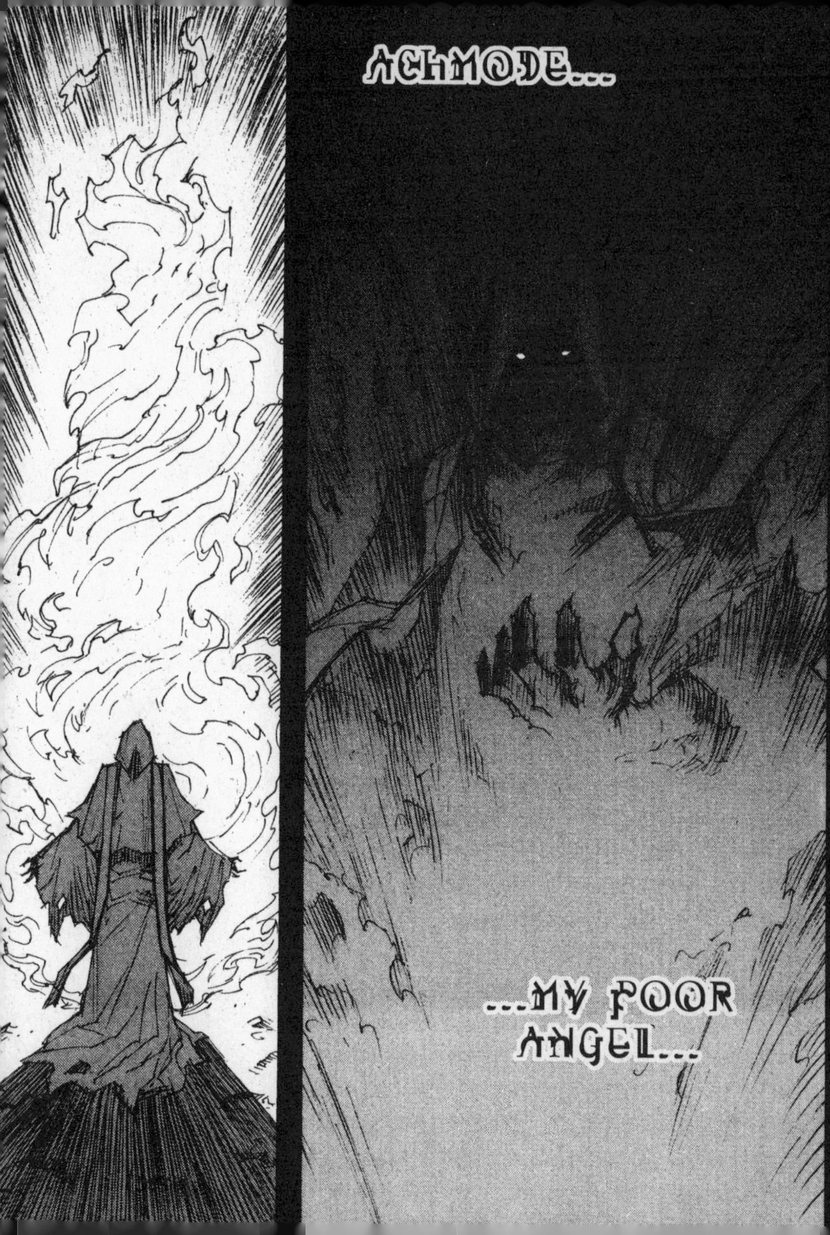
ACHMODE...
...MY POOR ANGEL...

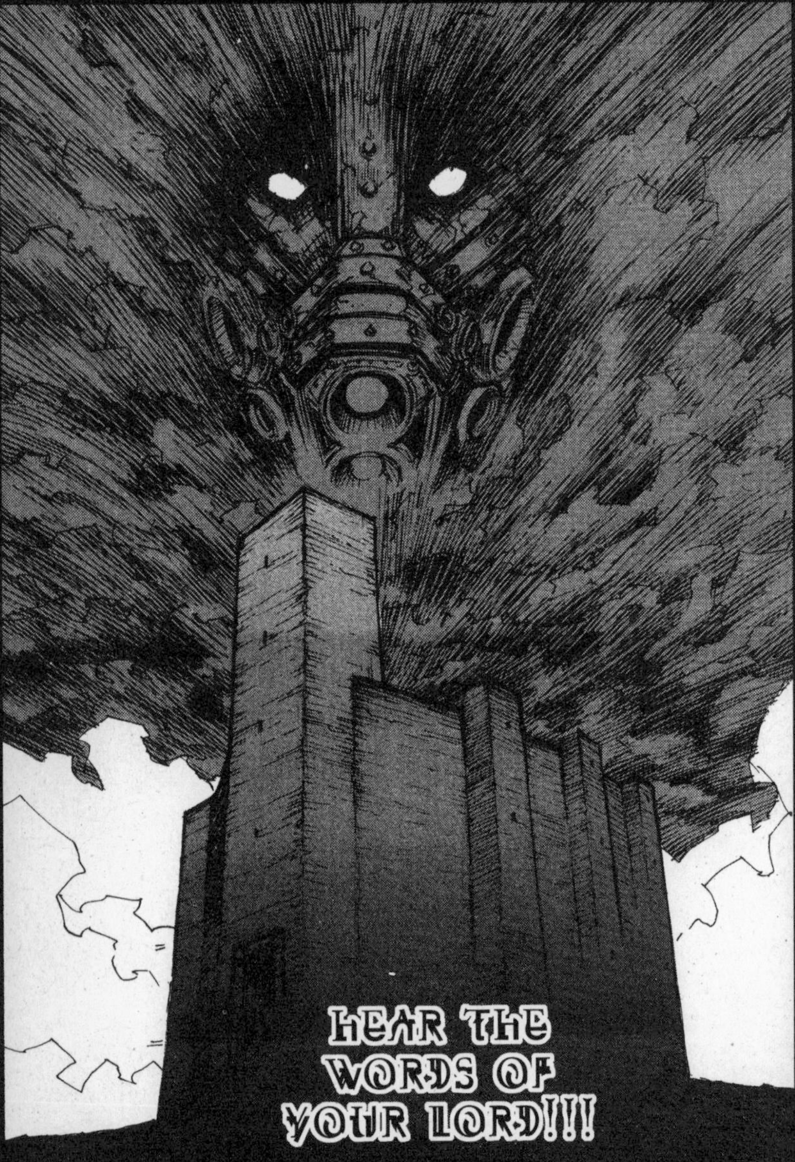
HEAR THE WORDS OF YOUR LORD!!!

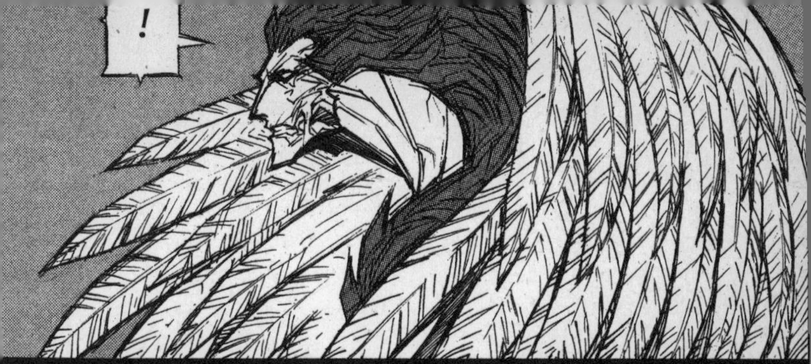
!
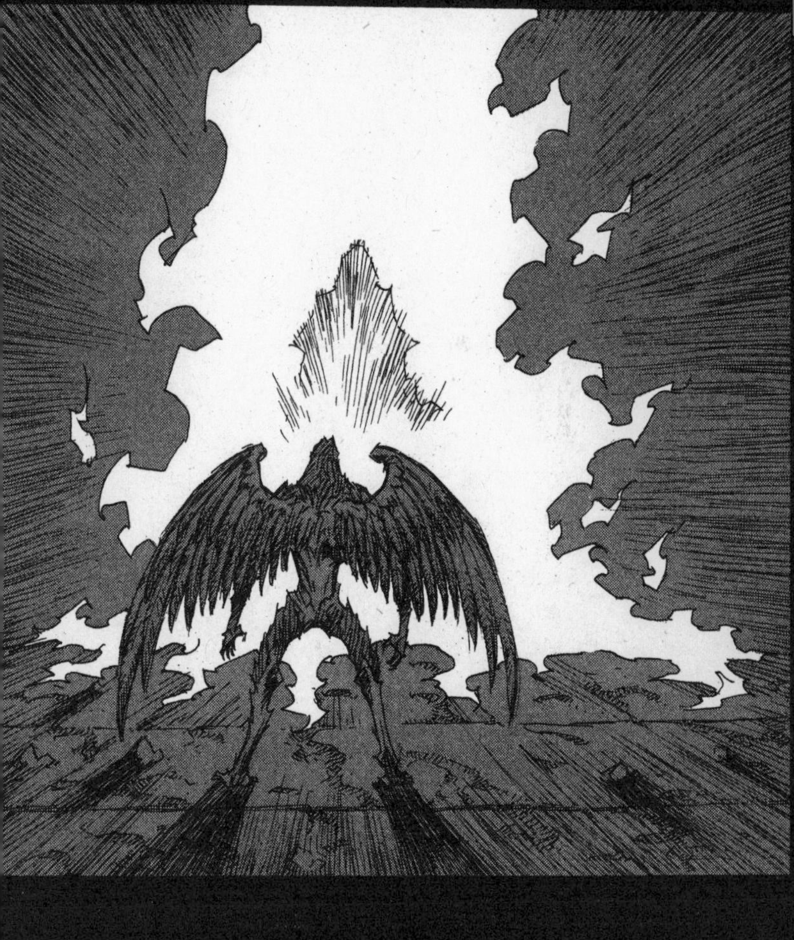

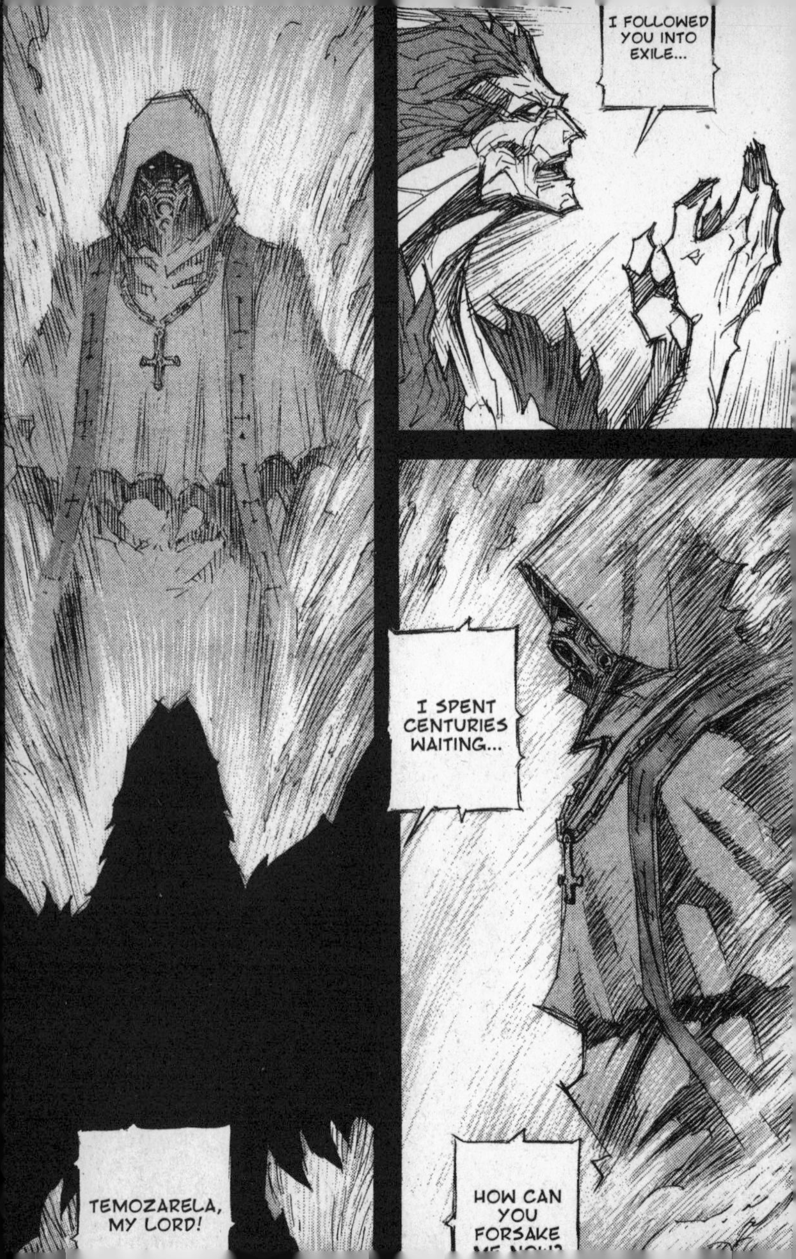
TEMOZARELA, MY LORD!
I FOLLOWED YOU INTO EXILE...
I SPENT CENTURIES WAITING...
HOW CAN YOU FORSAKE

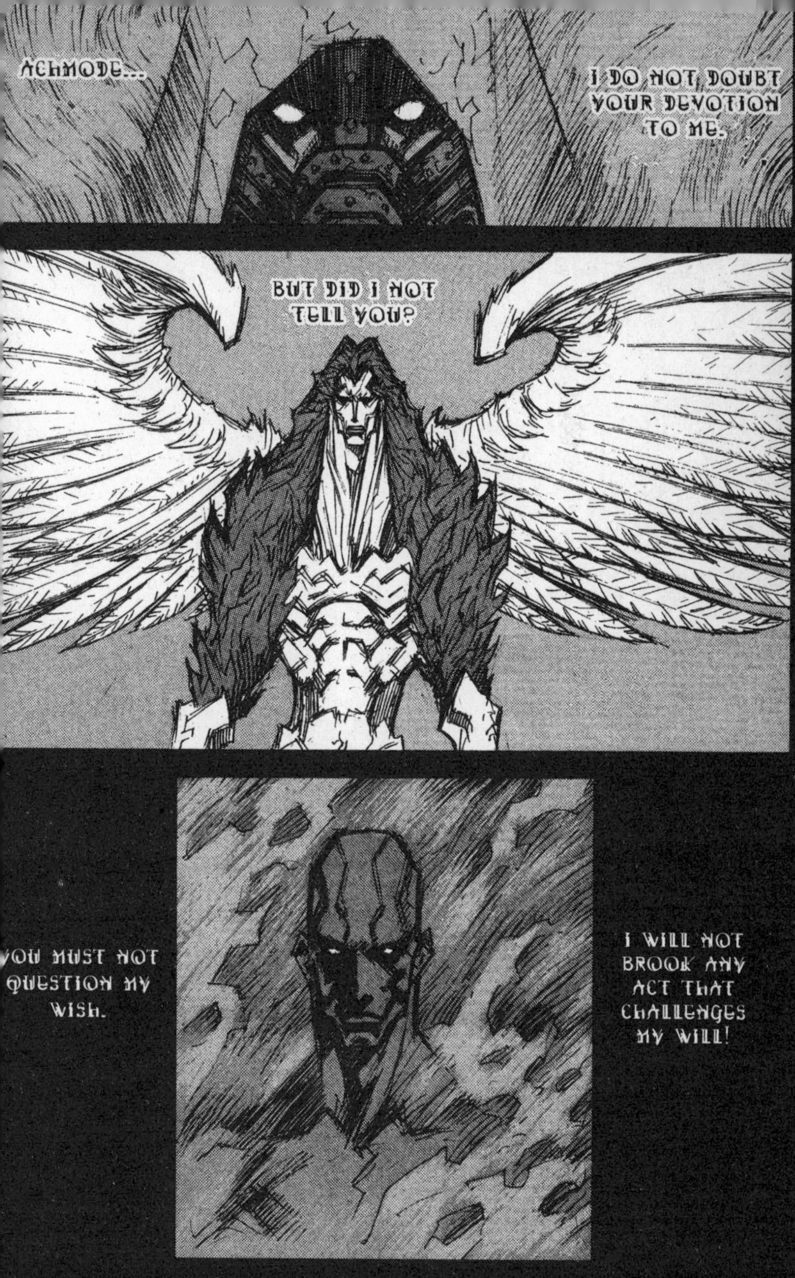
ACHMODE...
I DO NOT DOUBT YOUR DEVOTION TO ME.
BUT DID I NOT TELL YOU?
YOU MUST NOT QUESTION MY WISH.
I WILL NOT BROOK ANY ACT THAT CHALLENGES MY WILL!

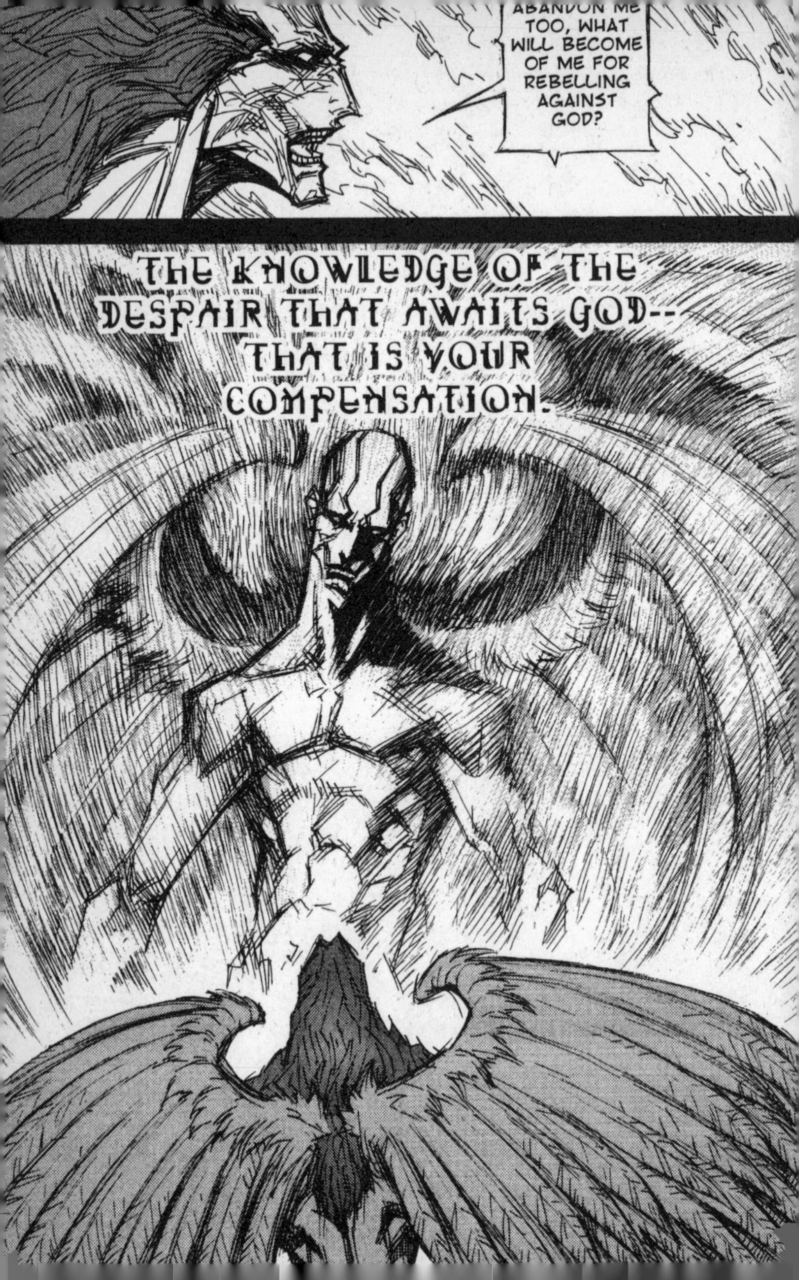
ABANDON ME TOO, WHAT WILL BECOME OF ME FOR REBELLING AGAINST GOD?
THE KNOWLEDGE OF THE DESPAIR THAT AWAITS GOD-- THAT IS YOUR COMPENSATION.

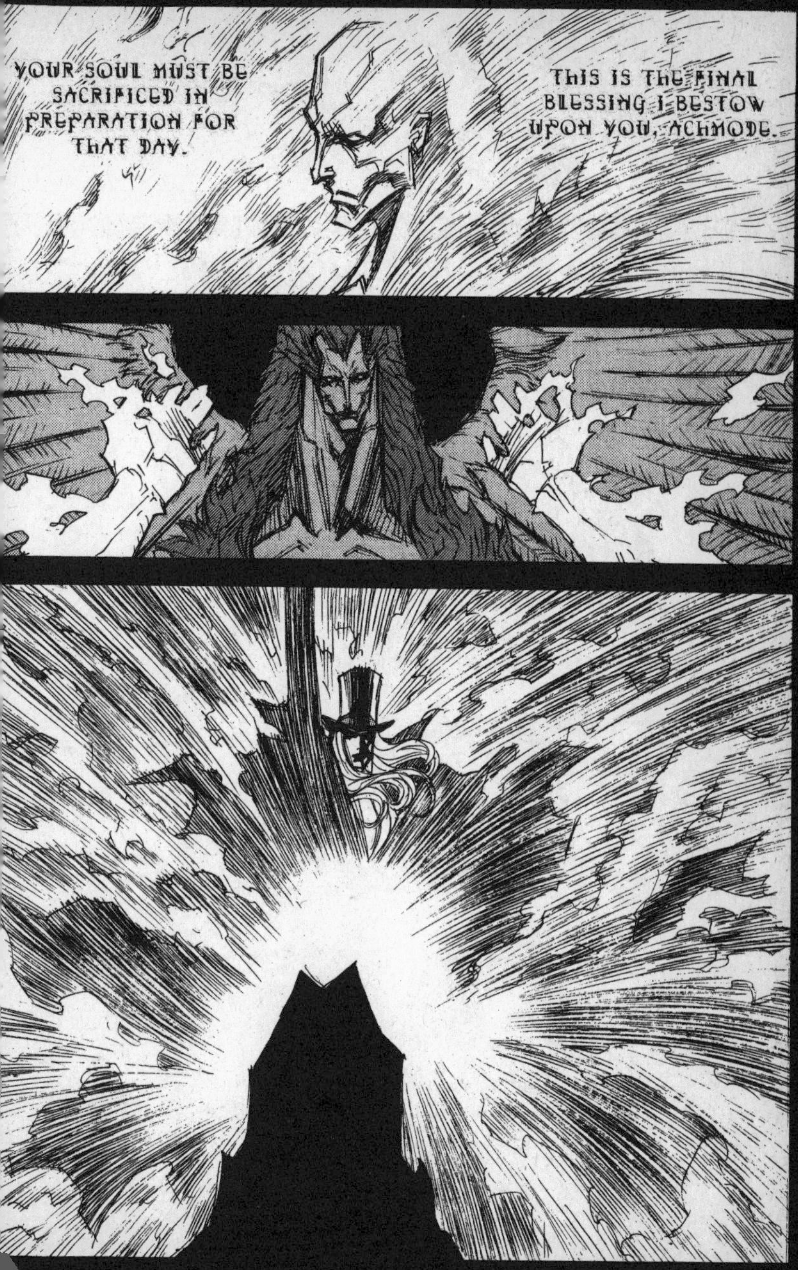
THIS IS THE FINAL BLESSING I BESTOW UPON YOU, ACHMODE.
YOUR SOUL MUST BE SACRIFICED IN PREPARATION FOR THAT DAY.

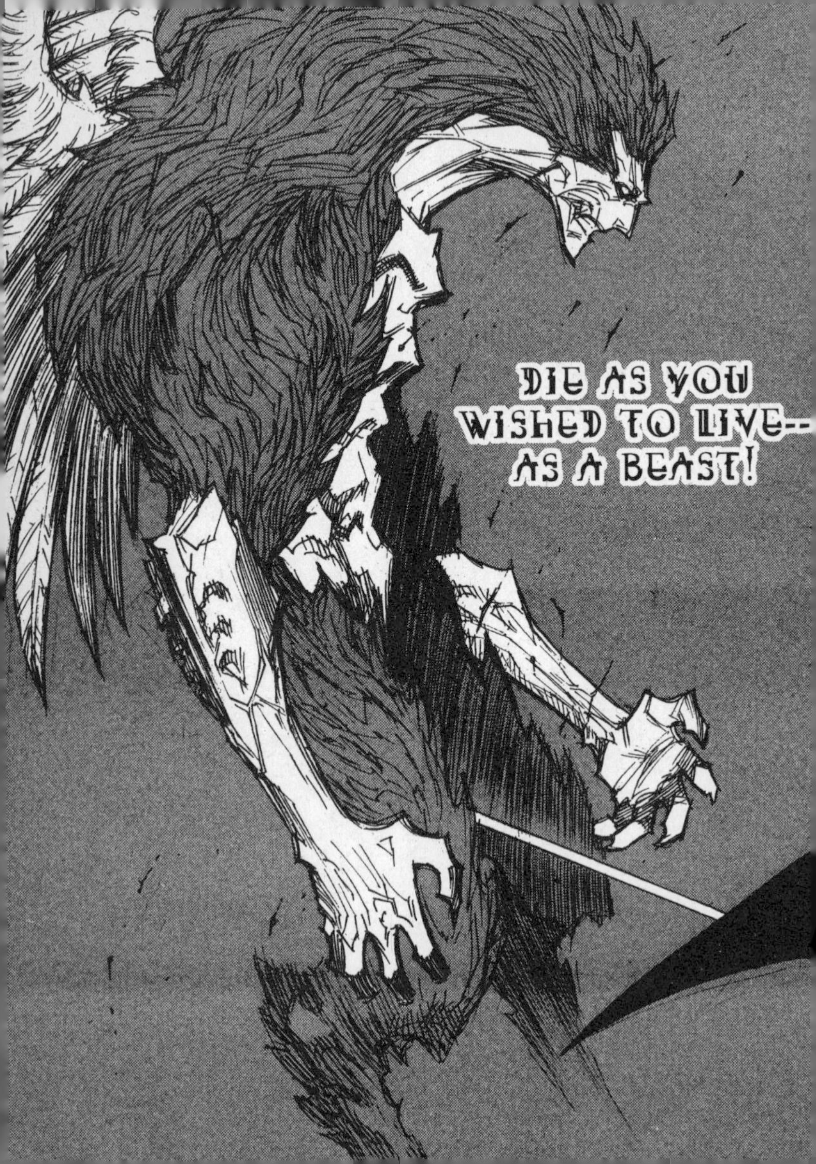
DIE AS YOU WISHED TO LIVE--AS A BEAST!

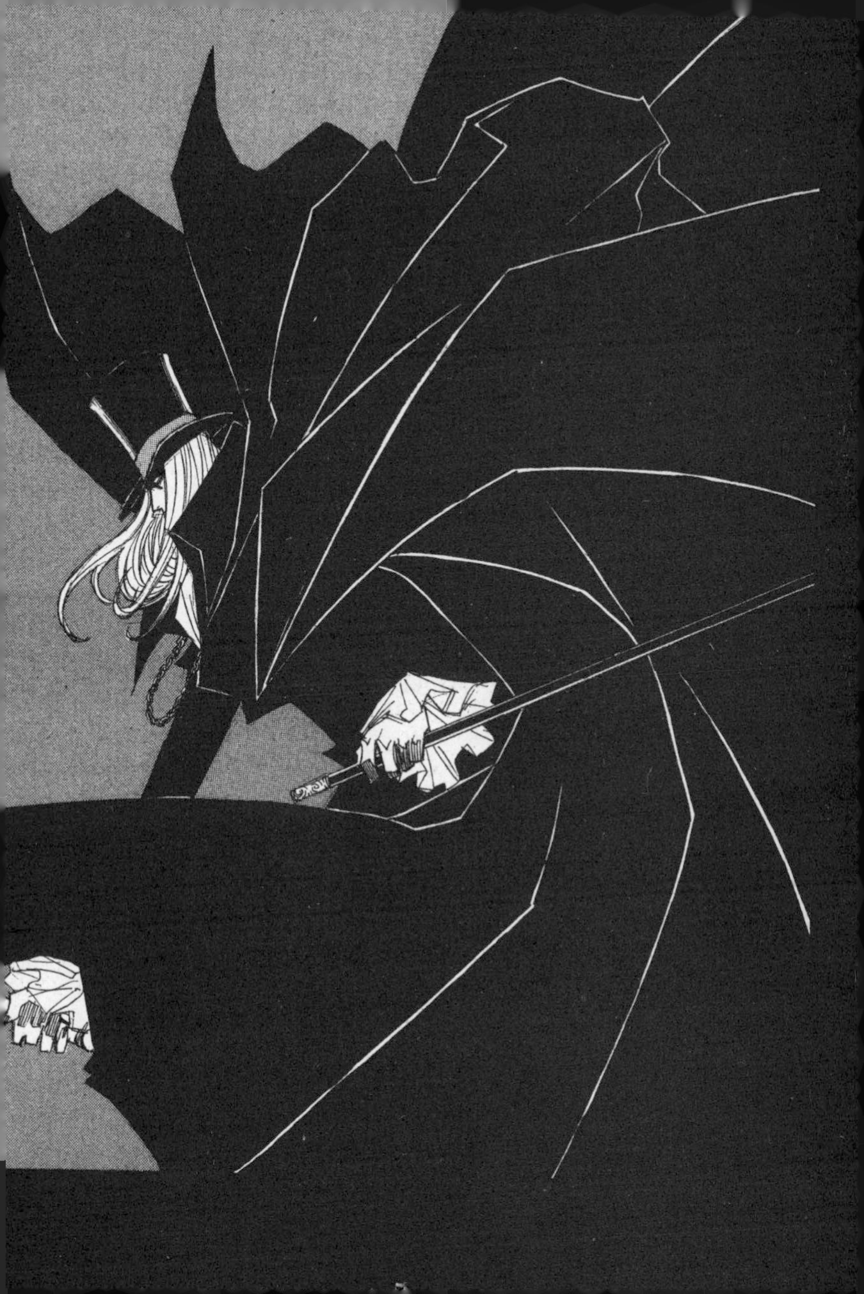

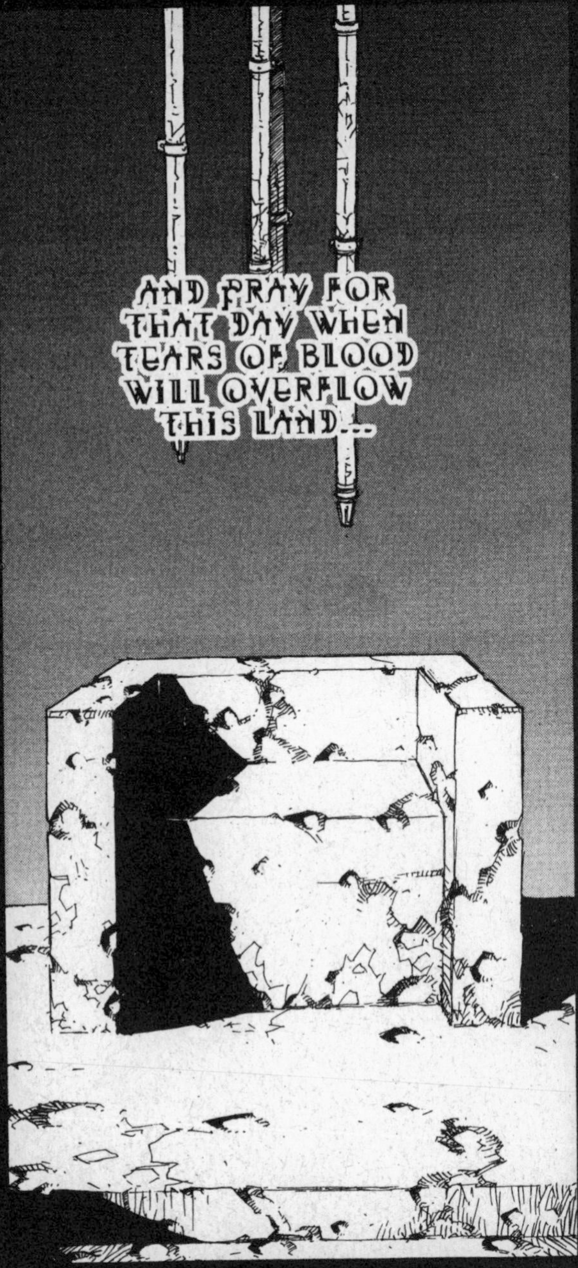
AND PRAY FOR THAT DAY WHEN TEARS OF BLOOD WILL OVERFLOW THIS LAND...

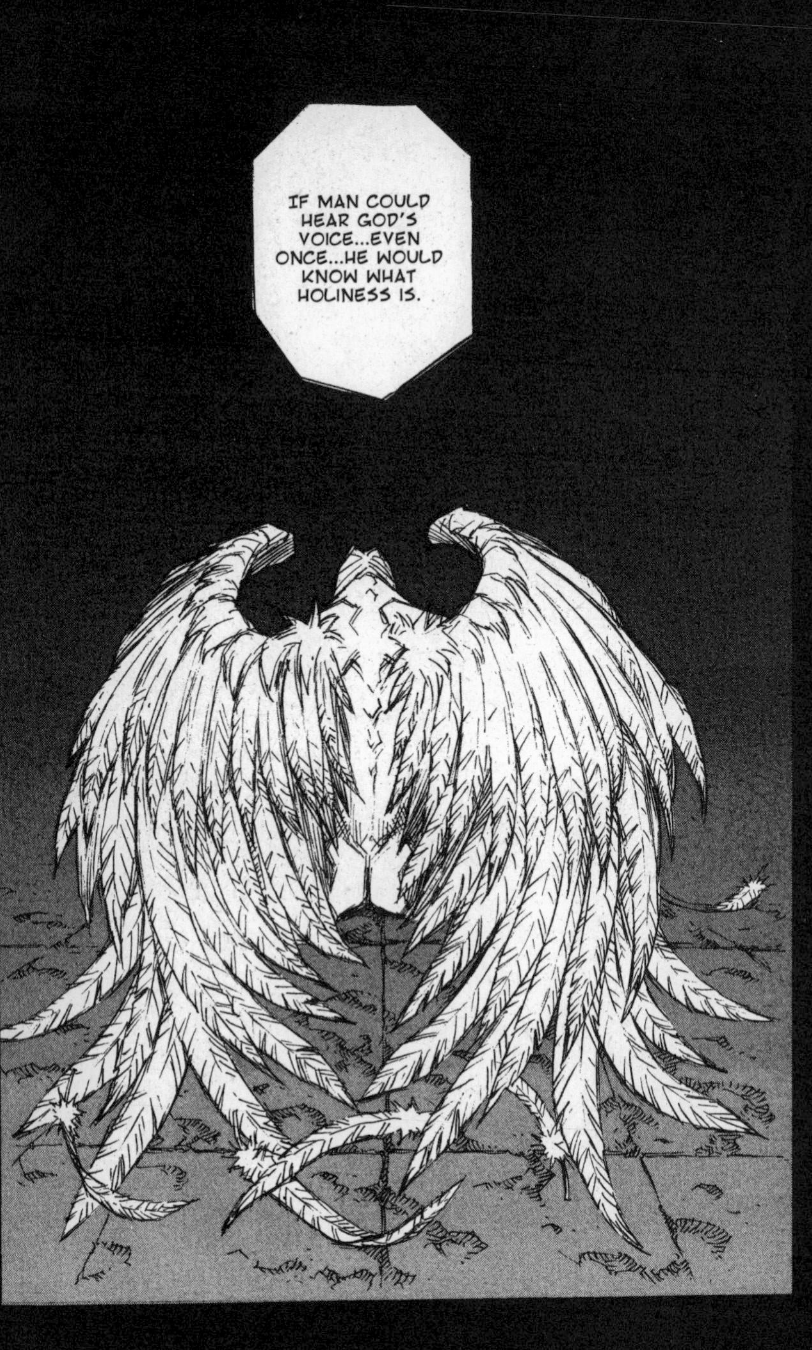
IF MAN COULD HEAR GOD'S VOICE...EVEN ONCE...HE WOULD KNOW WHAT HOLINESS IS.

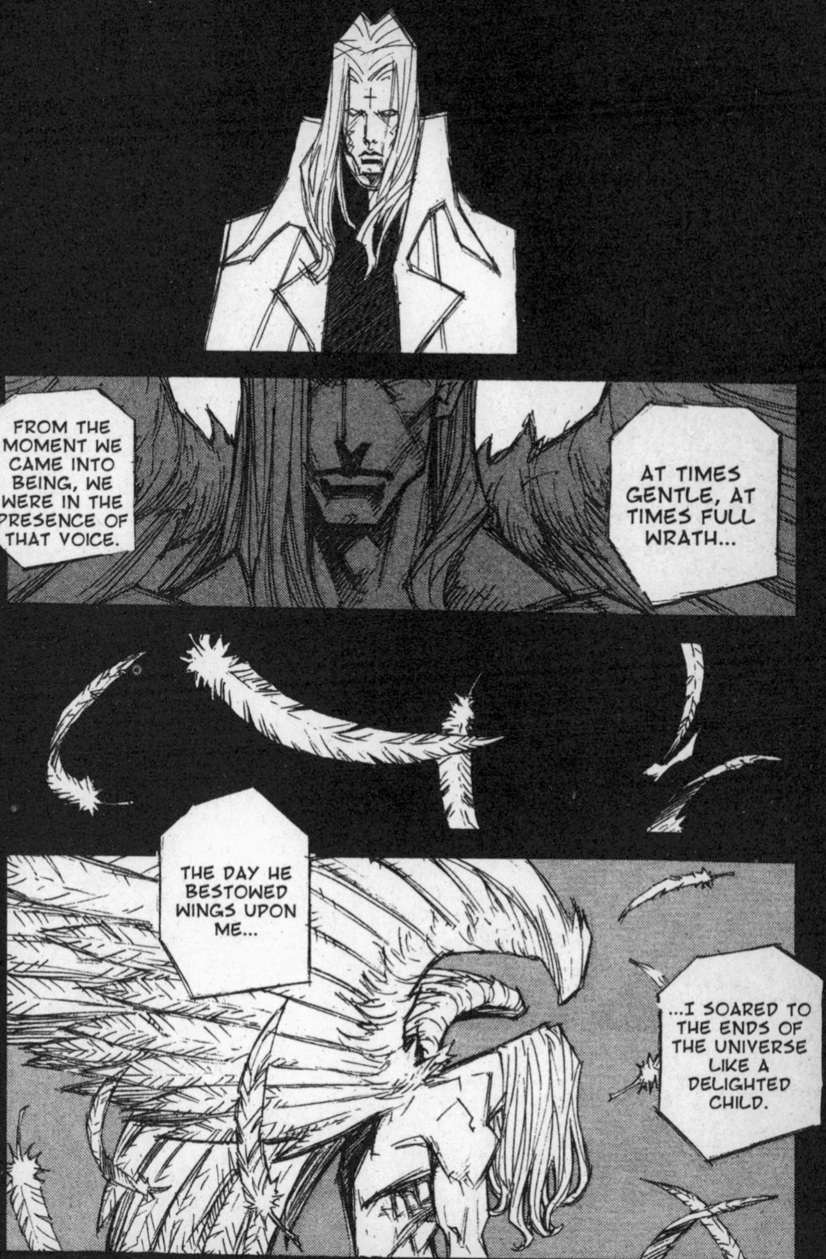
FROM THE MOMENT WE CAME INTO BEING, WE WERE IN THE PRESENCE OF THAT VOICE.
AT TIMES GENTLE, AT TIMES FULL WRATH...
THE DAY HE BESTOWED WINGS UPON ME...
...I SOARED TO THE ENDS OF THE UNIVERSE LIKE A DELIGHTED CHILD.

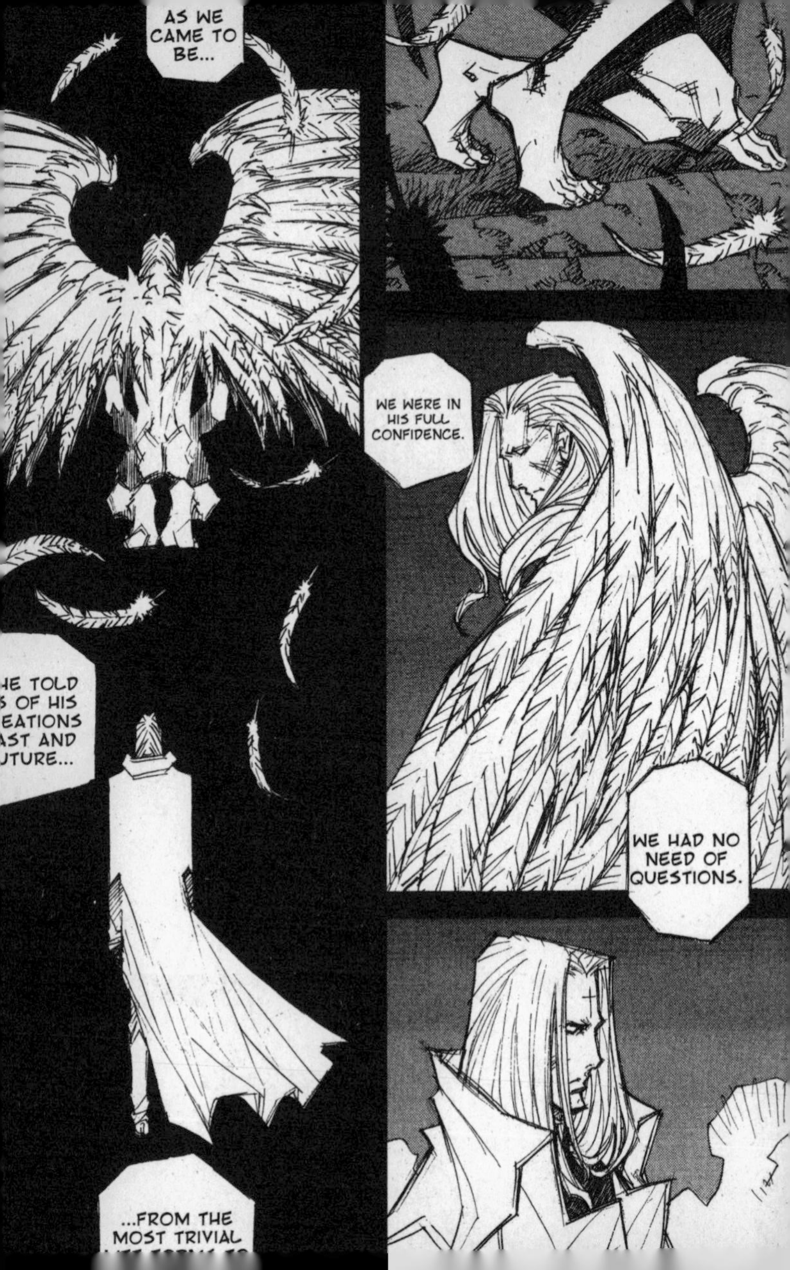
WE WERE IN HIS FULL CONFIDENCE.
WE HAD NO NEED OF QUESTIONS.
AS WE CAME TO BE...
HE TOLD
S OF HIS
EATIONS
AST AND
UTURE...
...FROM THE MOST TRIVIAL

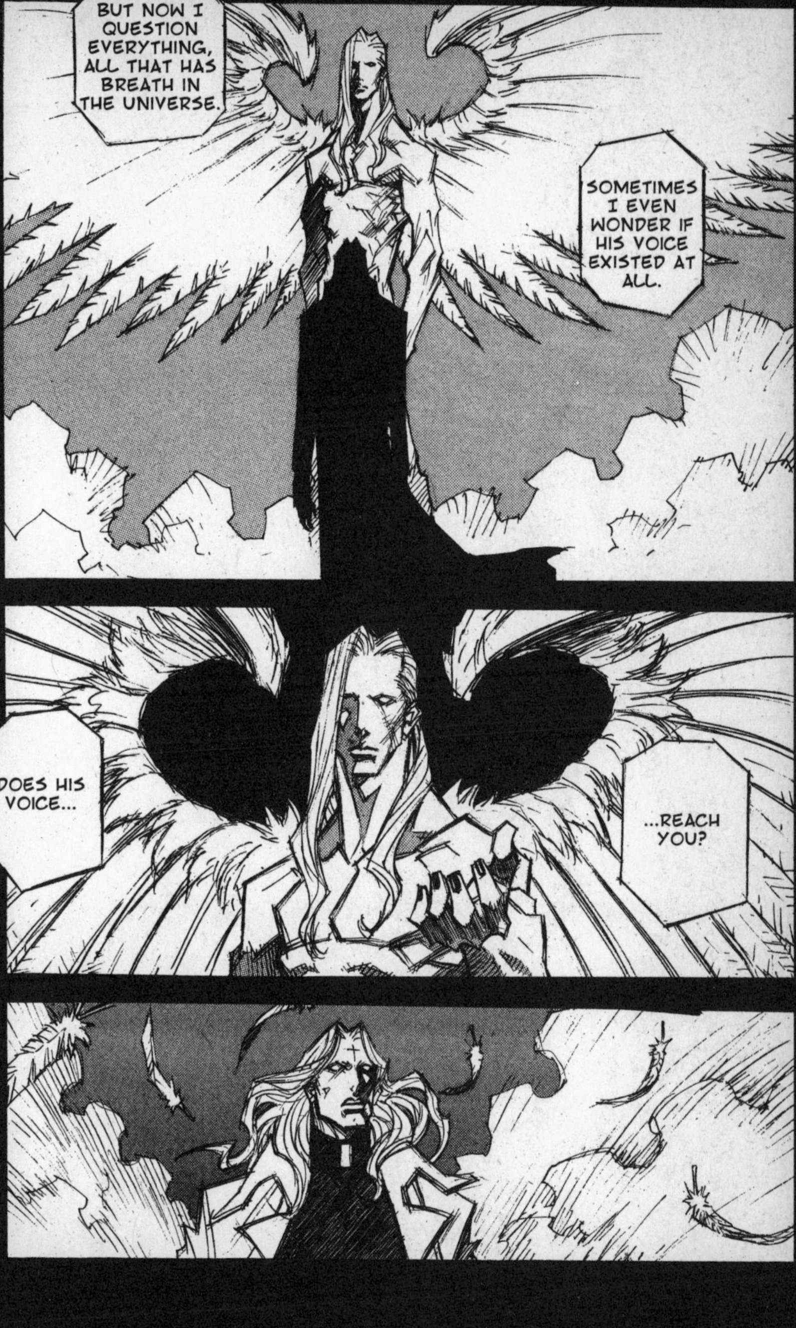
BUT NOW I QUESTION EVERYTHING, ALL THAT HAS BREATH IN THE UNIVERSE.
SOMETIMES I EVEN WONDER IF HIS VOICE EXISTED AT ALL.
DOES HIS VOICE...
...REACH YOU?

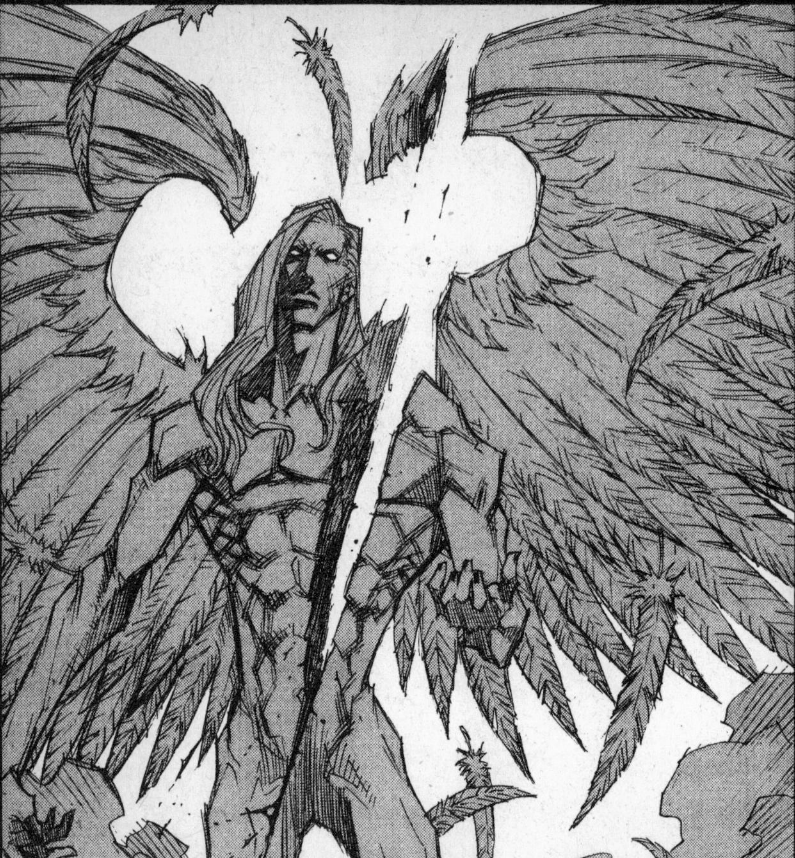

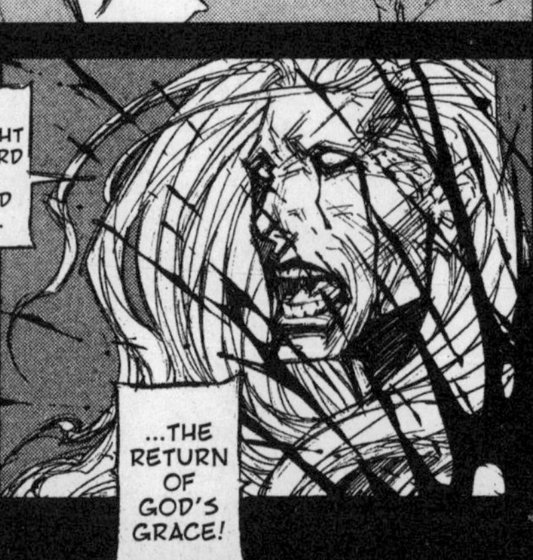
...THE RETURN OF GOD'S GRACE!

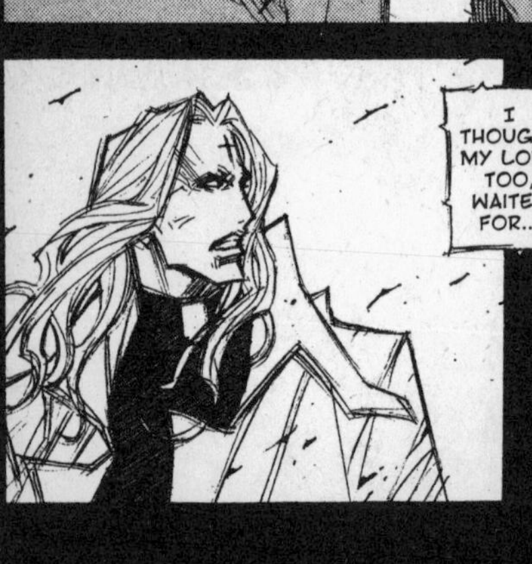
I THOUGHT MY LORD TOO, WAITED FOR...

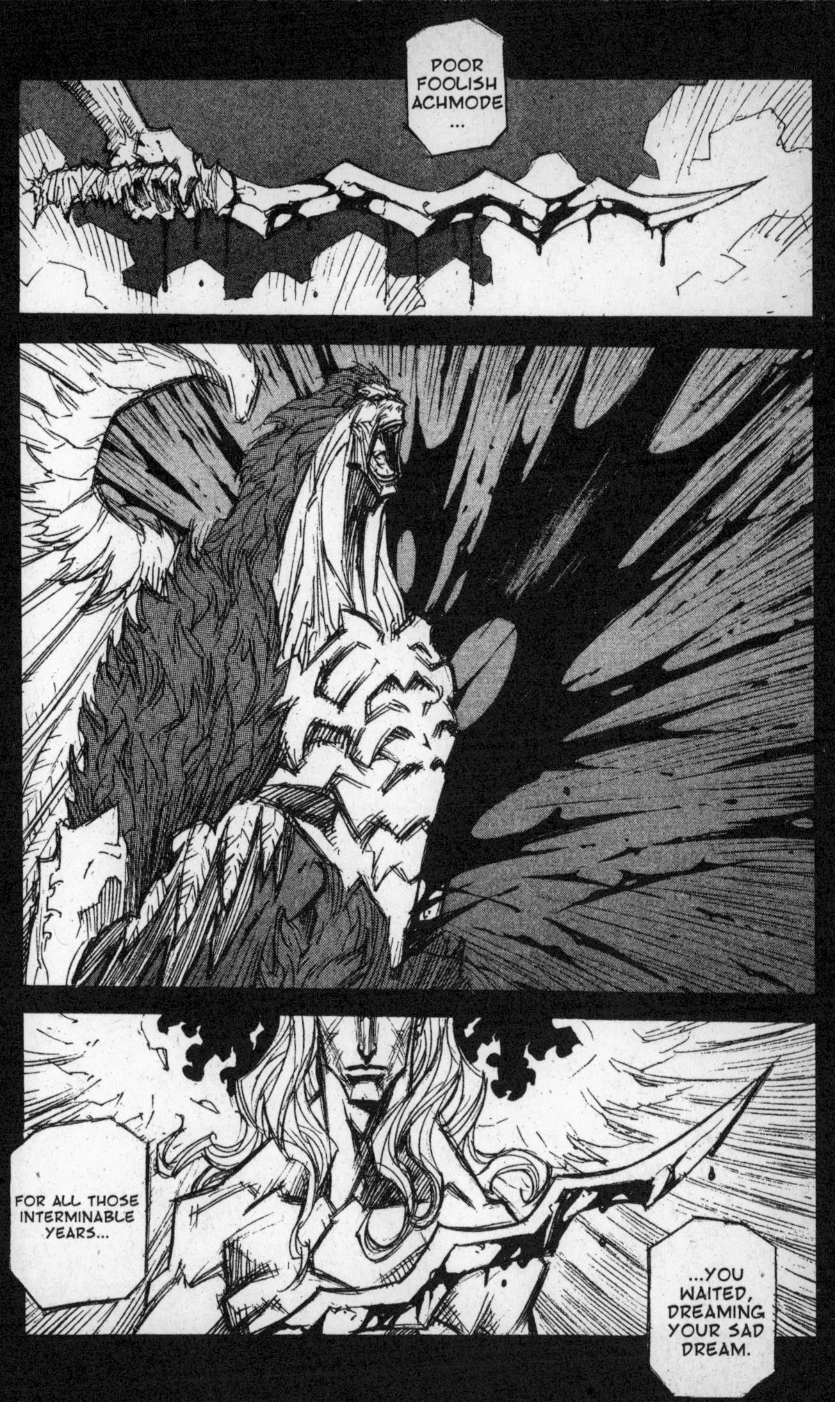
POOR FOOLISH ACHMODE ...
FOR ALL THOSE INTERMINABLE YEARS...
...YOU WAITED, DREAMING YOUR SAD DREAM.

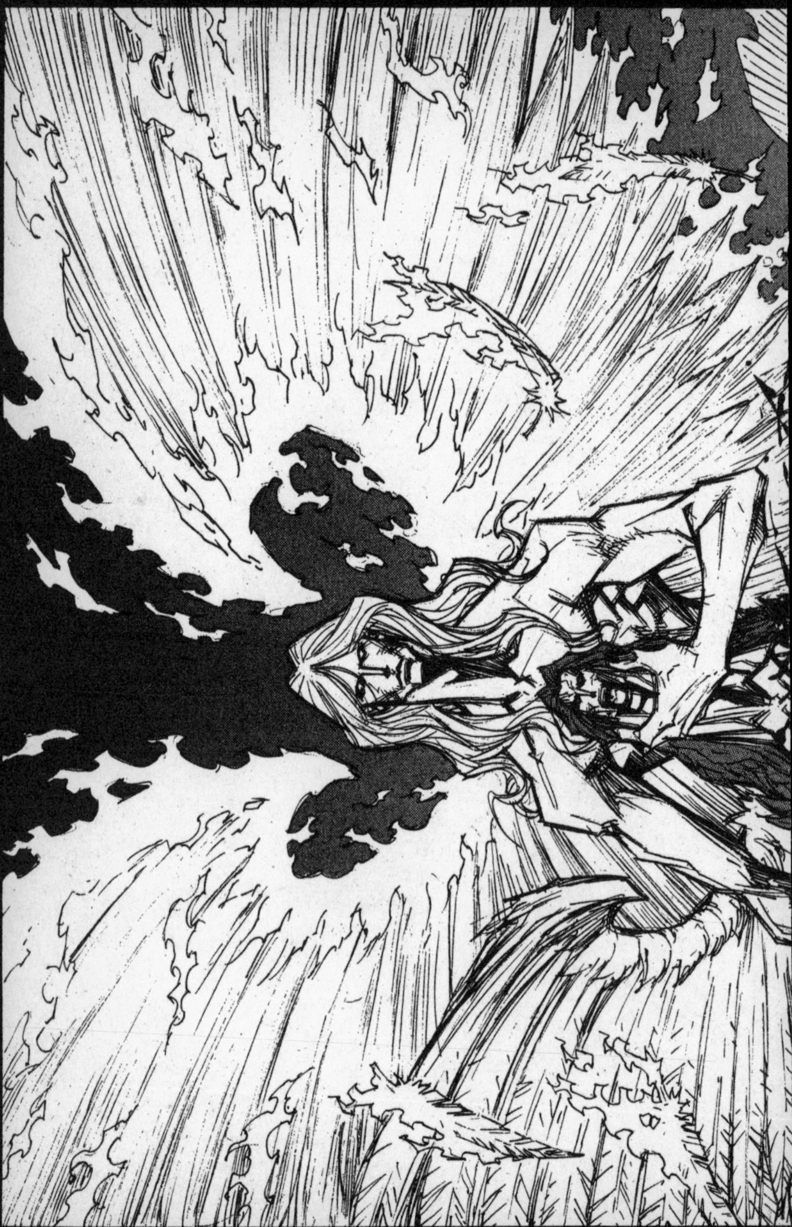

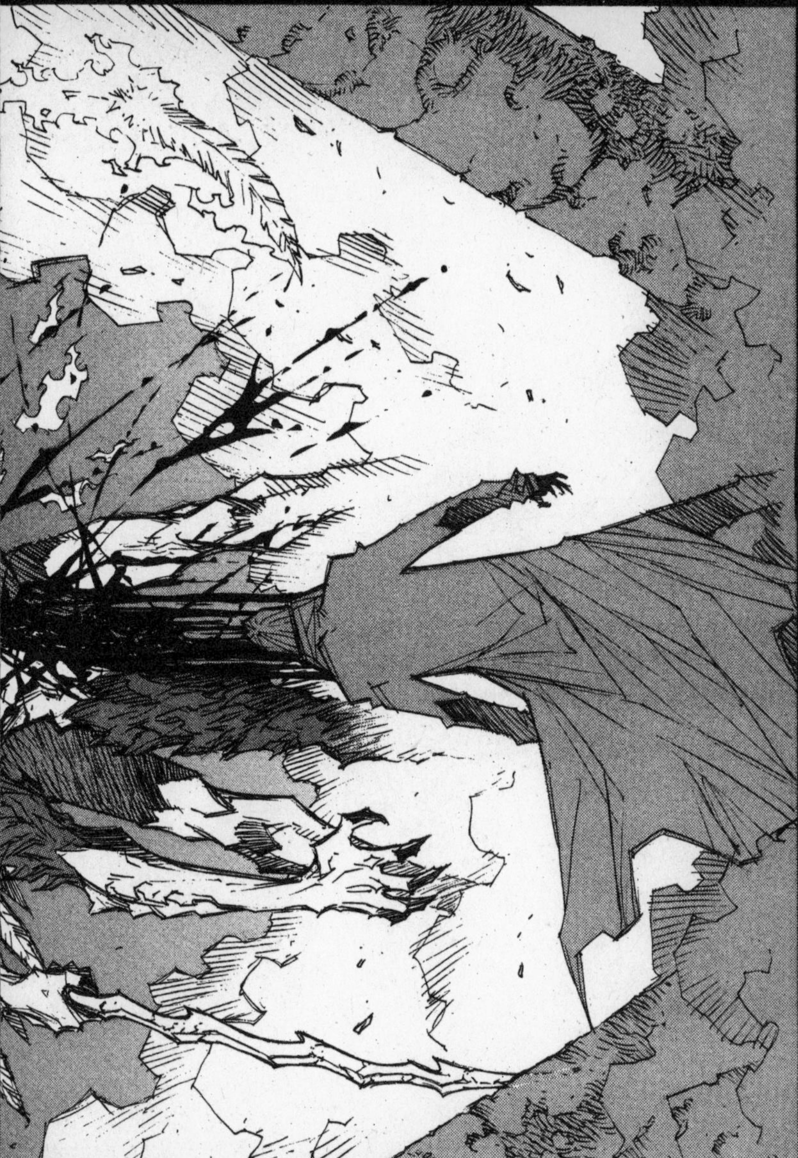

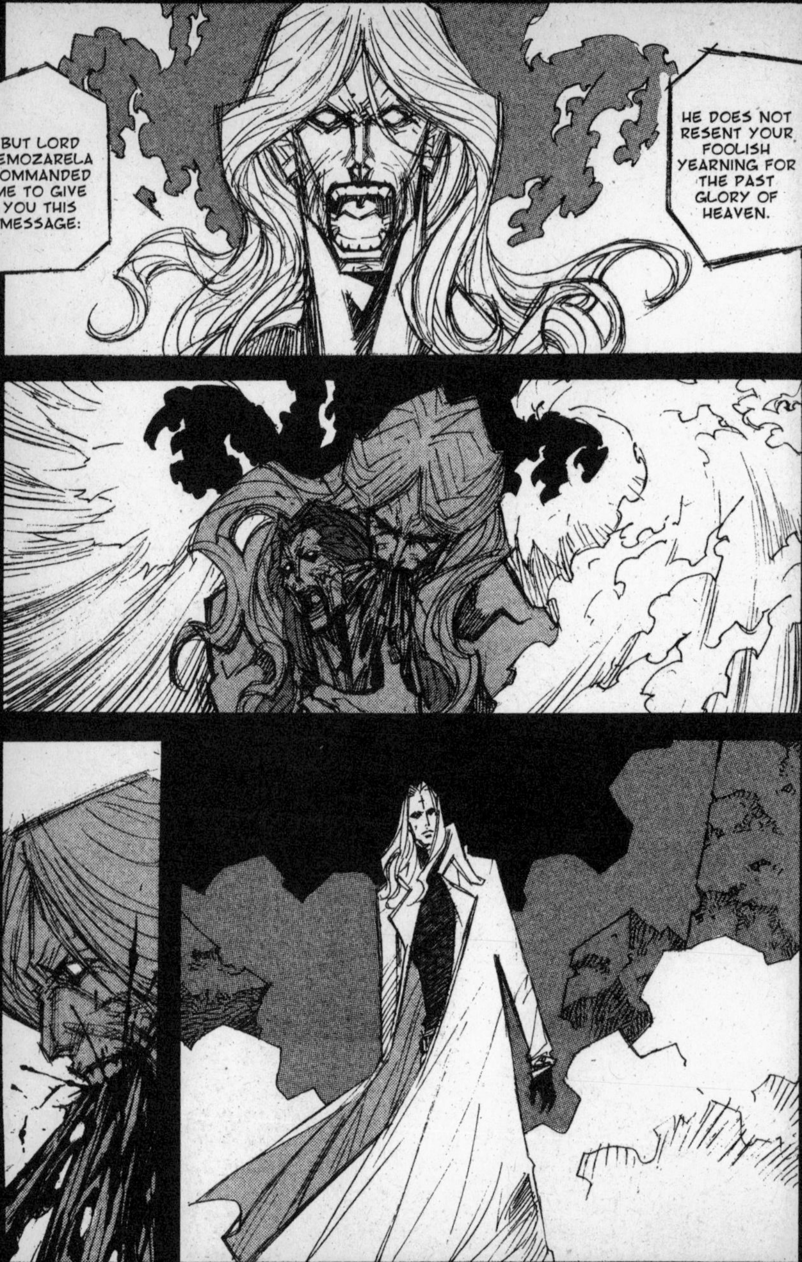
HE DOES NOT RESENT YOUR FOOLISH YEARNING FOR THE PAST GLORY OF HEAVEN.
BUT LORD TEMOZARELA COMMANDED ME TO GIVE YOU THIS MESSAGE:

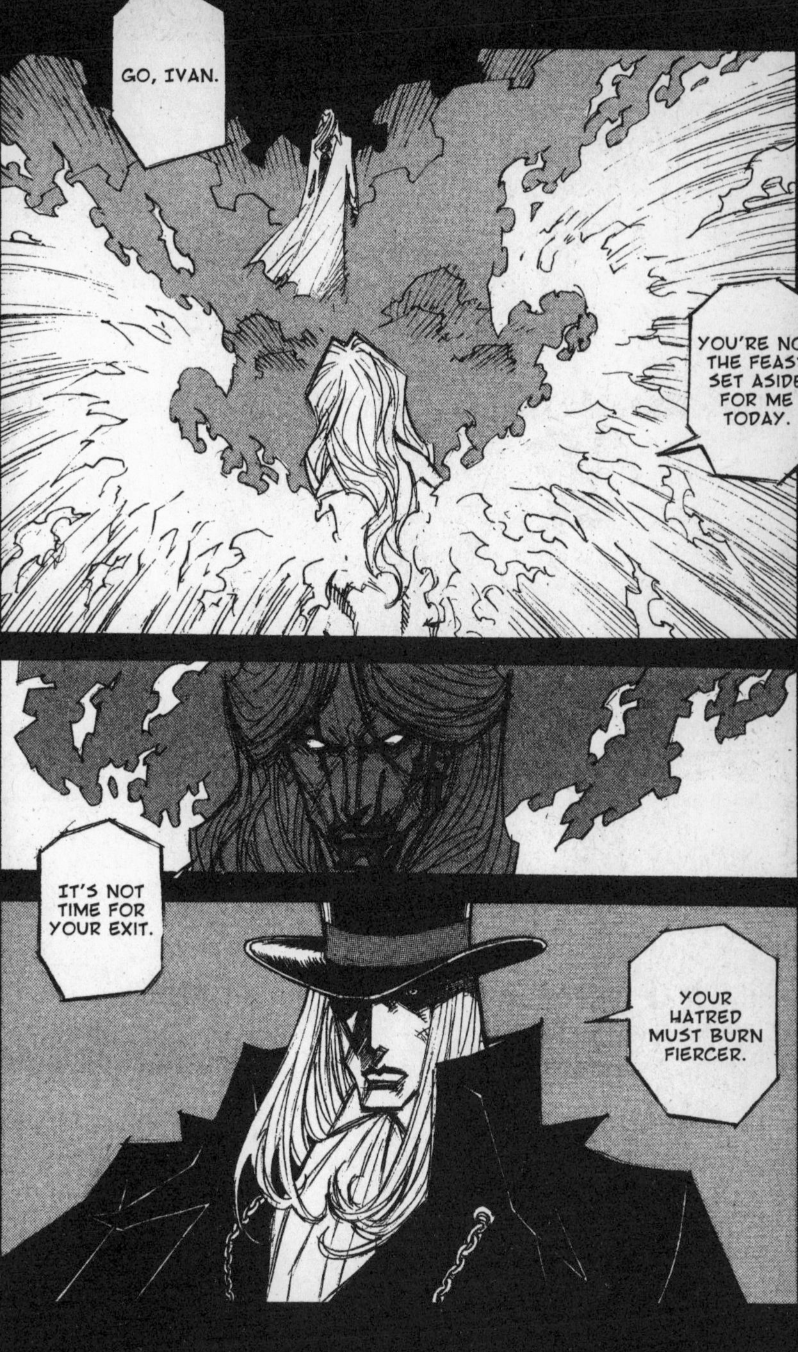
GO, IVAN.
YOU'RE NOT THE FEAST SET ASIDE FOR ME TODAY.
IT'S NOT TIME FOR YOUR EXIT.
YOUR HATRED MUST BURN FIERCER.

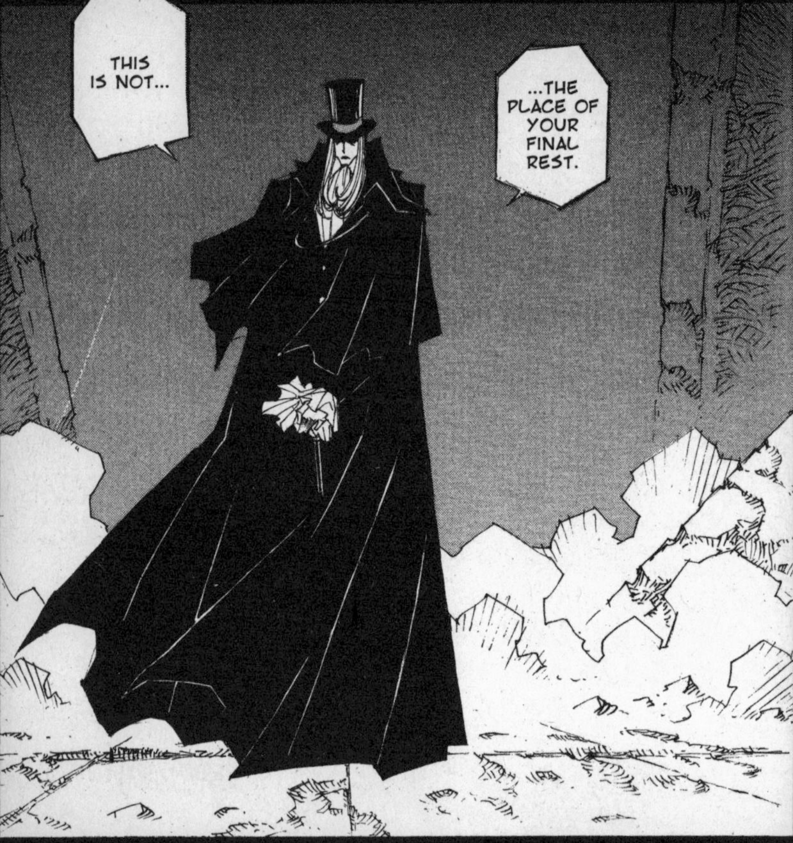
THIS IS NOT...
...THE PLACE OF YOUR FINAL REST.
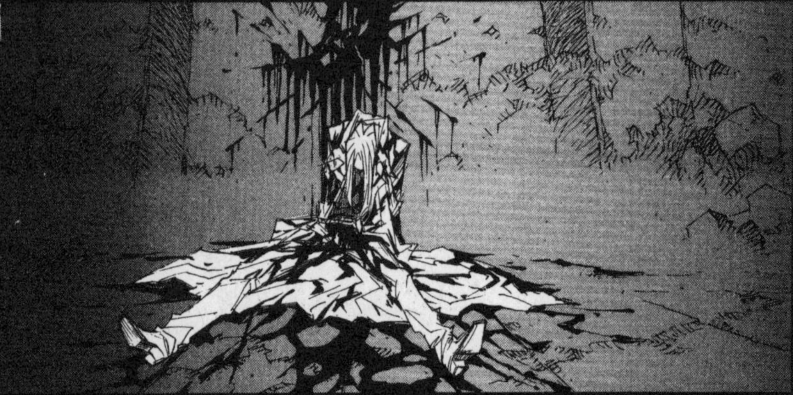

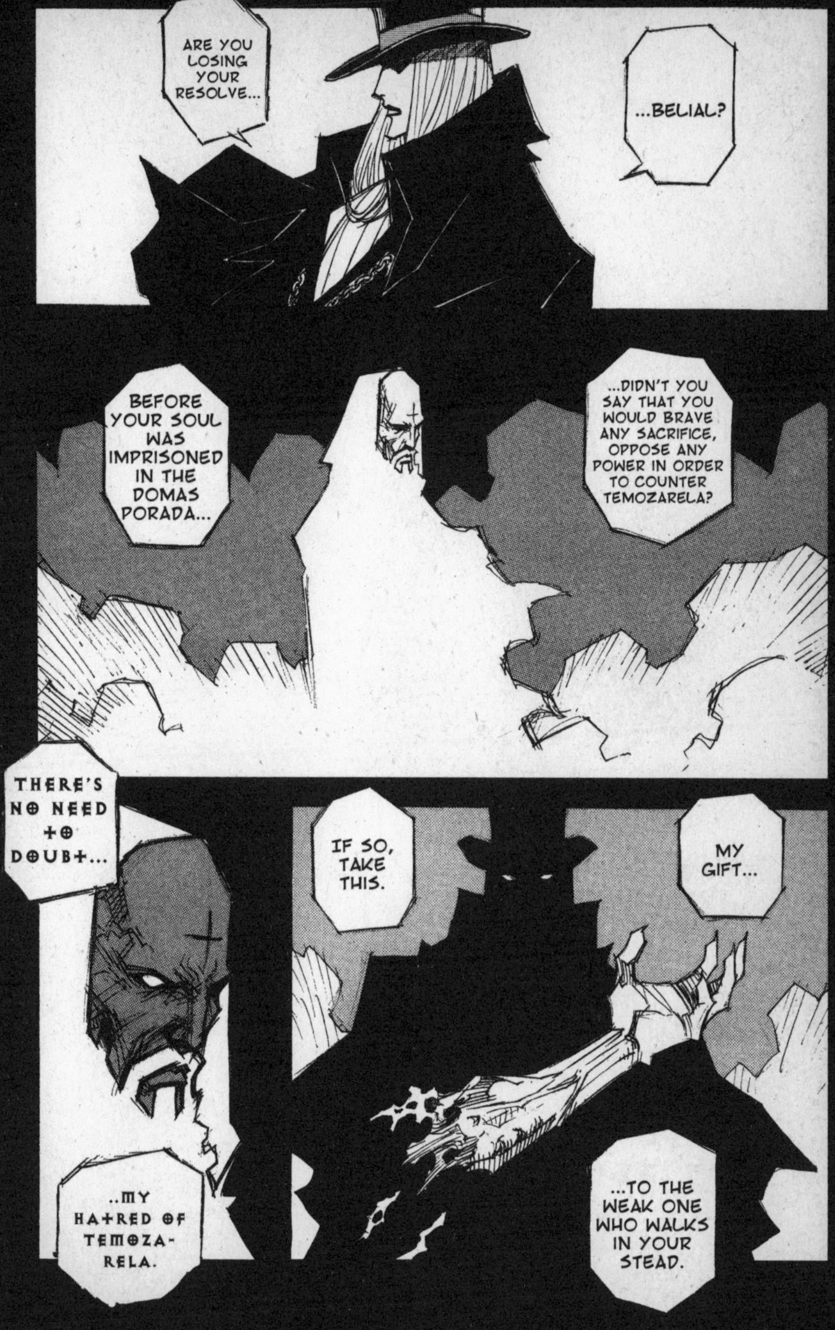
ARE YOU LOSING YOUR RESOLVE...
...BELIAL?
BEFORE YOUR SOUL WAS IMPRISONED IN THE DOMAS PORADA...
...DIDN'T YOU SAY THAT YOU WOULD BRAVE ANY SACRIFICE, OPPOSE ANY POWER IN ORDER TO COUNTER TEMOZARELA?
THERE'S NO NEED TO DOUBT...
..MY HATRED OF TEMOZA-RELA.
IF SO, TAKE THIS.
MY GIFT...
...TO THE WEAK ONE WHO WALKS IN YOUR STEAD.

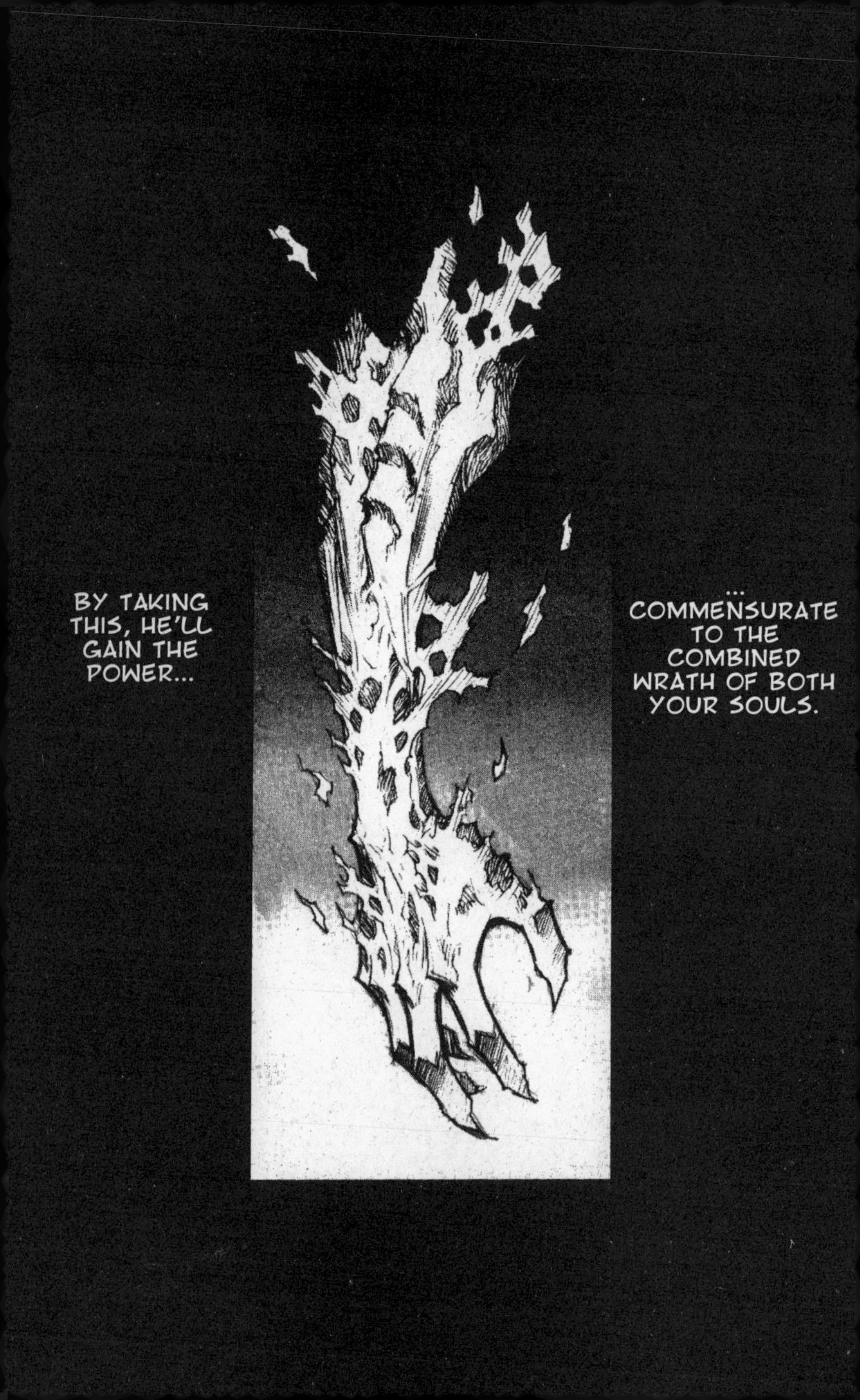
BY TAKING THIS, HE'LL GAIN THE POWER...
...COMMENSURATE TO THE COMBINED WRATH OF BOTH YOUR SOULS.

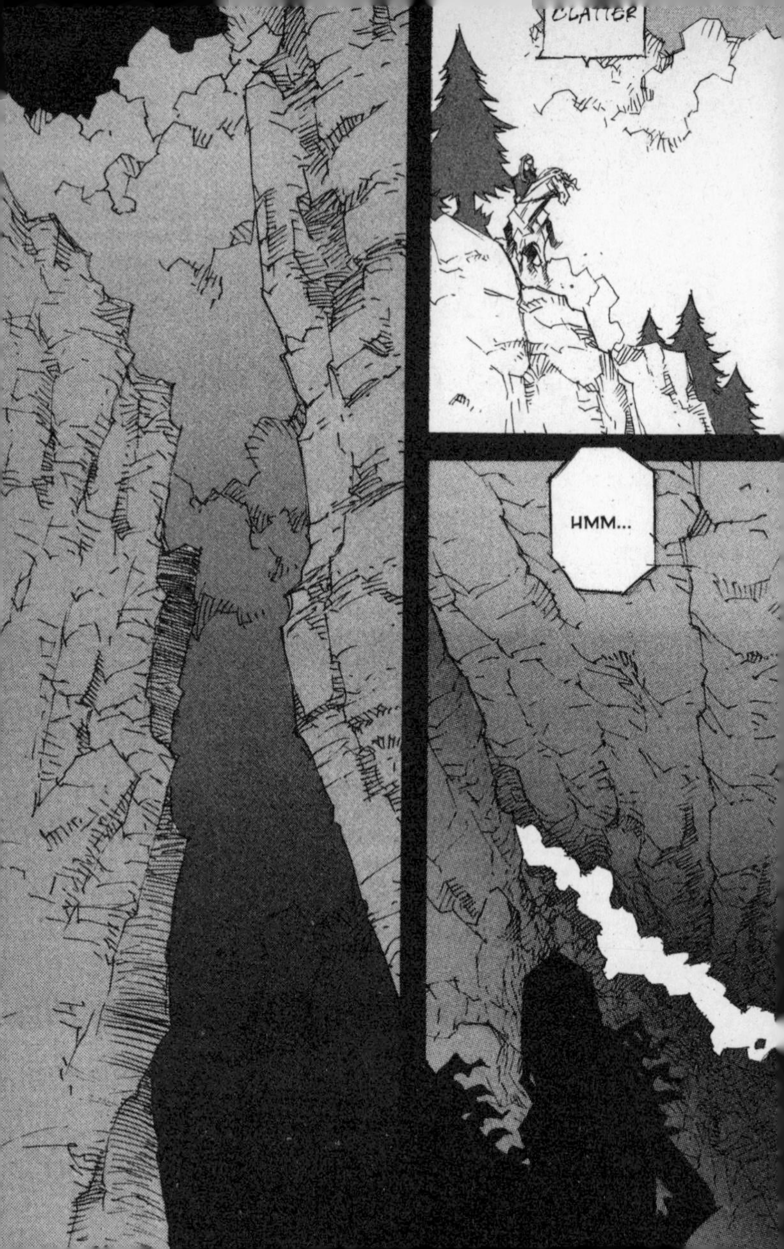
CLATTER
HMM...

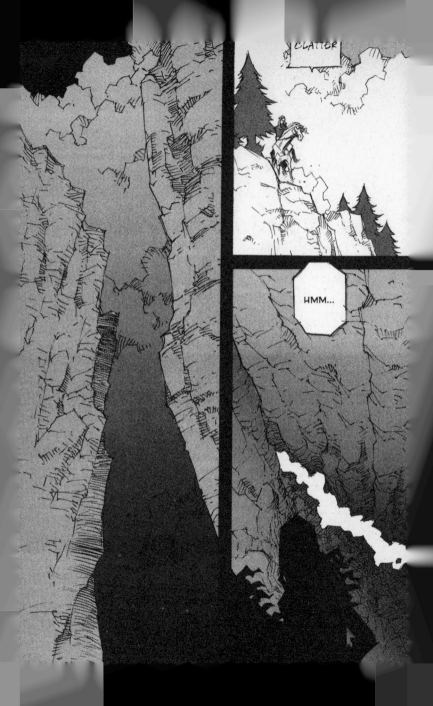

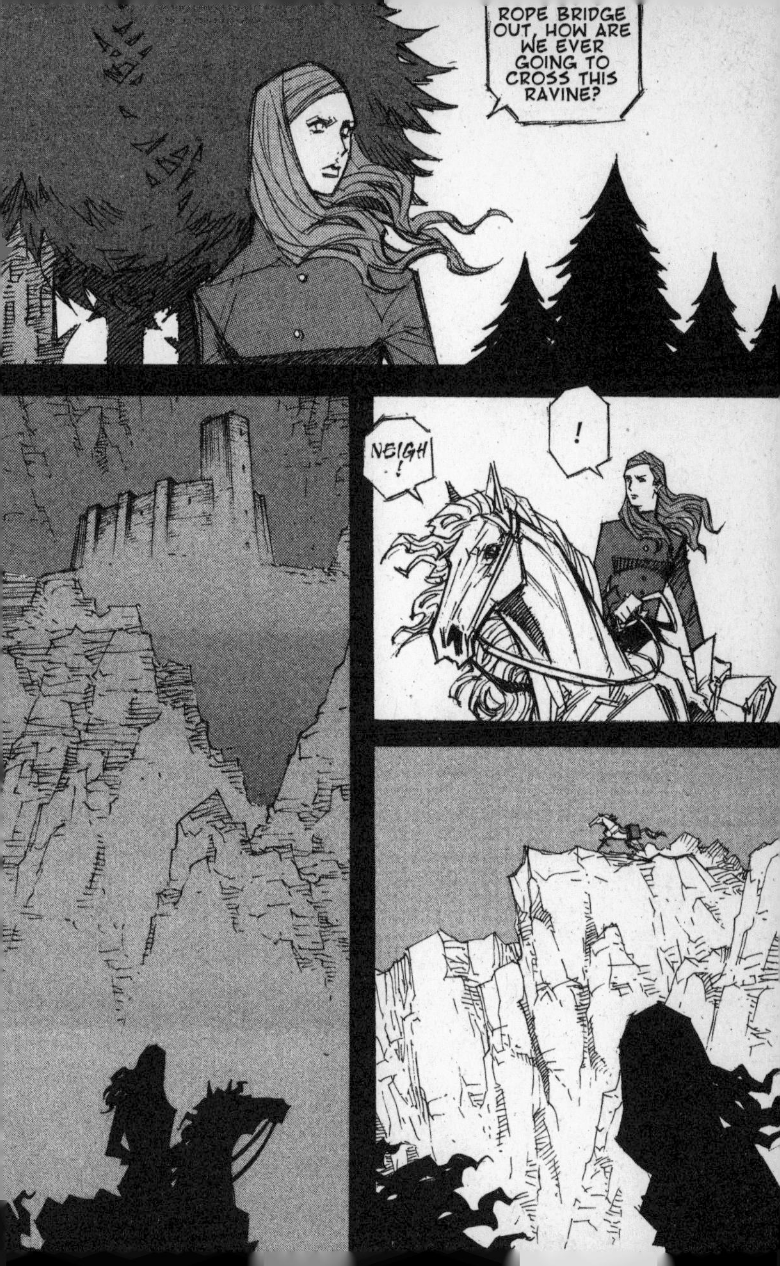
ROPE BRIDGE OUT, HOW ARE WE EVER GOING TO CROSS THIS RAVINE?
!
NEIGH!

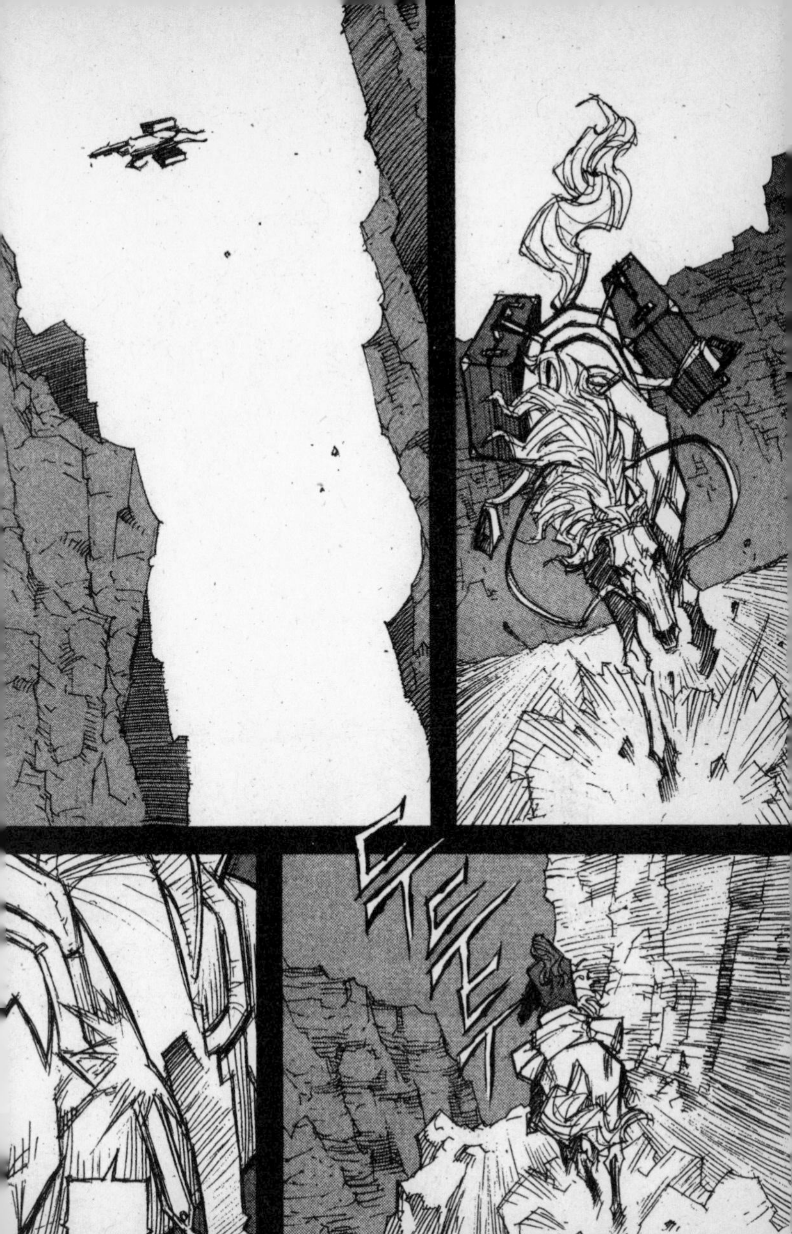
HUP!

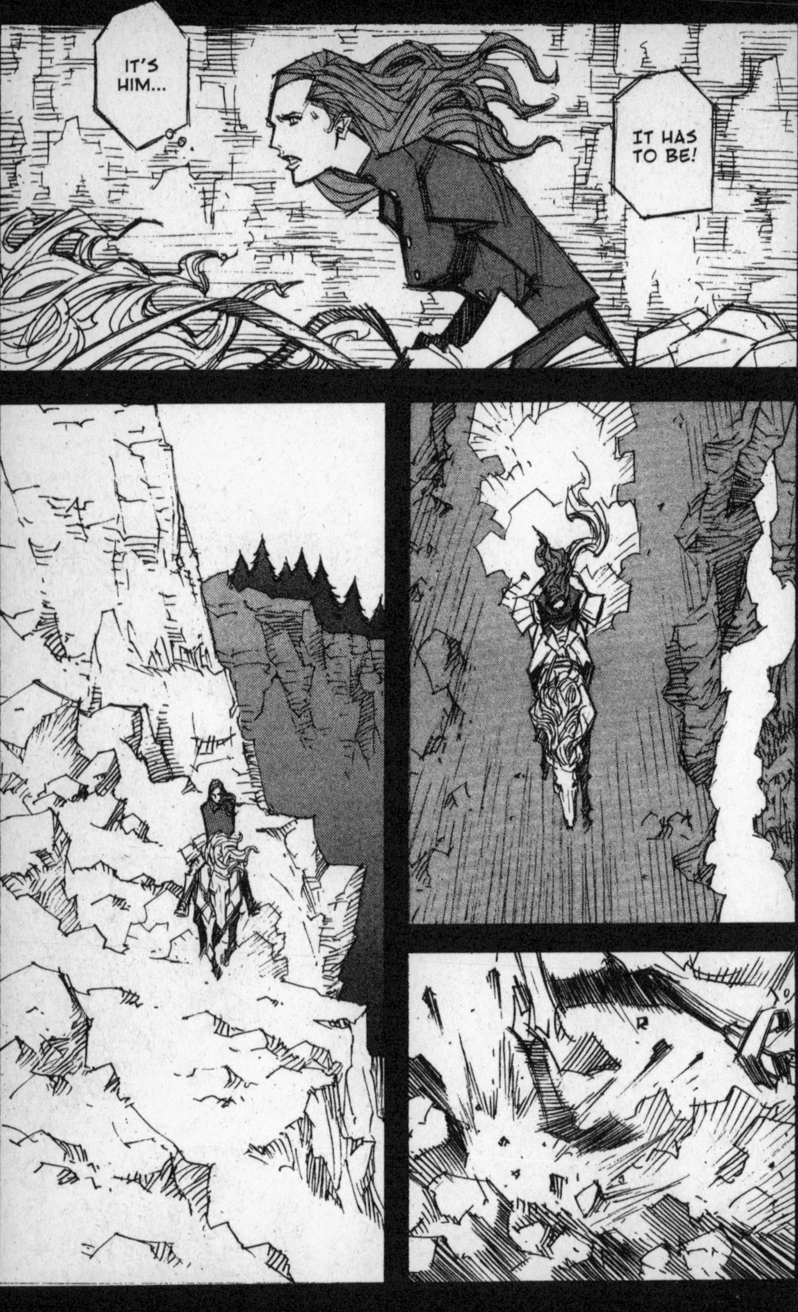
IT HAS TO BE!
IT'S HIM...

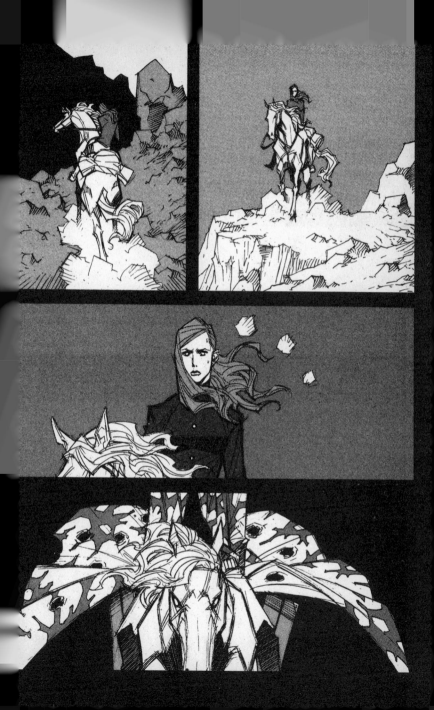

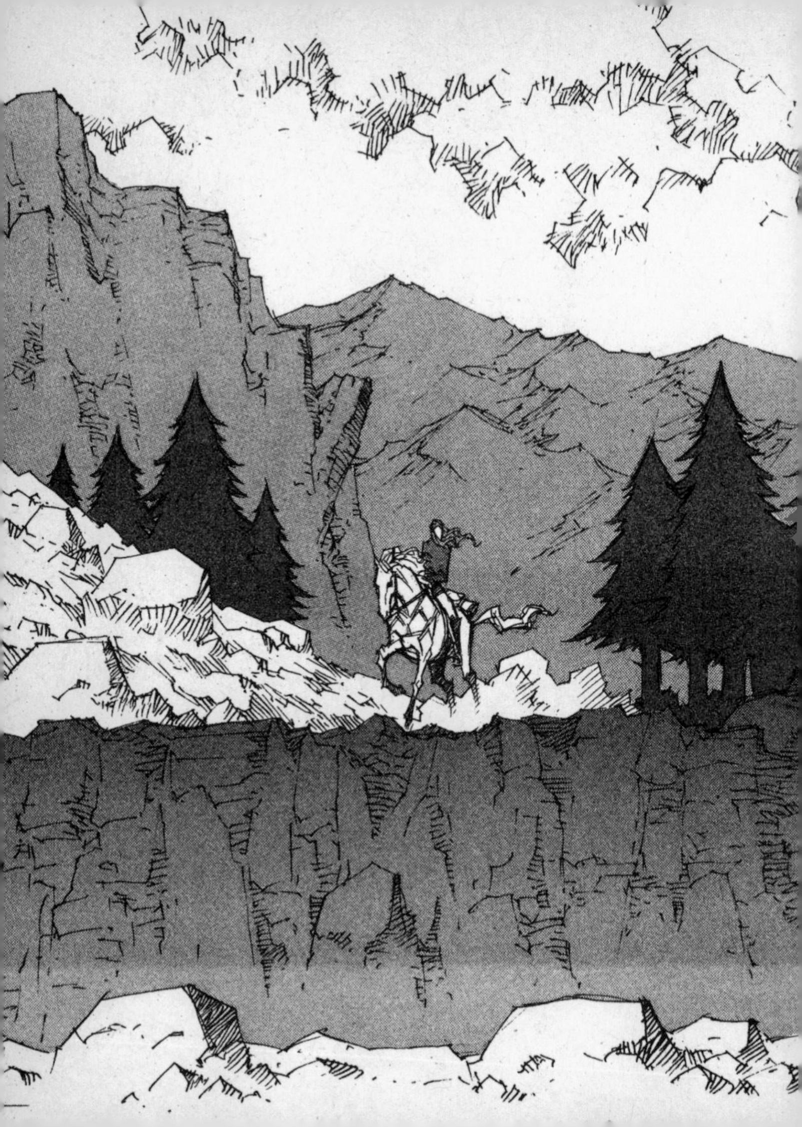

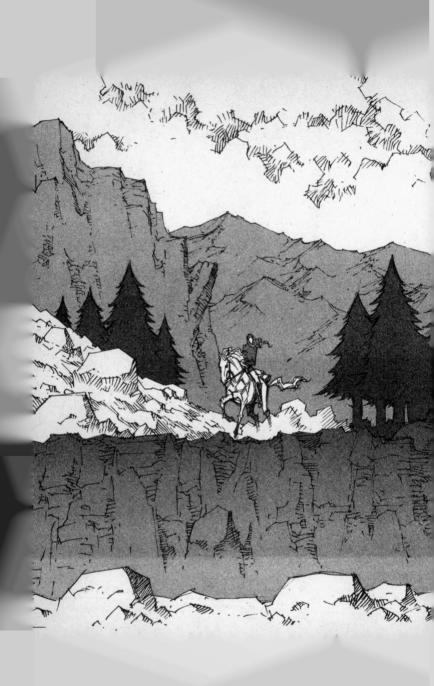

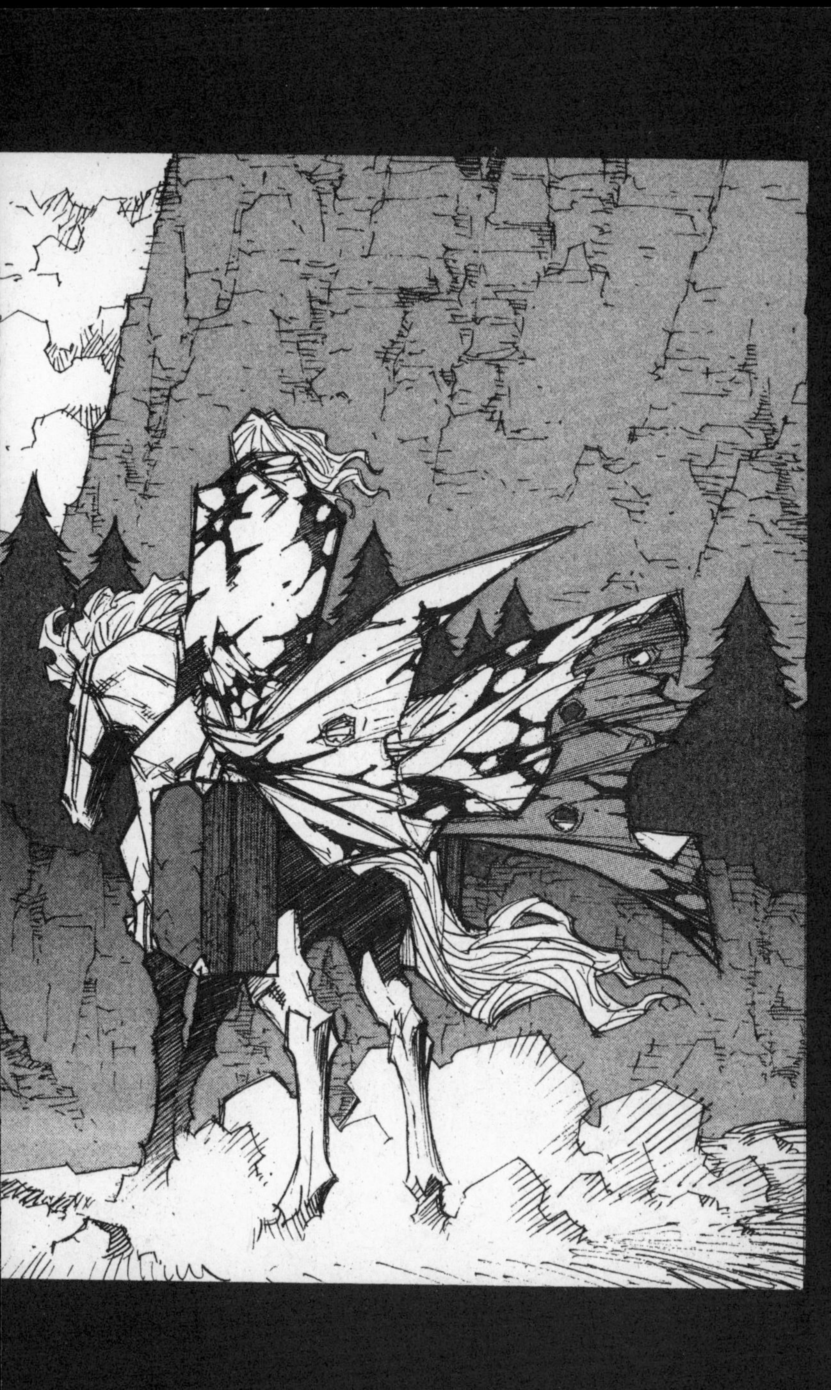

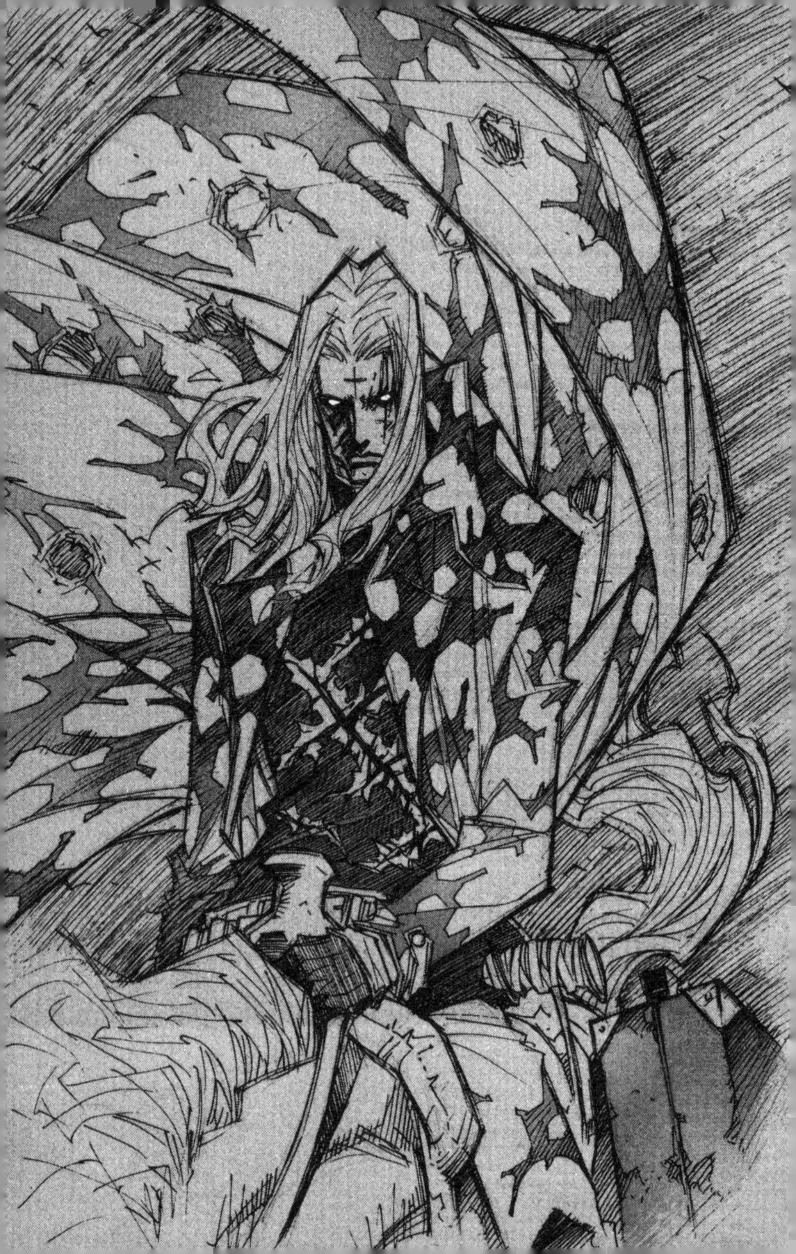

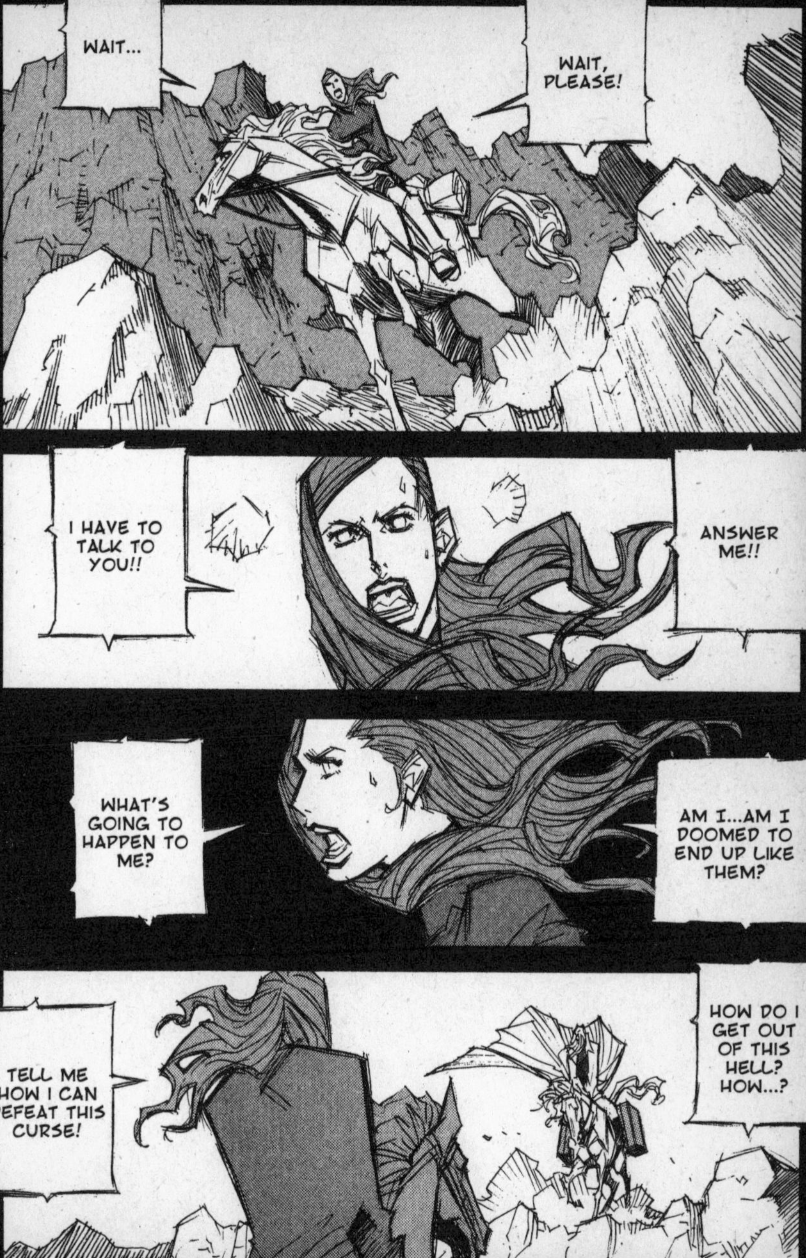
WAIT...
WAIT, PLEASE!
I HAVE TO TALK TO YOU!!
ANSWER ME!!
WHAT'S GOING TO HAPPEN TO ME?
AM I...AM I DOOMED TO END UP LIKE THEM?
TELL ME HOW I CAN DEFEAT THIS CURSE!
HOW DO I GET OUT OF THIS HELL? HOW...?

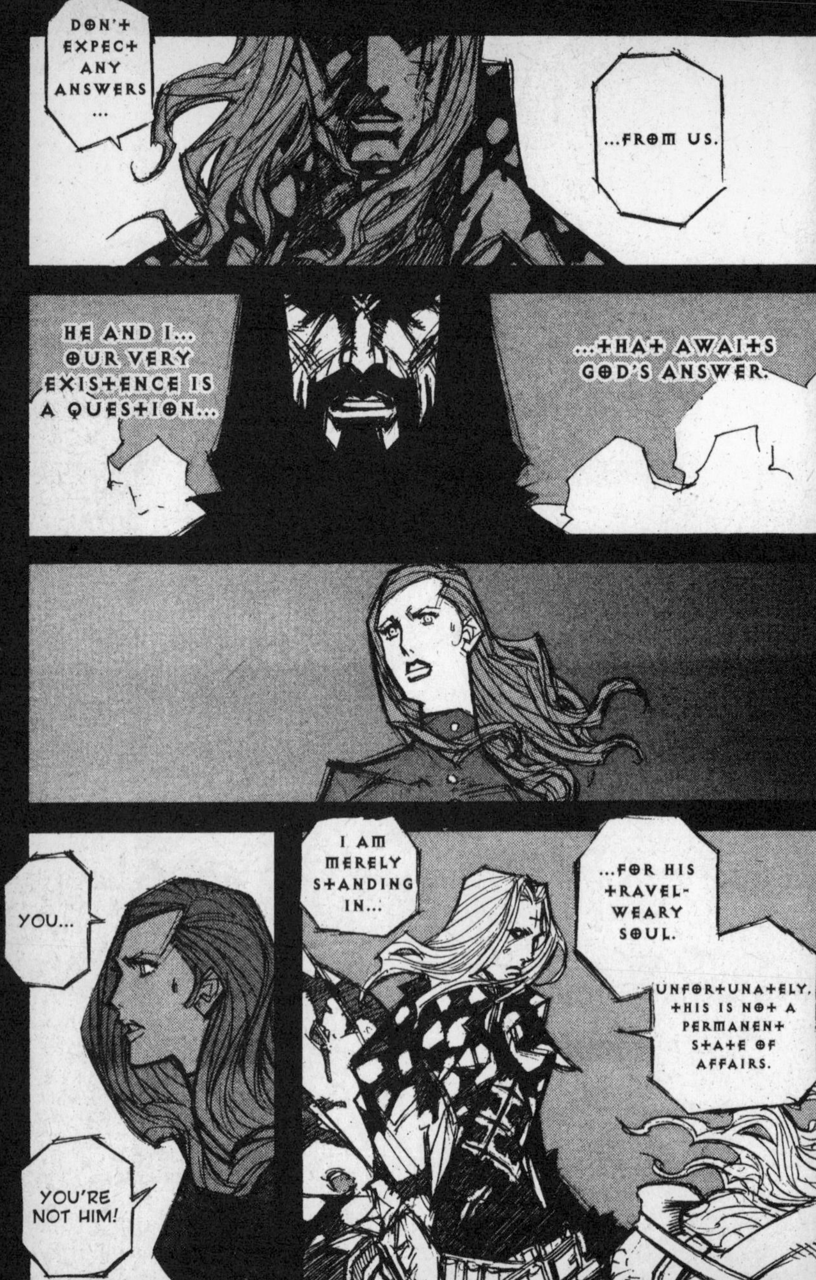
DON'T EXPECT ANY ANSWERS ...
...FROM US.
HE AND I... OUR VERY EXISTENCE IS A QUESTION...
...THAT AWAITS GOD'S ANSWER.
YOU...
YOU'RE NOT HIM!
I AM MERELY STANDING IN...
...FOR HIS TRAVEL-WEARY SOUL.
UNFORTUNATELY, THIS IS NOT A PERMANENT STATE OF AFFAIRS.

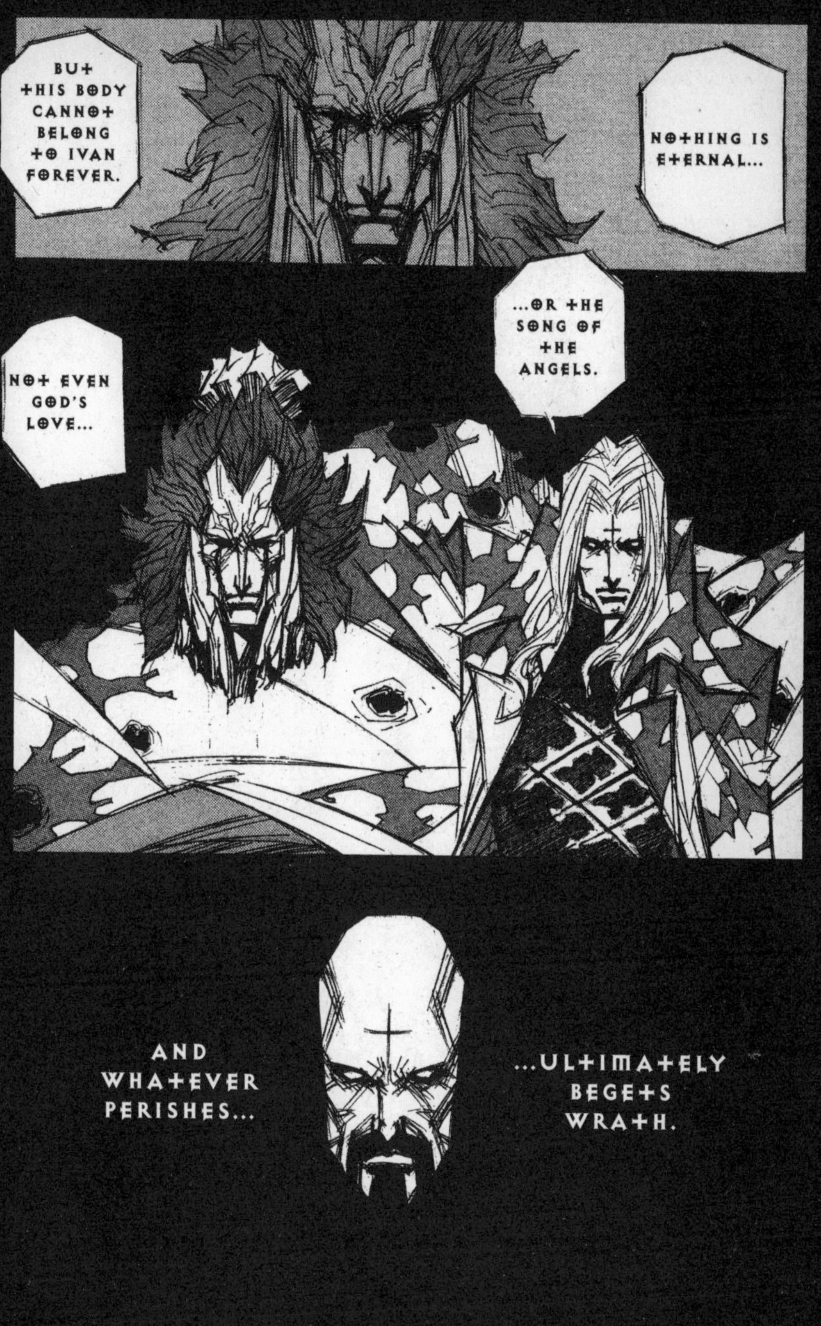
BUT THIS BODY CANNOT BELONG TO IVAN FOREVER.
NOTHING IS ETERNAL...
NOT EVEN GOD'S LOVE...
...OR THE SONG OF THE ANGELS.
AND WHATEVER PERISHES...
...ULTIMATELY BEGETS WRATH.

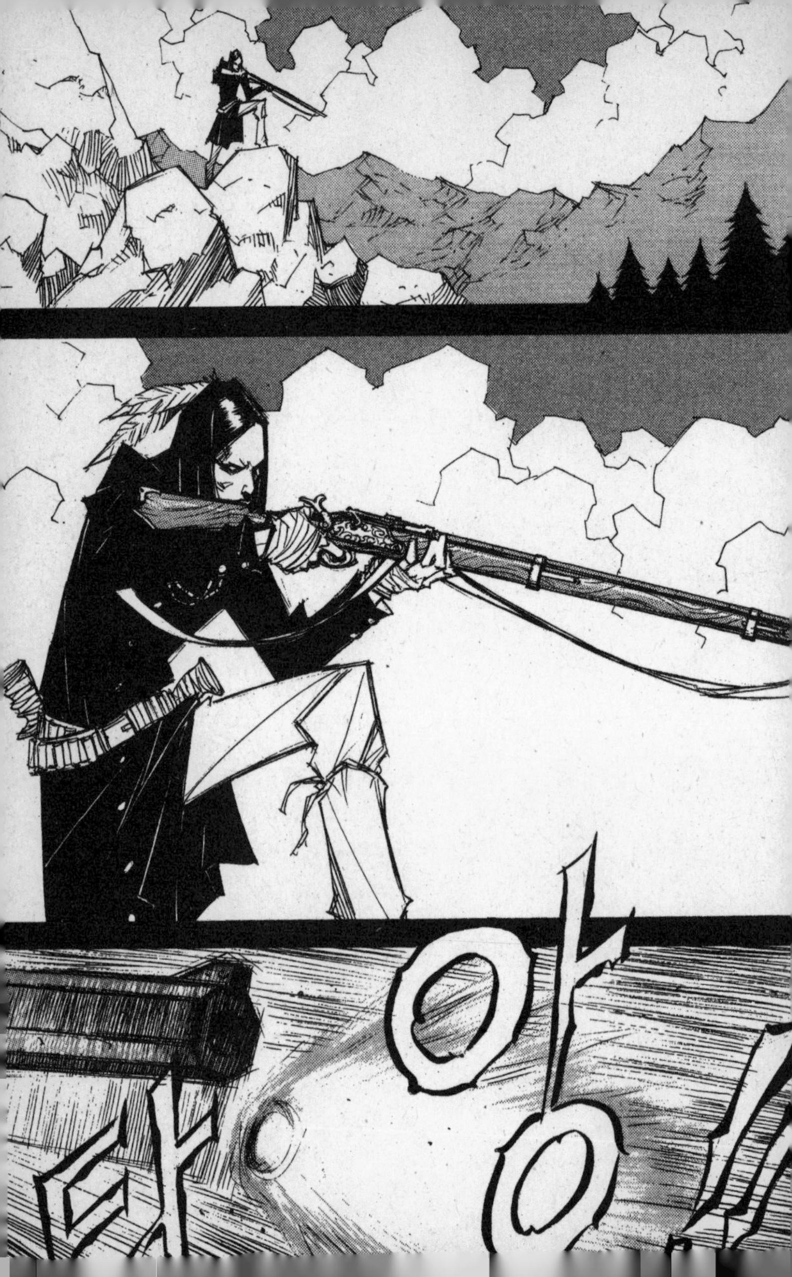
타앙!!

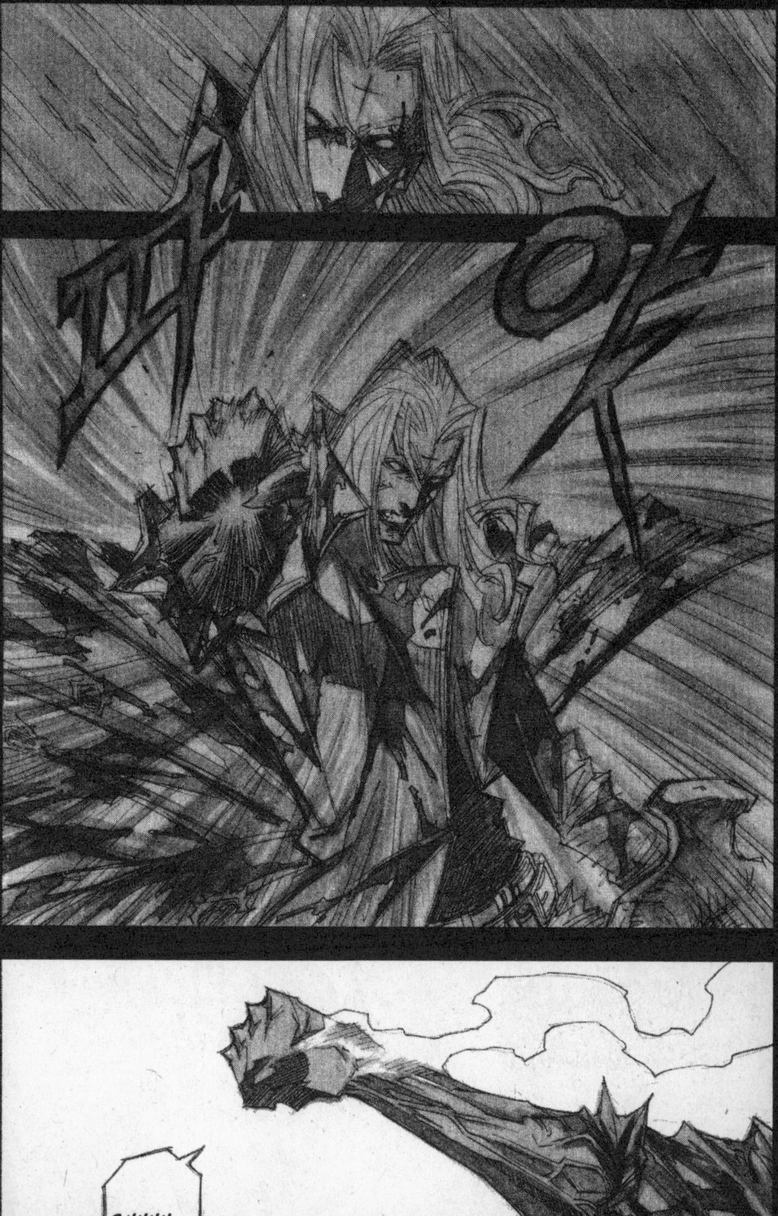
SHHHH...

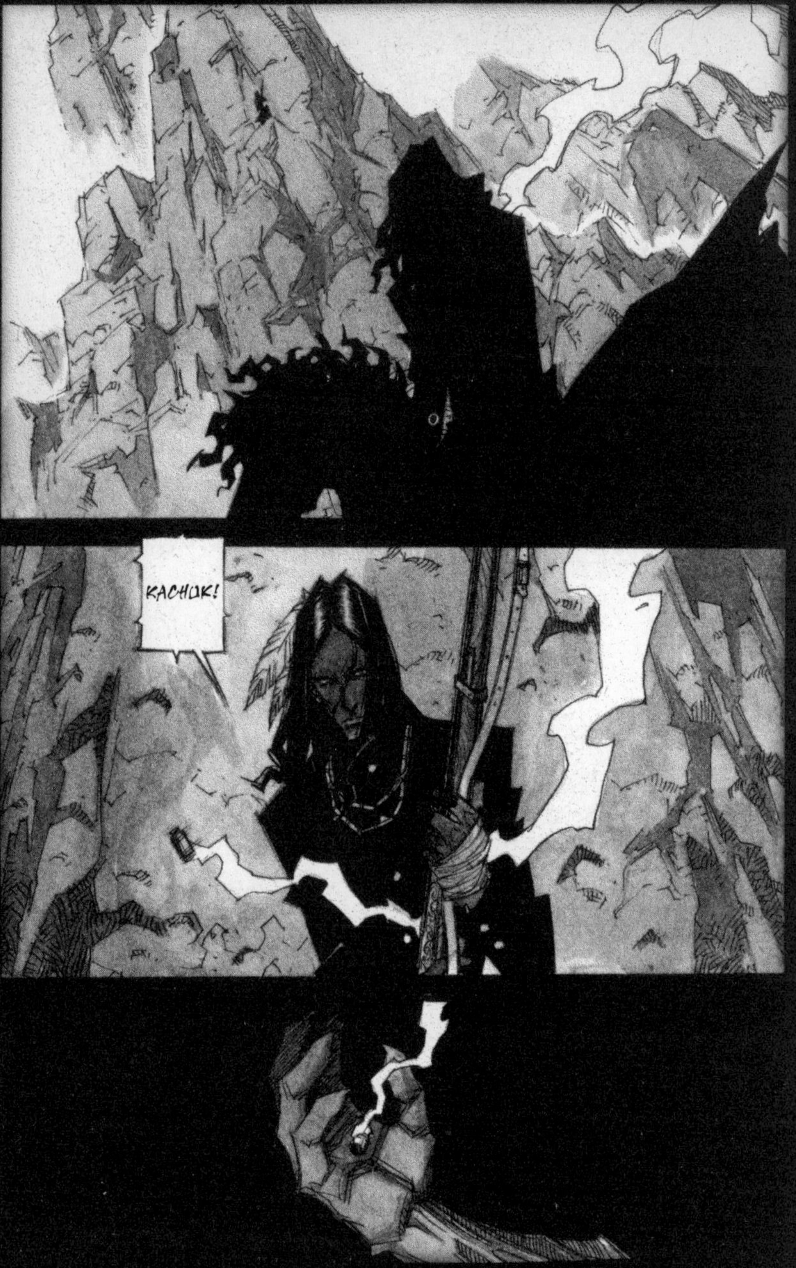
KACHUK!

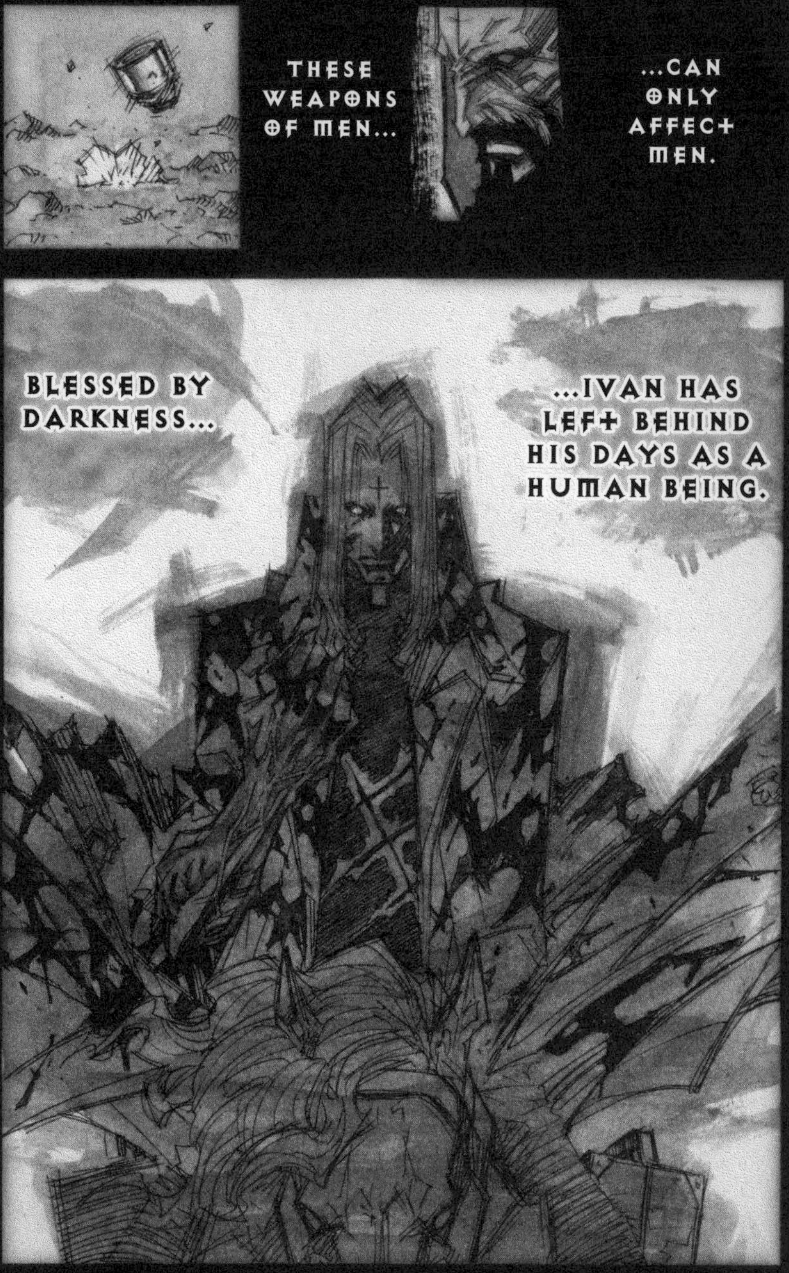
THESE WEAPONS OF MEN...
...CAN ONLY AFFECT MEN.
BLESSED BY DARKNESS...
...IVAN HAS LEFT BEHIND HIS DAYS AS A HUMAN BEING.

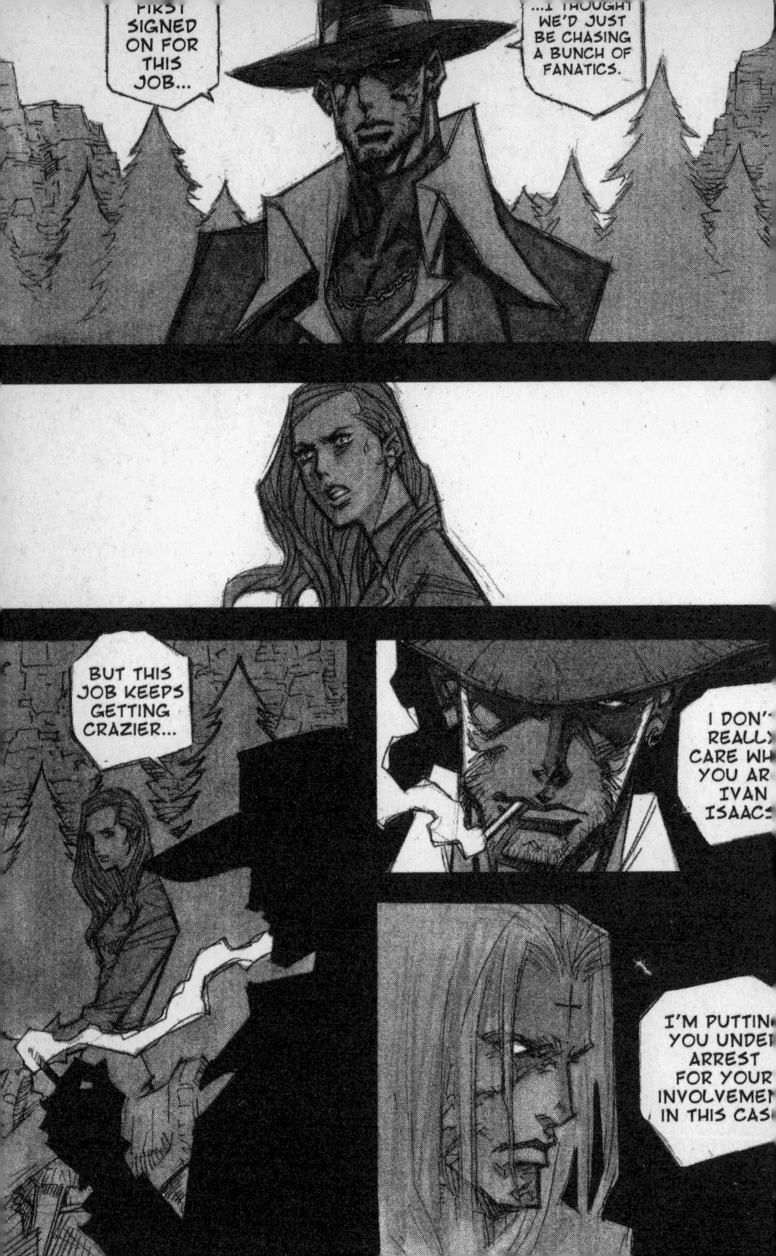
FIRST SIGNED ON FOR THIS JOB...
...I THOUGHT WE'D JUST BE CHASING A BUNCH OF FANATICS.
BUT THIS JOB KEEPS GETTING CRAZIER...
I DON' REALL CARE WH YOU AR IVAN ISAACS
I'M PUTTIN YOU UNDE ARREST FOR YOUR INVOLVEME IN THIS CAS

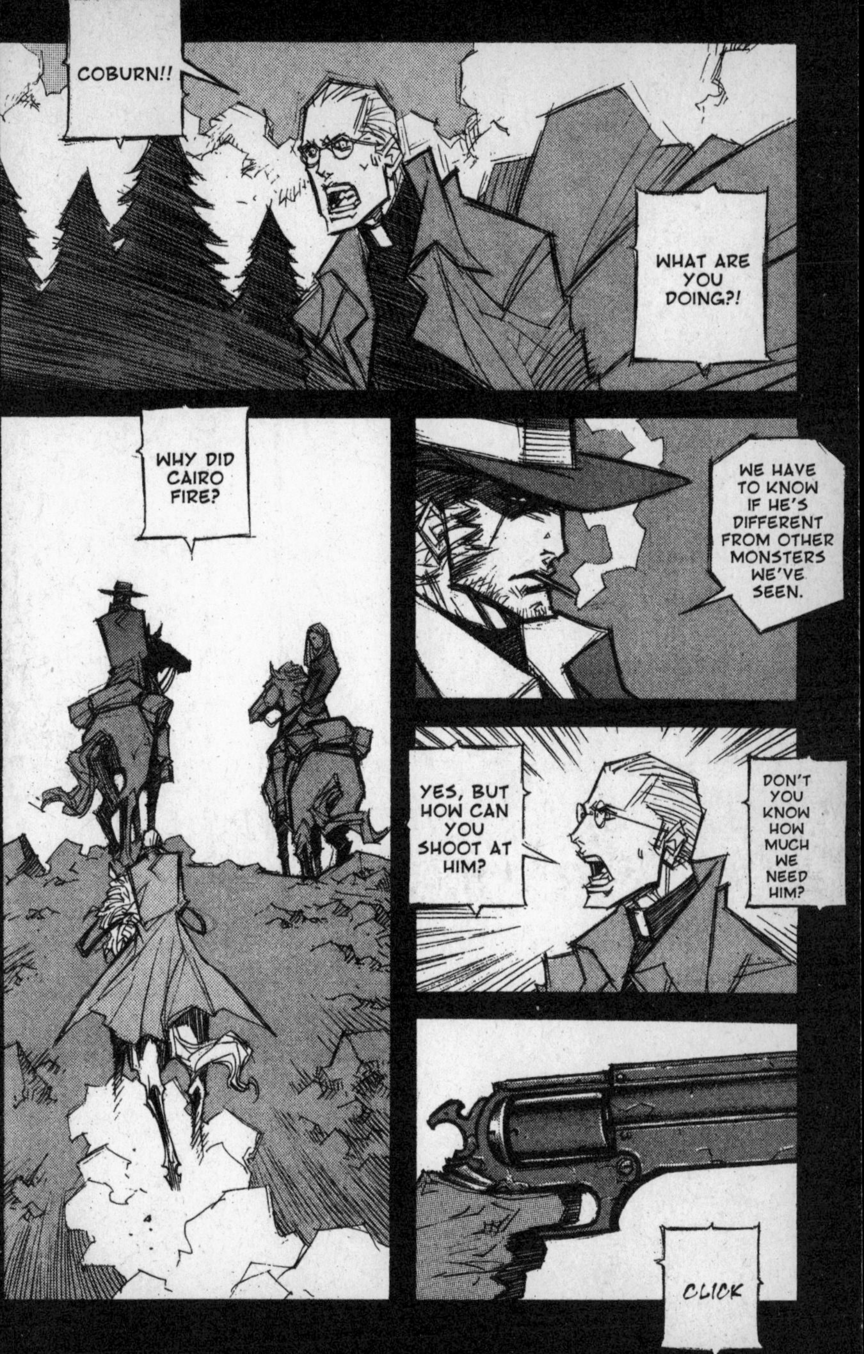
COBURN!!
WHAT ARE YOU DOING?!
WHY DID CAIRO FIRE?
WE HAVE TO KNOW IF HE'S DIFFERENT FROM OTHER MONSTERS WE'VE SEEN.
YES, BUT HOW CAN YOU SHOOT AT HIM?
DON'T YOU KNOW HOW MUCH WE NEED HIM?
CLICK

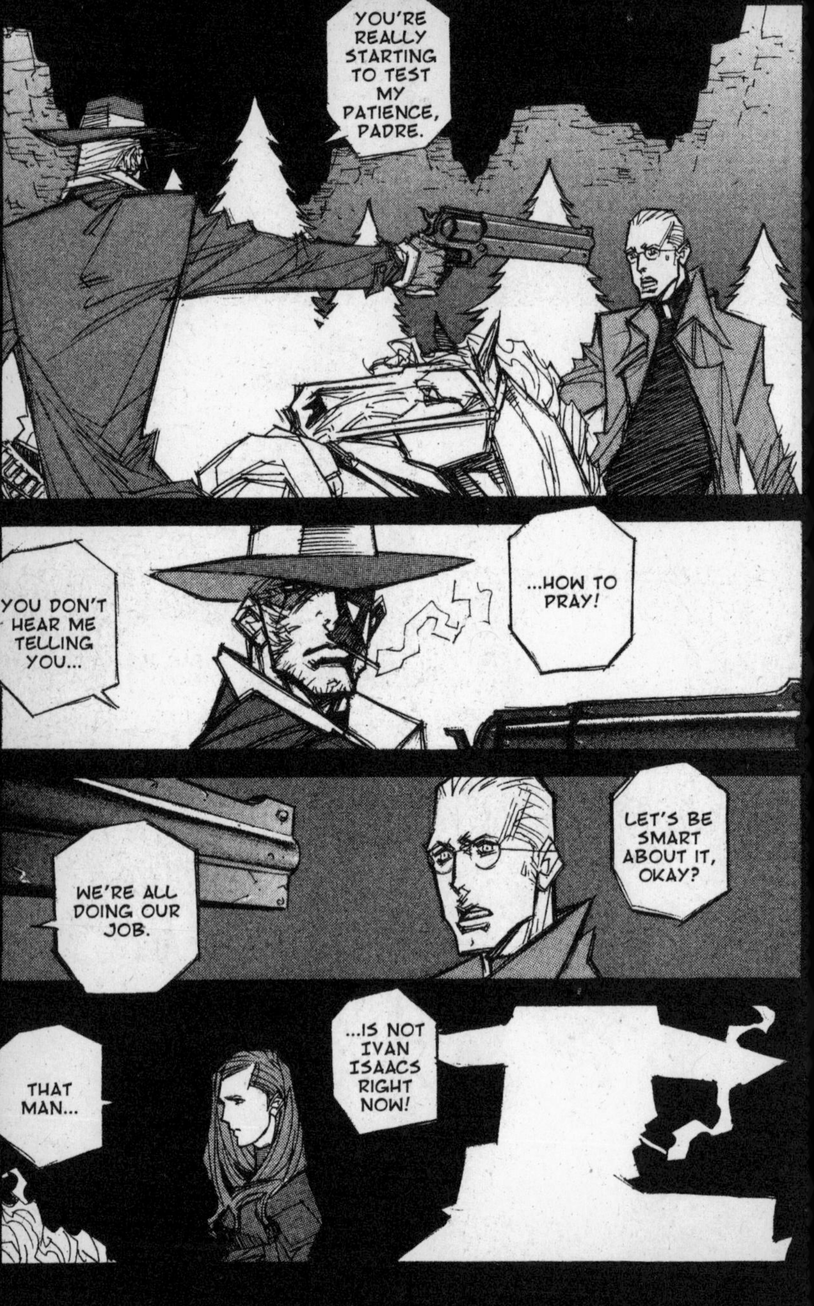
YOU'RE REALLY STARTING TO TEST MY PATIENCE, PADRE.
YOU DON'T HEAR ME TELLING YOU...
...HOW TO PRAY!
WE'RE ALL DOING OUR JOB.
LET'S BE SMART ABOUT IT, OKAY?
THAT MAN...
...IS NOT IVAN ISAACS RIGHT NOW!

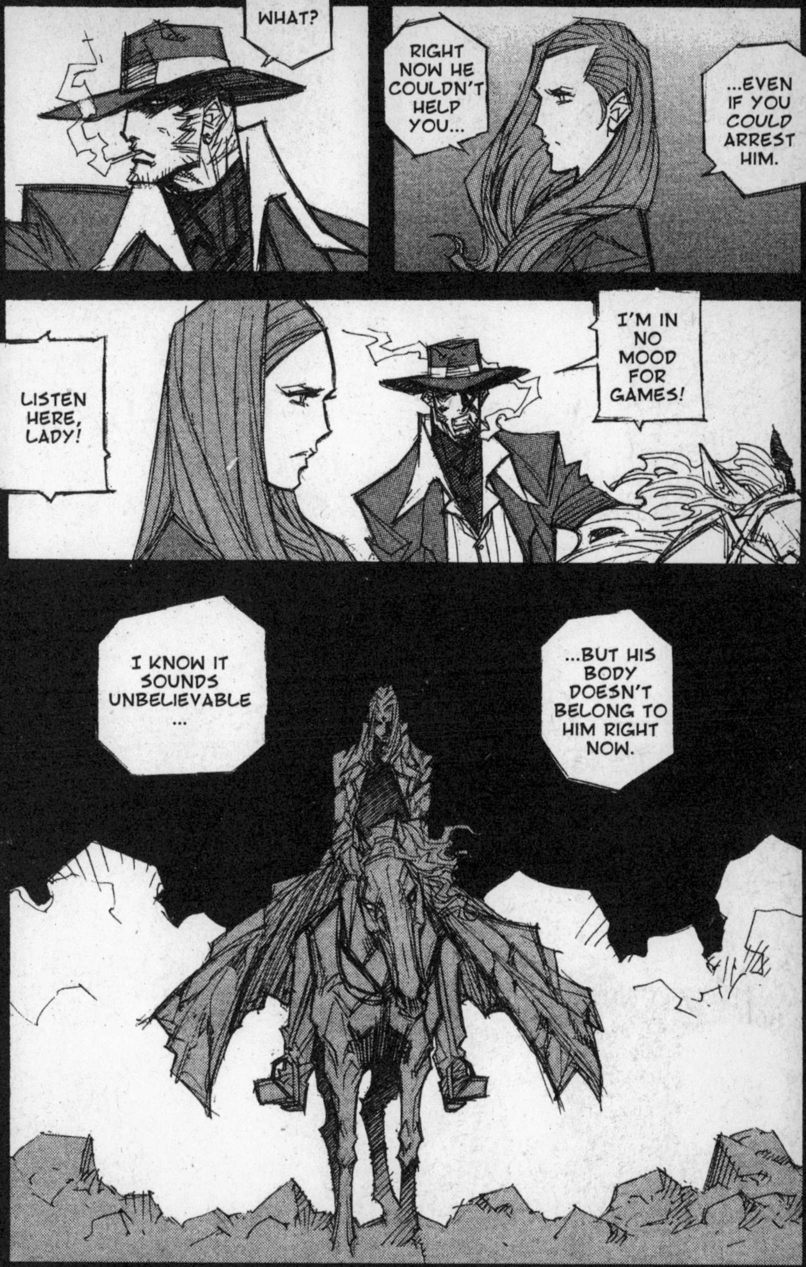
WHAT?
RIGHT NOW HE COULDN'T HELP YOU...
...EVEN IF YOU COULD ARREST HIM.
LISTEN HERE, LADY!
I'M IN NO MOOD FOR GAMES!
I KNOW IT SOUNDS UNBELIEVABLE ...
...BUT HIS BODY DOESN'T BELONG TO HIM RIGHT NOW.

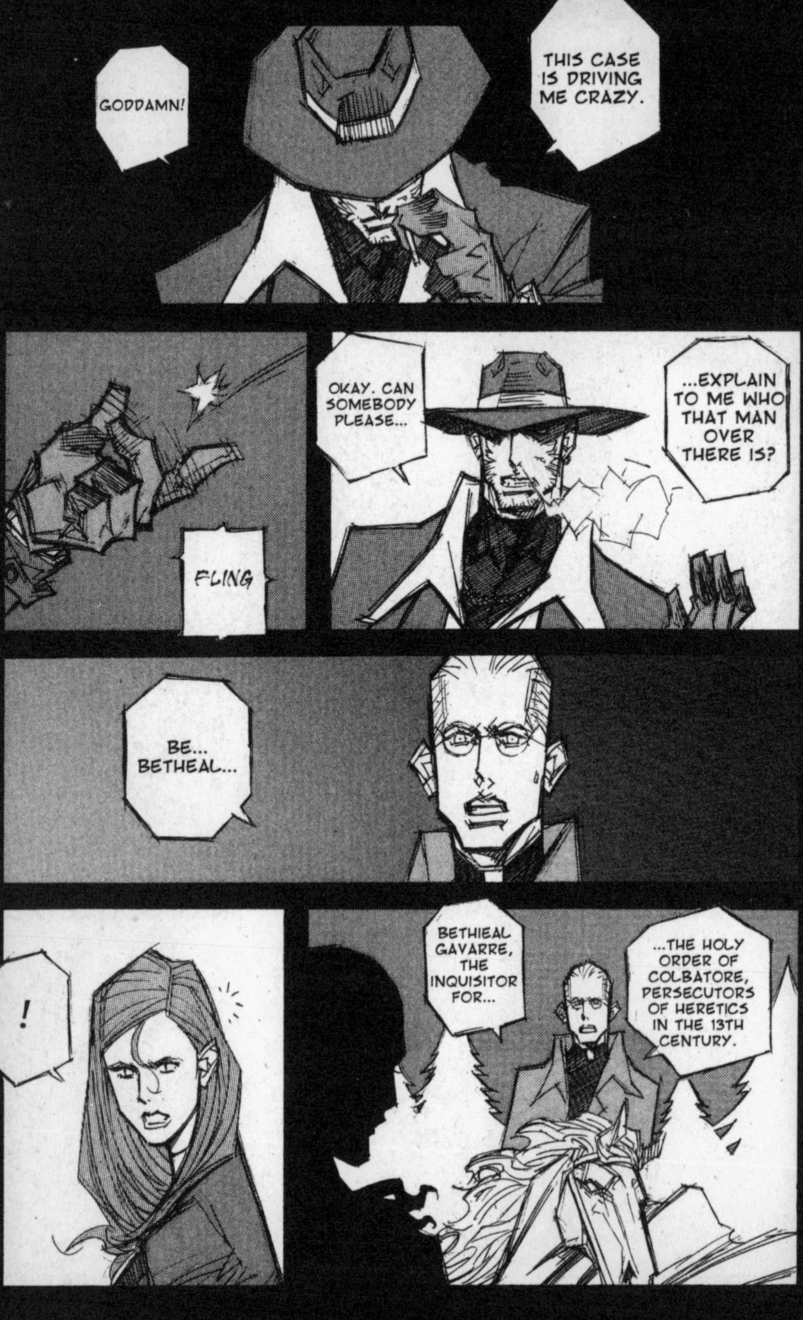
GODDAMN!
THIS CASE IS DRIVING ME CRAZY.
FLING
OKAY. CAN SOMEBODY PLEASE...
...EXPLAIN TO ME WHO THAT MAN OVER THERE IS?
BE... BETHEAL...
!
BETHIEAL GAVARRE, THE INQUISITOR FOR...
...THE HOLY ORDER OF COLBATORE, PERSECUTORS OF HERETICS IN THE 13TH CENTURY.

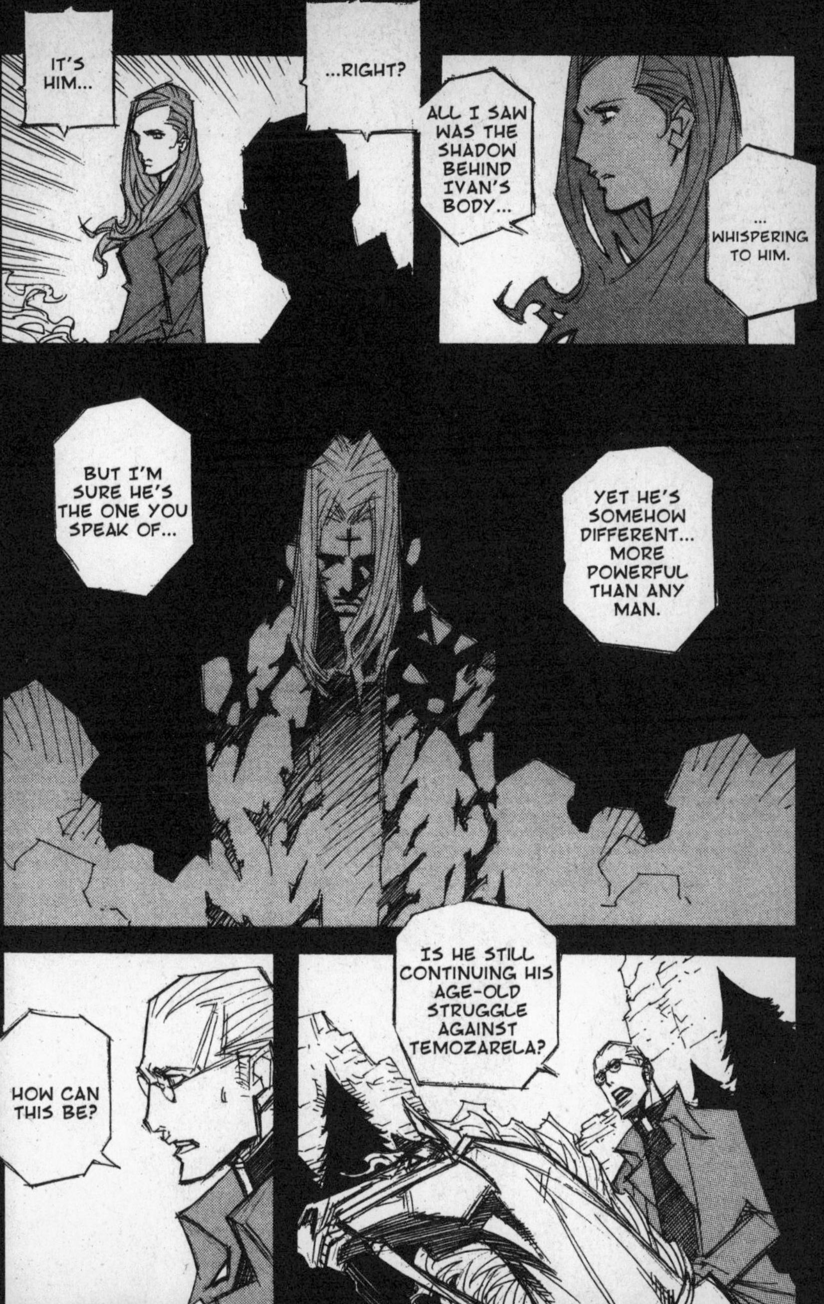
IT'S HIM...
...RIGHT?
ALL I SAW WAS THE SHADOW BEHIND IVAN'S BODY...
...WHISPERING TO HIM.
BUT I'M SURE HE'S THE ONE YOU SPEAK OF...
YET HE'S SOMEHOW DIFFERENT... MORE POWERFUL THAN ANY MAN.
HOW CAN THIS BE?
IS HE STILL CONTINUING HIS AGE-OLD STRUGGLE AGAINST TEMOZARELA?

WHAT I DO COULD BE DONE...

...BY ANY CREATURE OF GOD.

DRIP

DRIP

DRIP

DRIP

CLANG

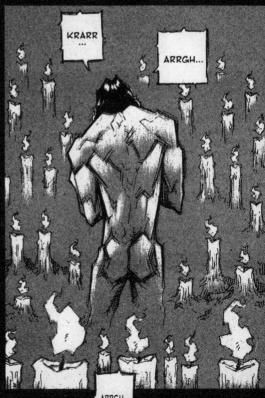

KRARR...

ARRGH...

ARRGH...

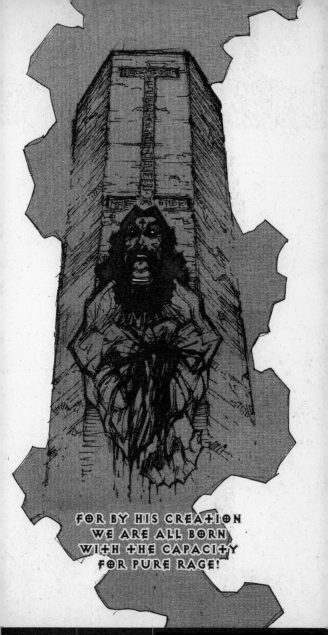

FOR BY HIS CREATION
WE ARE ALL BORN
WITH THE CAPACITY
FOR PURE RAGE!

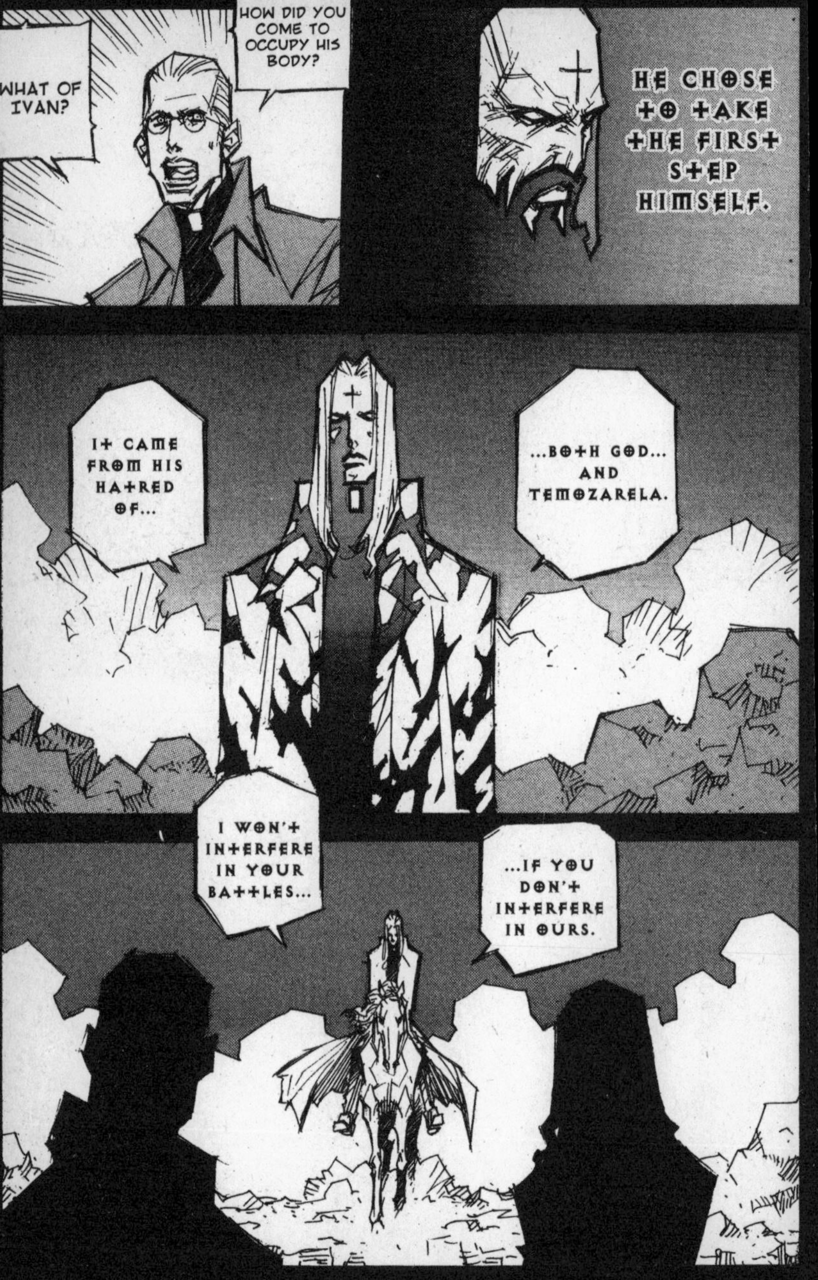
WHAT OF IVAN?
HOW DID YOU COME TO OCCUPY HIS BODY?
HE CHOSE TO TAKE THE FIRST STEP HIMSELF.
IT CAME FROM HIS HATRED OF...
...BOTH GOD... AND TEMOZARELA.
I WON'T INTERFERE IN YOUR BATTLES...
...IF YOU DON'T INTERFERE IN OURS.

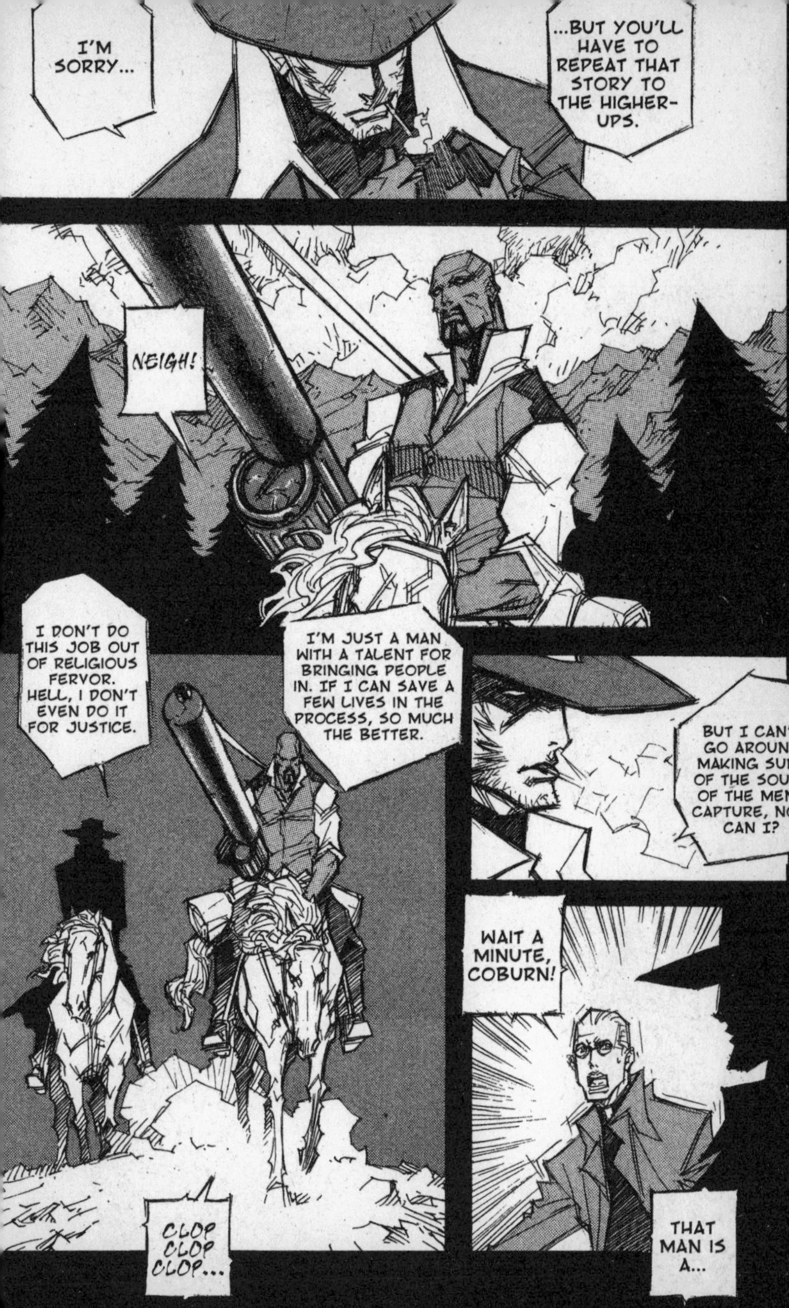
I'M SORRY...
...BUT YOU'LL HAVE TO REPEAT THAT STORY TO THE HIGHER-UPS.
NEIGH!
I DON'T DO THIS JOB OUT OF RELIGIOUS FERVOR. HELL, I DON'T EVEN DO IT FOR JUSTICE.
I'M JUST A MAN WITH A TALENT FOR BRINGING PEOPLE IN. IF I CAN SAVE A FEW LIVES IN THE PROCESS, SO MUCH THE BETTER.
CLOP CLOP CLOP...
BUT I CAN'T GO AROUND MAKING SURE OF THE SOULS OF THE MEN I CAPTURE, NOW CAN I?
WAIT A MINUTE, COBURN!
THAT MAN IS A...

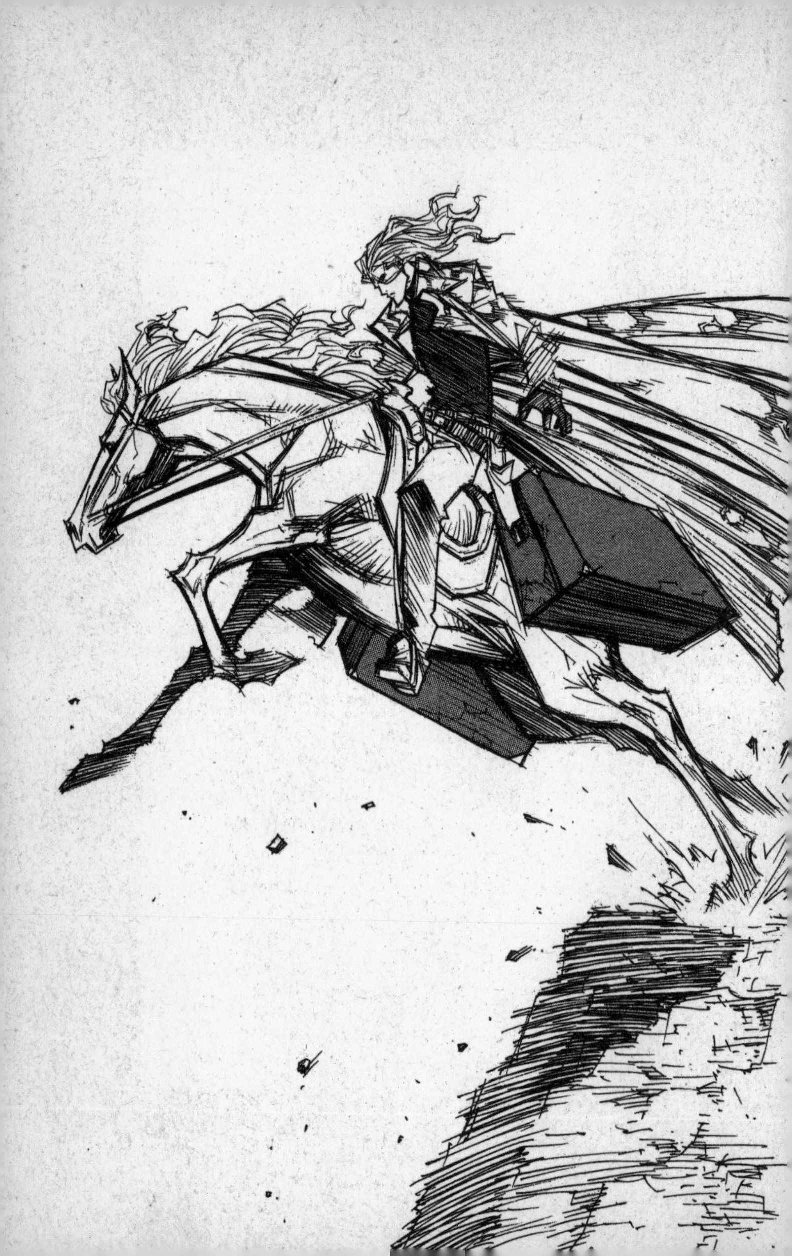

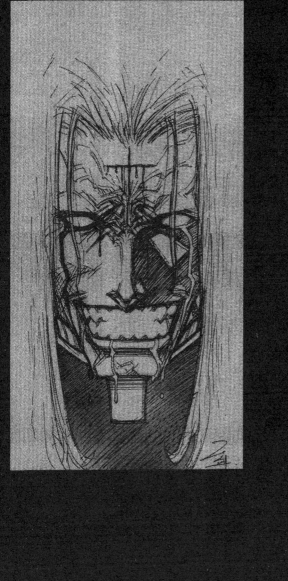

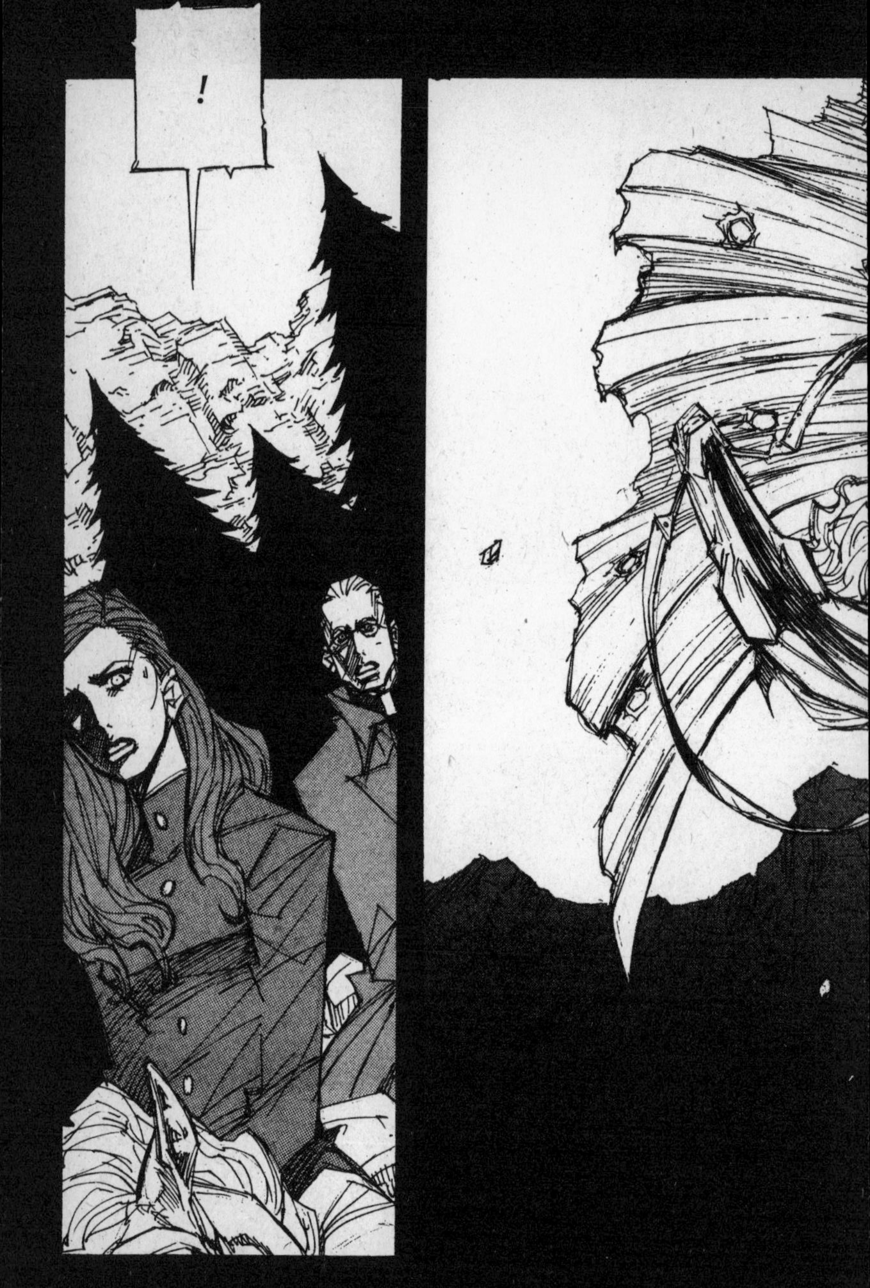
!

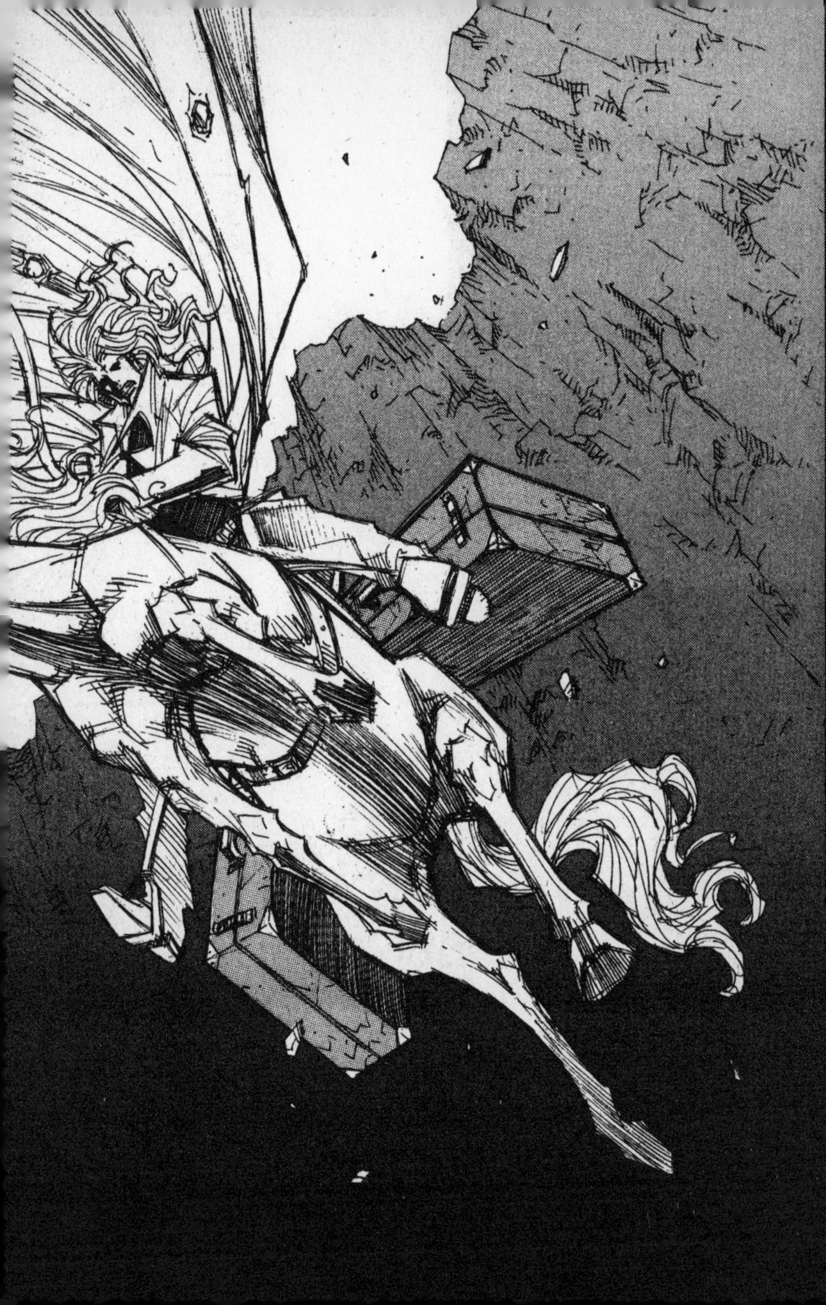

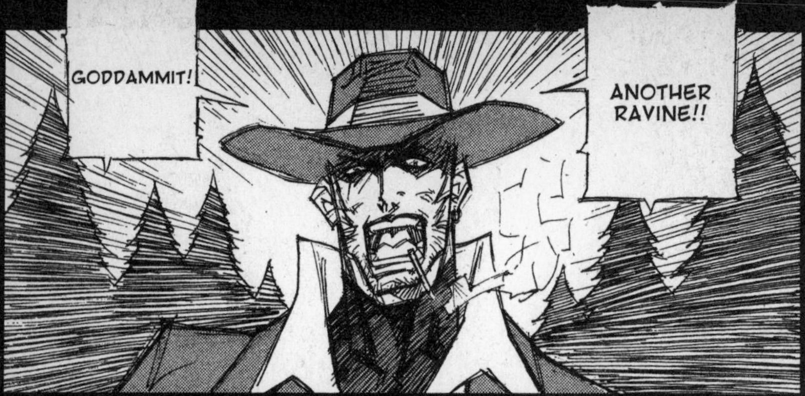
GODDAMMIT!
ANOTHER RAVINE!!
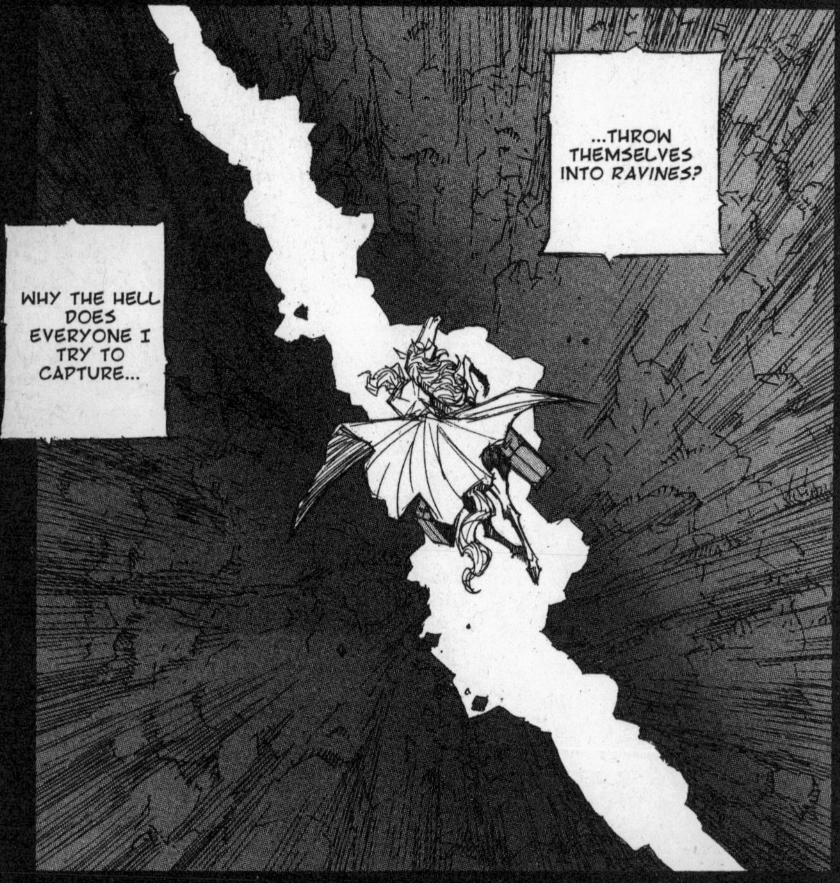
WHY THE HELL DOES EVERYONE I TRY TO CAPTURE...
...THROW THEMSELVES INTO RAVINES?

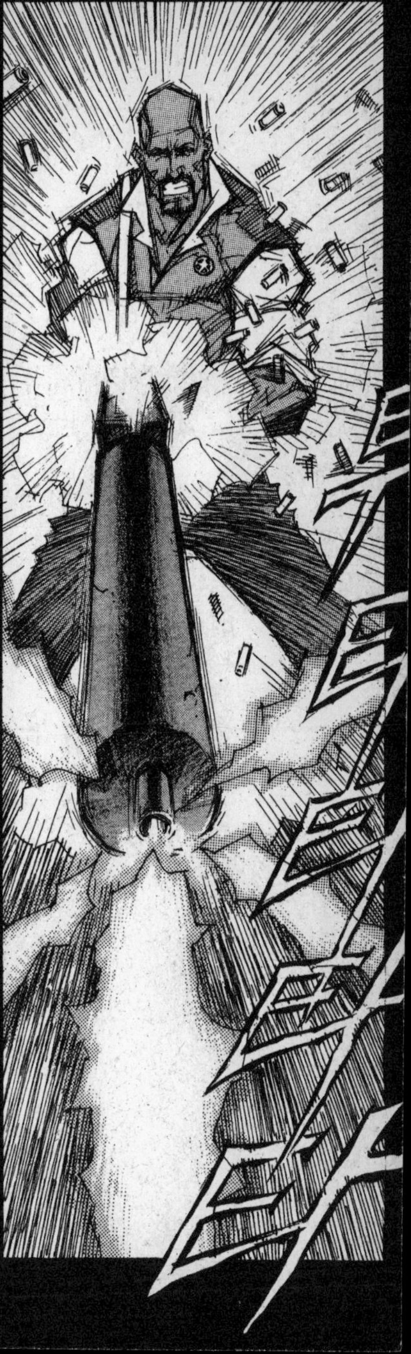
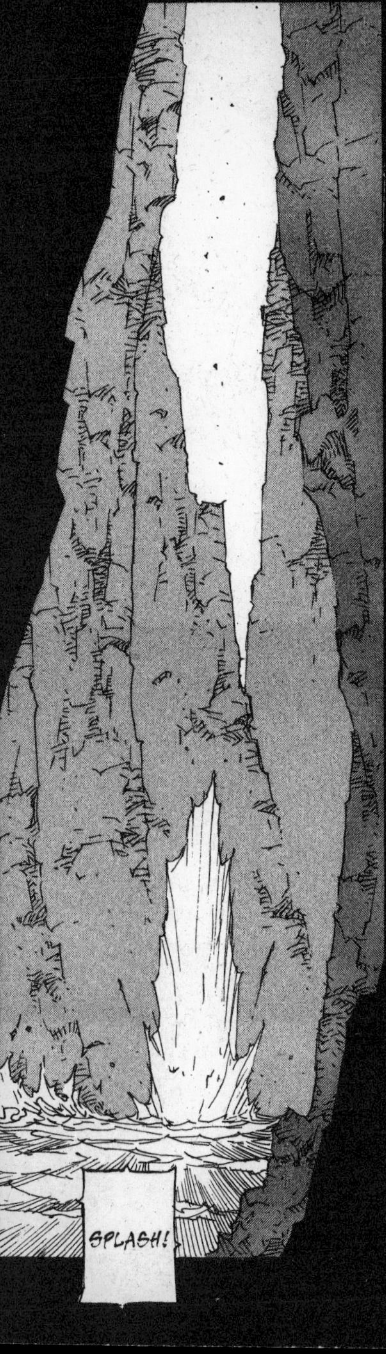
SPLASH!

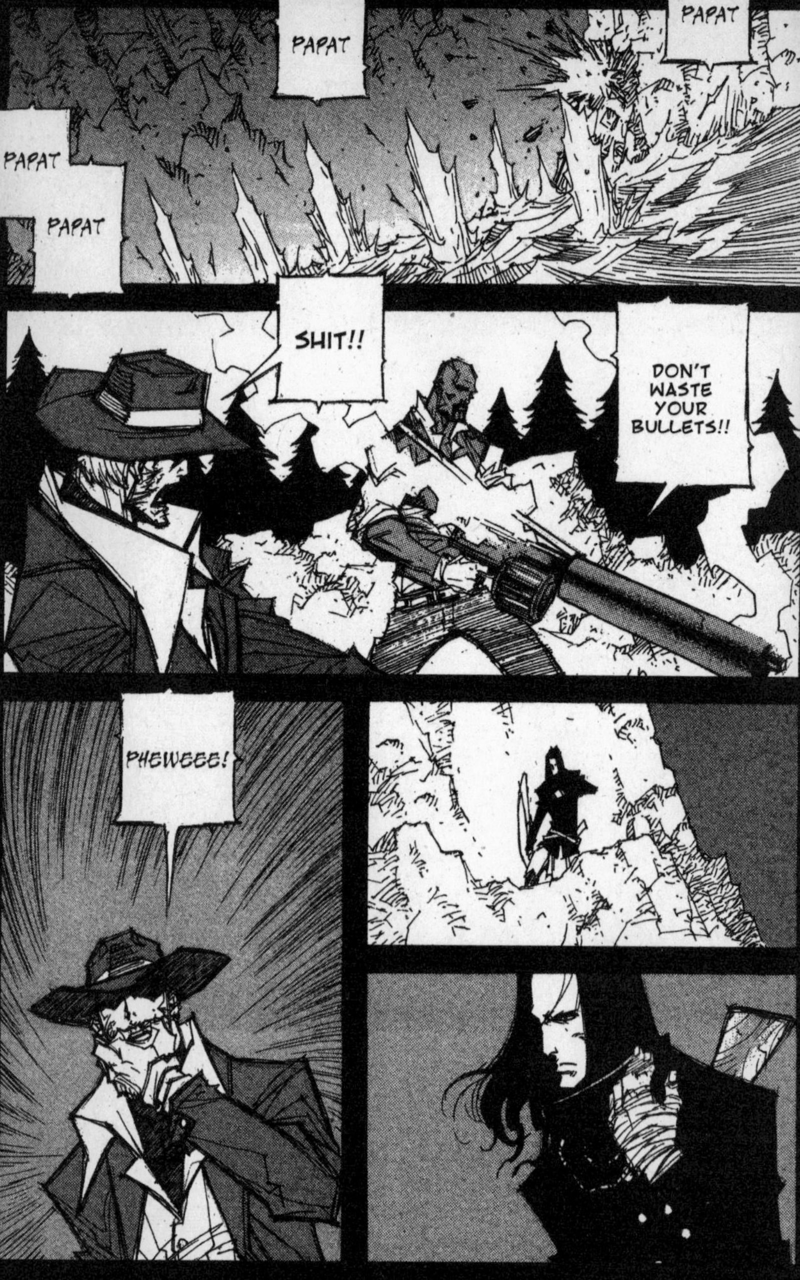
PAPAT
PAPAT
PAPAT
PAPAT
DON'T WASTE YOUR BULLETS!!
SHIT!!
PHEWEEE!

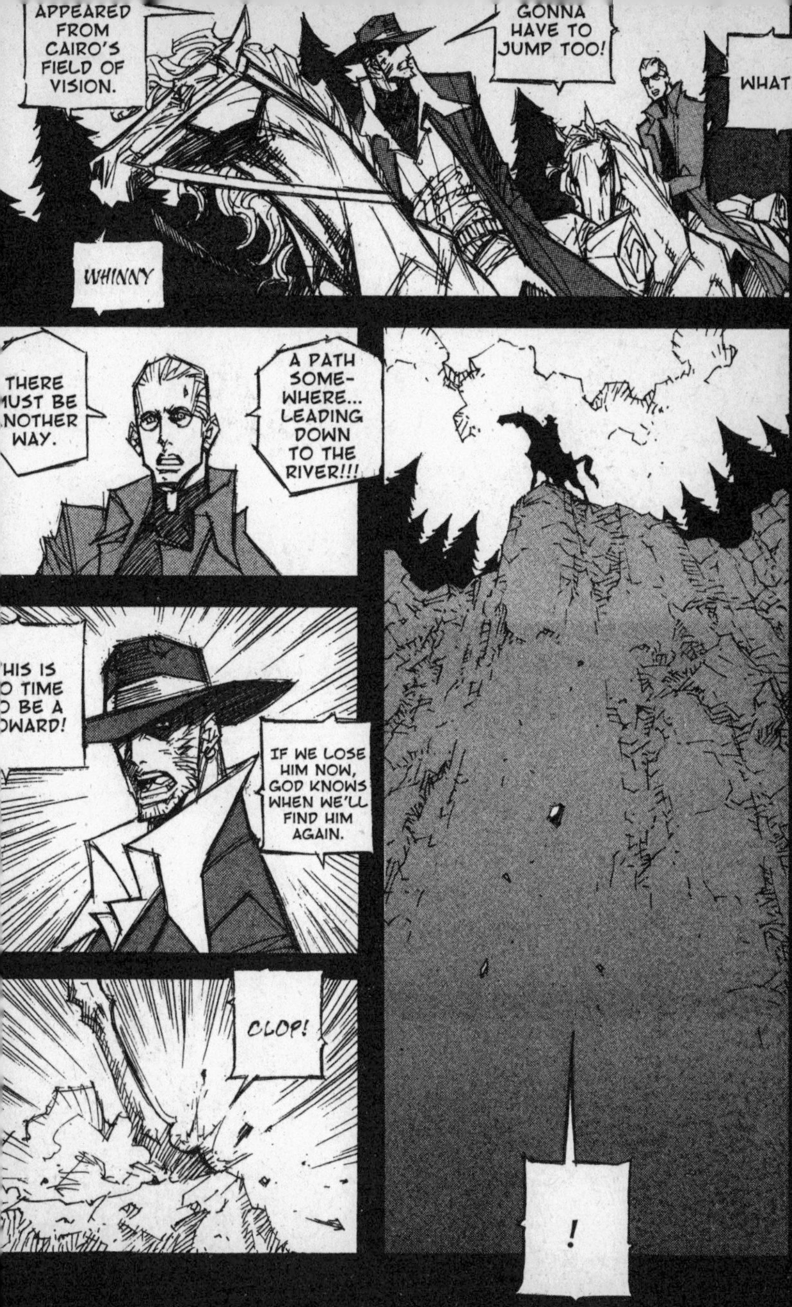
APPEARED FROM CAIRO'S FIELD OF VISION.
GONNA HAVE TO JUMP TOO!
WHAT?
WHINNY
THERE MUST BE NOTHER WAY.
A PATH SOME-WHERE... LEADING DOWN TO THE RIVER!!!
HIS IS O TIME O BE A OWARD!
IF WE LOSE HIM NOW, GOD KNOWS WHEN WE'LL FIND HIM AGAIN.
CLOP!
!

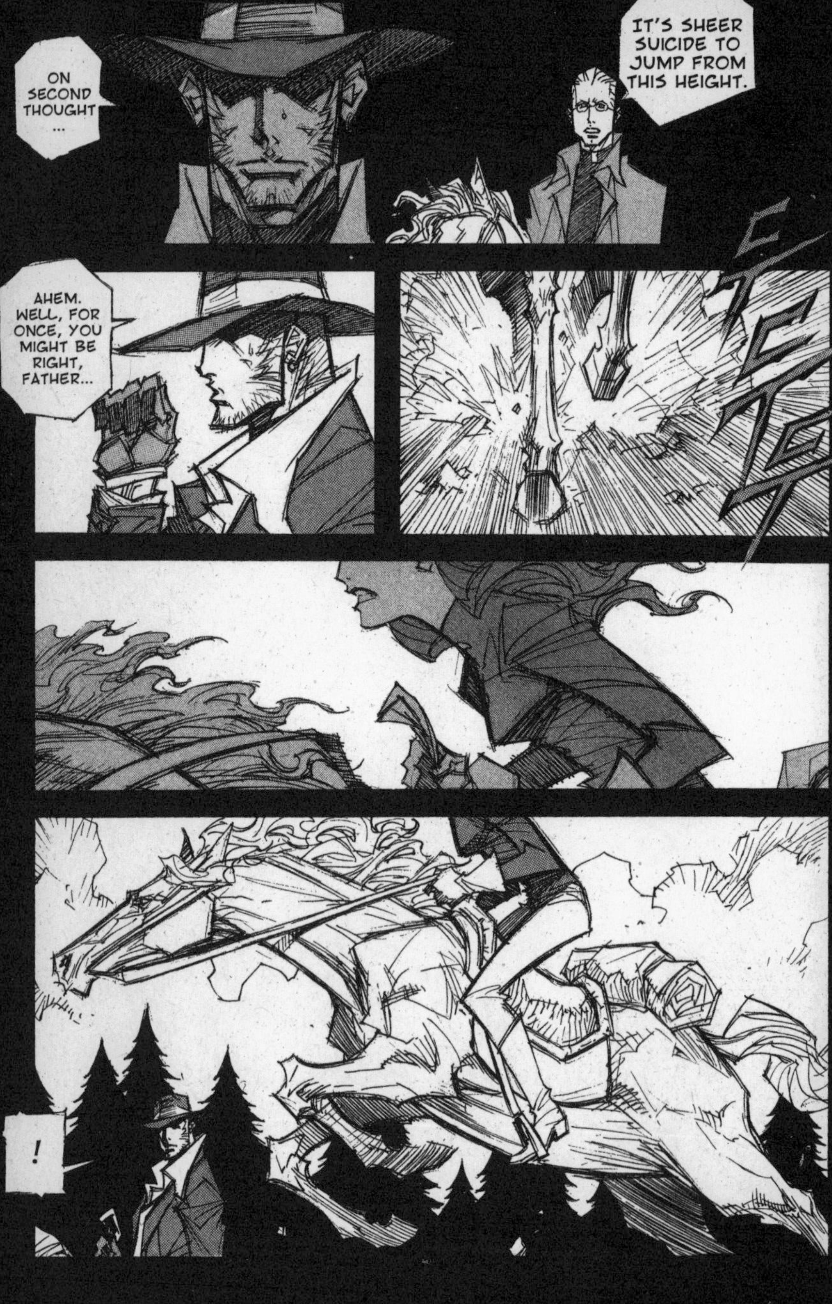
IT'S SHEER SUICIDE TO JUMP FROM THIS HEIGHT.
ON SECOND THOUGHT ...
AHEM. WELL, FOR ONCE, YOU MIGHT BE RIGHT, FATHER...
!

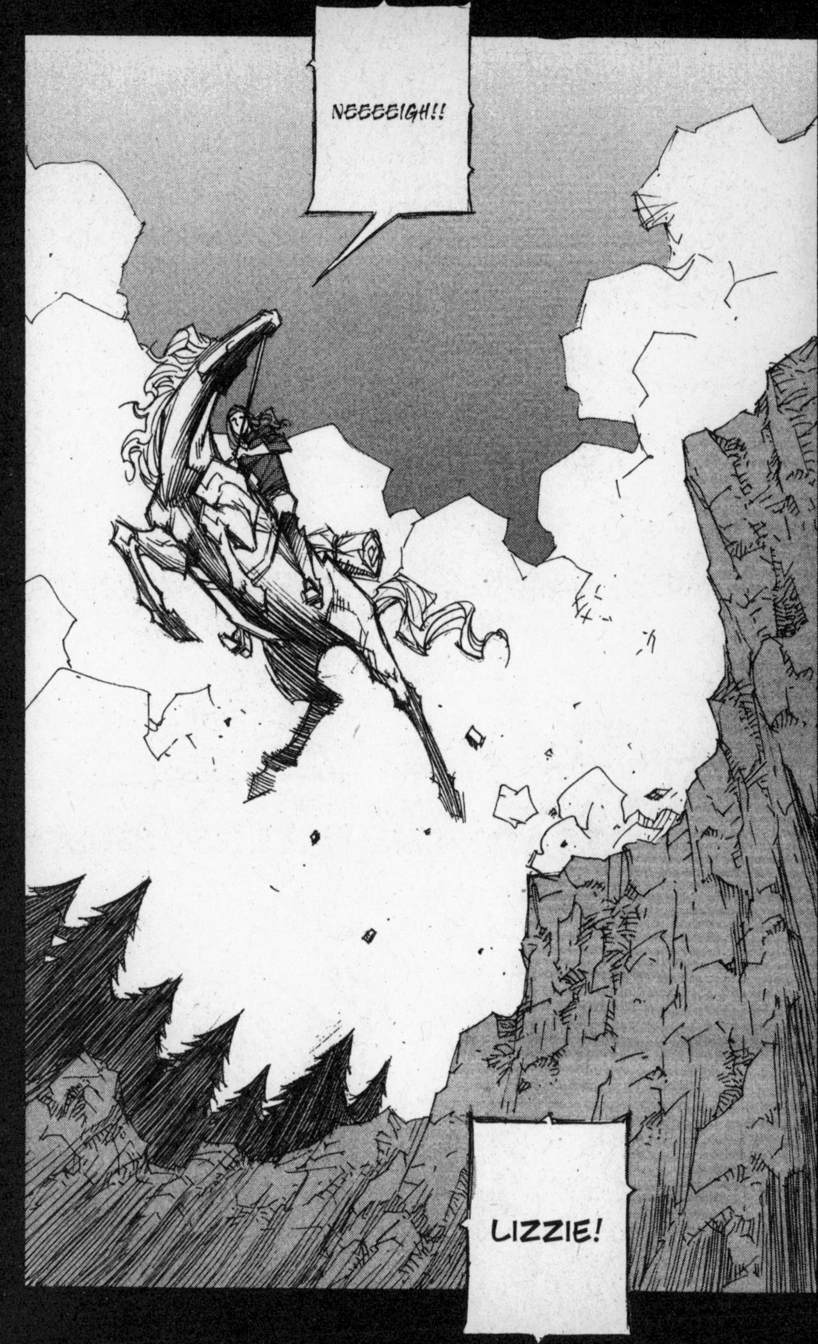
NEEEEIGH!!
LIZZIE!

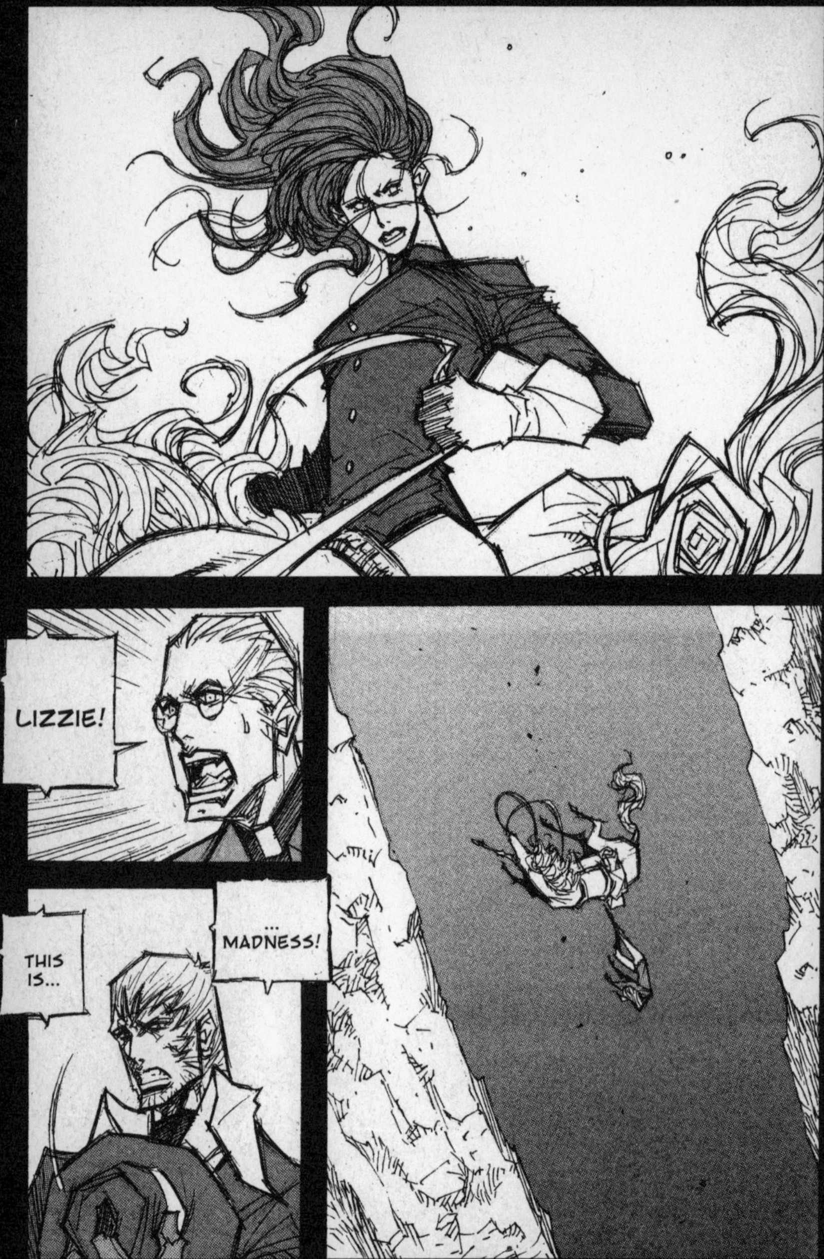
LIZZIE!
THIS IS...
...MADNESS!

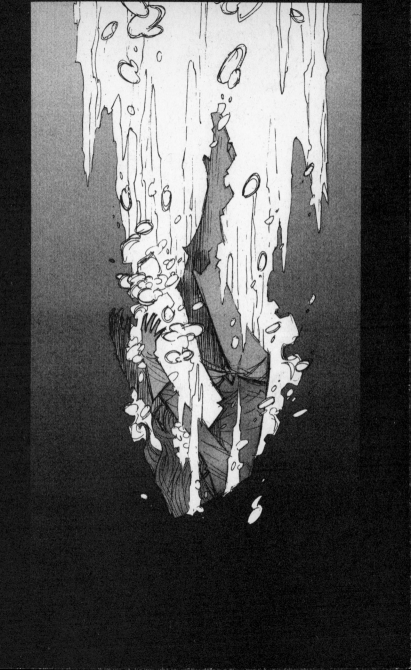

WHAT AM I
DOING?

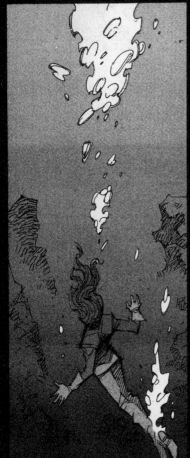

HE WON'T GIVE
ME ANY ANSWERS
ANYWAY...

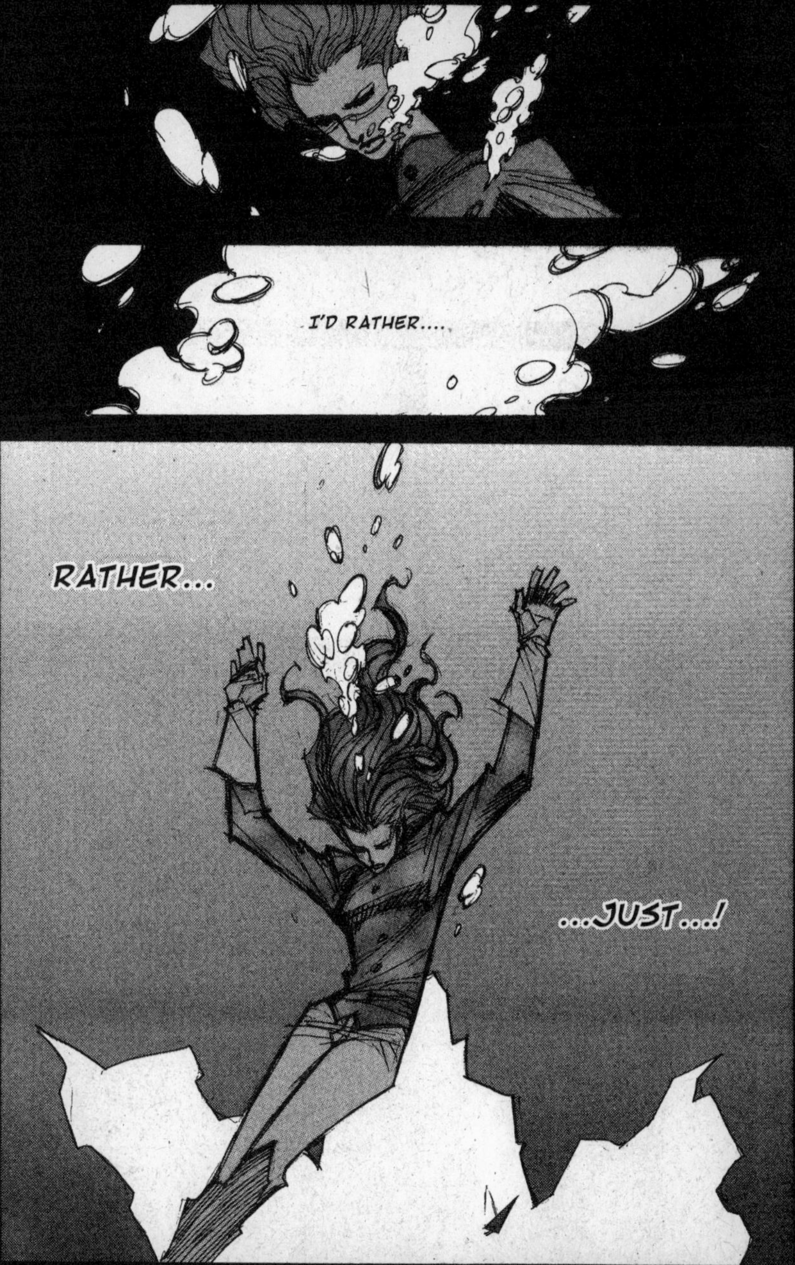
I'D RATHER....
RATHER...
...JUST...!

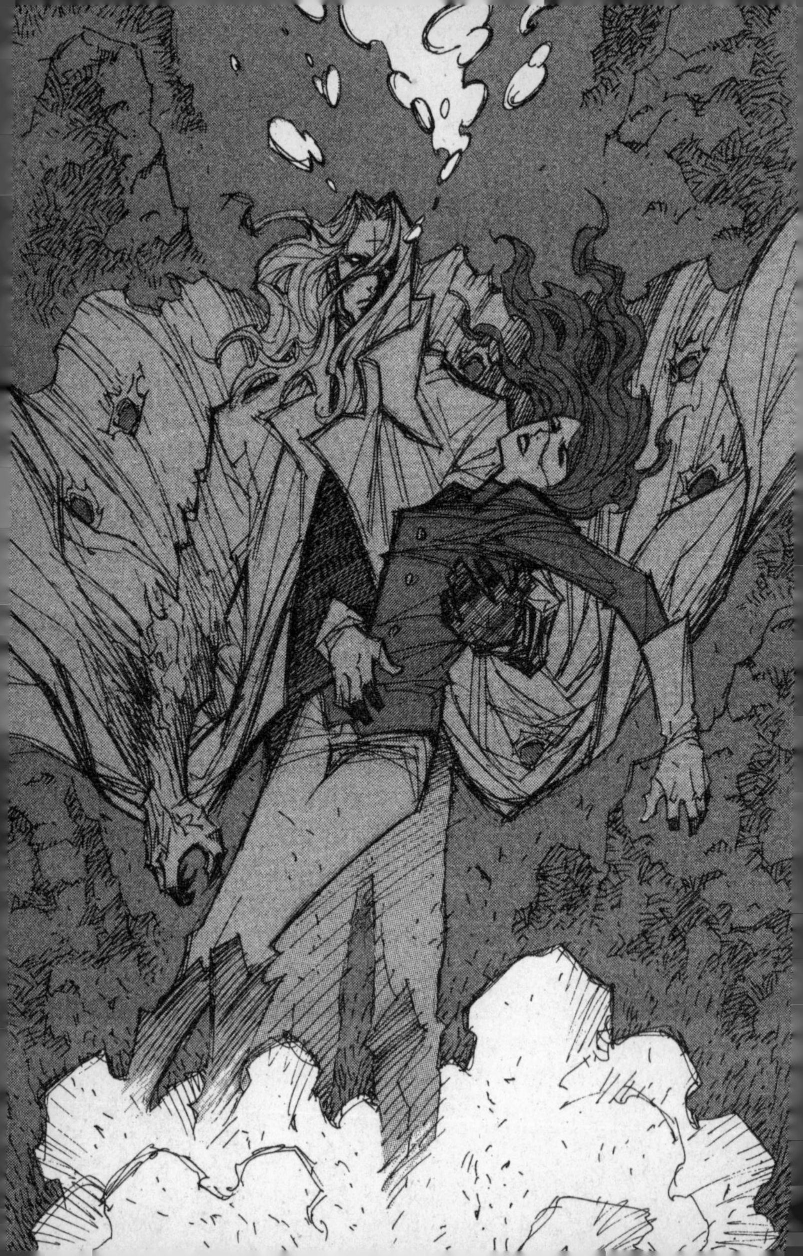

IVAN ISAACS WILL RETURN IN

PRIEST VOLUME II: CANTICLE OF THE SWORD

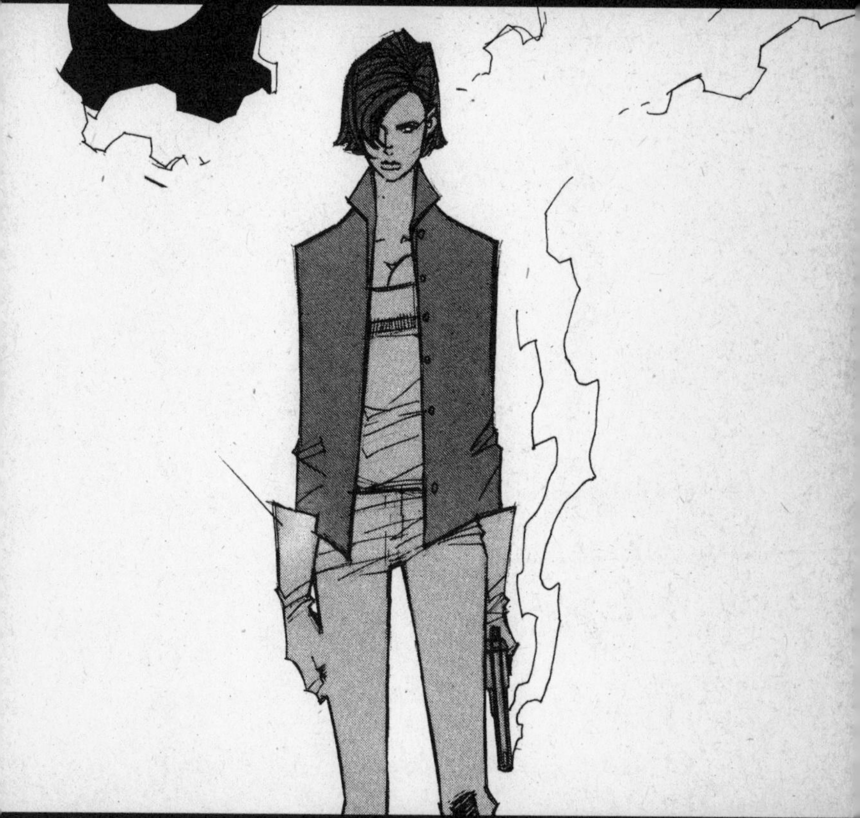

IN WHICH LIZZIE RETURNS TO HER OUTLAW ROOTS AND THE VATICAN ATTEMPTS TO CLEAN UP THE MESS IT MADE.

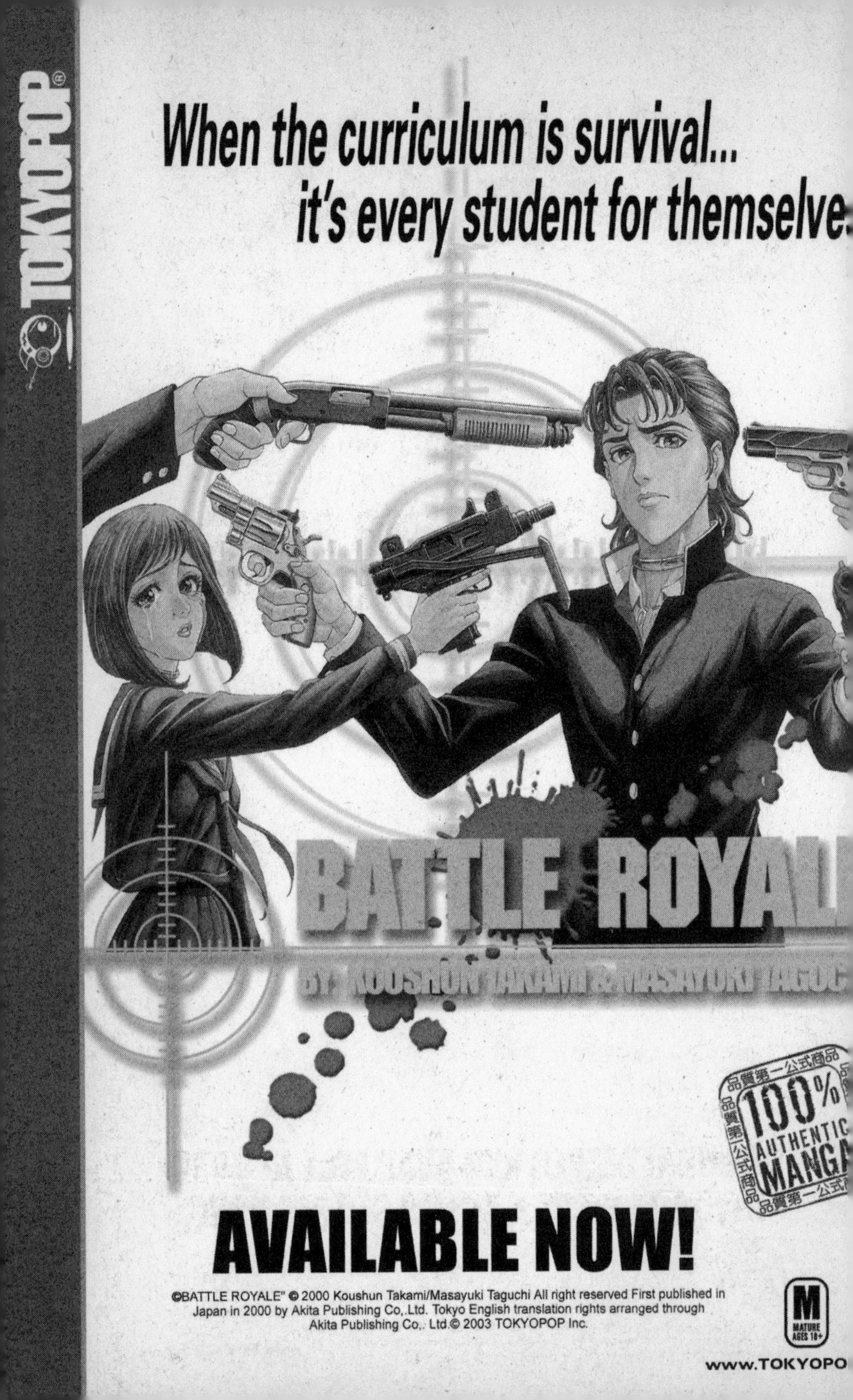
TOKYOPOP
When the curriculum is survival...
it's every student for themselve
BATTLE ROYAL
BY KOUSHUN TAKAMI & MASAYUKI TAGUC
品質第一公式商品
100%
AUTHENTIC
MANGA
AVAILABLE NOW!
©BATTLE ROYALE" © 2000 Koushun Takami/Masayuki Taguchi All right reserved First published in Japan in 2000 by Akita Publishing Co,.Ltd. Tokyo English translation rights arranged through Akita Publishing Co,. Ltd.© 2003 TOKYOPOP Inc.
M
MATURE
AGES 18+
www.TOKYOPO

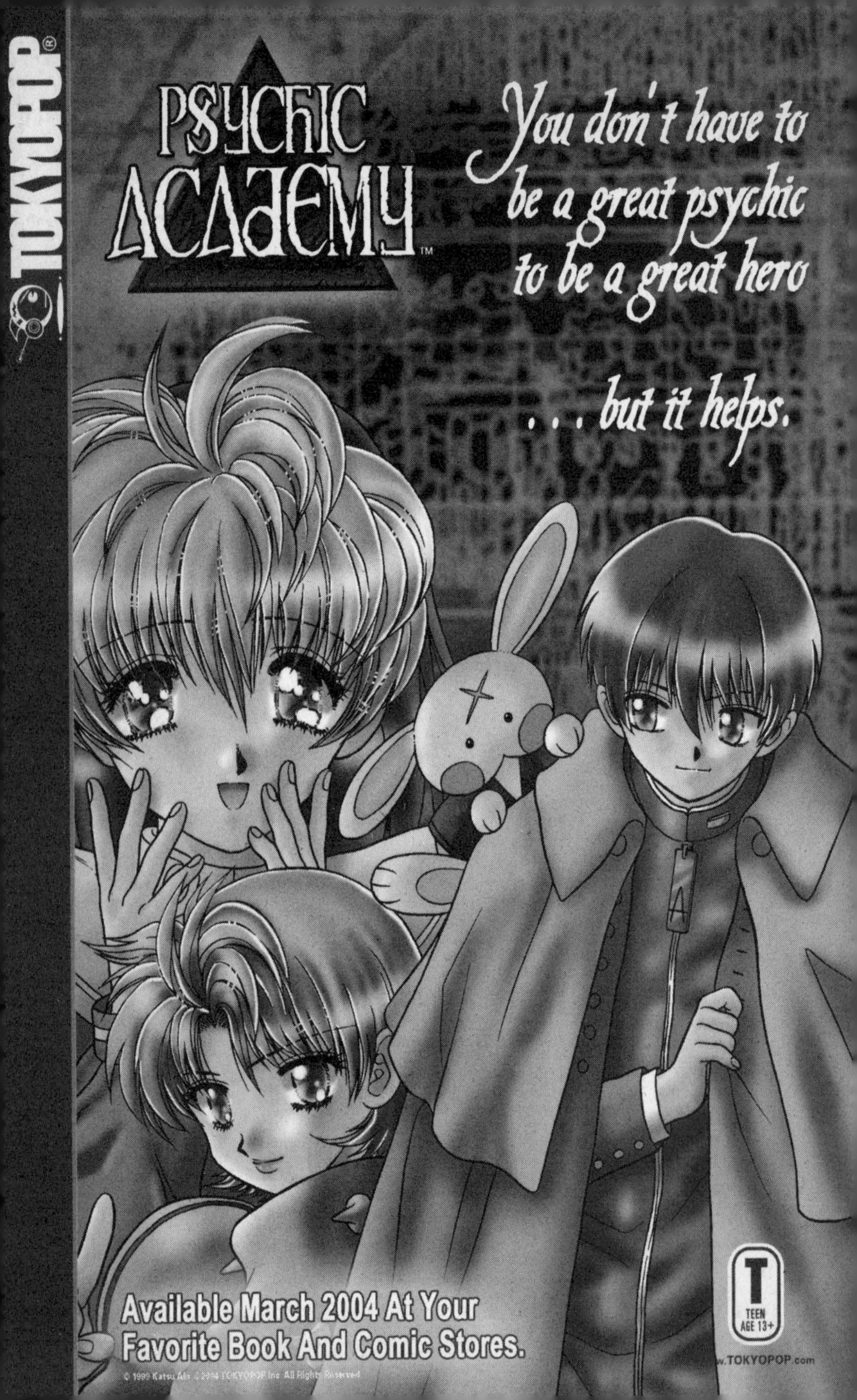
TOKYOPOP
PSYCHIC ACADEMY™
You don't have to be a great psychic to be a great hero
. . . but it helps.
Available March 2004 At Your Favorite Book And Comic Stores.
T TEEN AGE 13+
w.TOKYOPOP.com
© 1999 Katsu Aki ©2004 TOKYOPOP Inc. All Rights Reserved

LAMENT OF THE LAMB ™

MANGA

.HACK//LEGEND OF THE TWILIGHT
@LARGE
A.I. LOVE YOU February 2004
AI YORI AOSHI
ANGELIC LAYER
BABY BIRTH
BATTLE ROYALE
BATTLE VIXENS April 2004
BIRTH May 2004
BRAIN POWERED
BRIGADOON
B'TX
CARDCAPTOR SAKURA
CARDCAPTOR SAKURA: MASTER OF THE CLOW
CARDCAPTOR SAKURA: BOXED SET COLLECTION 1
CARDCAPTOR SAKURA: BOXED SET COLLECTION 2
  March 2004
CHOBITS
CHRONICLES OF THE CURSED SWORD
CLAMP SCHOOL DETECTIVES
CLOVER
COMIC PARTY June 2004
CONFIDENTIAL CONFESSIONS
CORRECTOR YUI
COWBOY BEBOP: BOXED SET THE COMPLETE
  COLLECTION
CRESCENT MOON May 2004
CREST OF THE STARS June 2004
CYBORG 009
DEMON DIARY
DIGIMON
DIGIMON SERIES 3 April 2004
DIGIMON ZERO TWO February 2004
DNANGEL April 2004
DOLL May 2004
DRAGON HUNTER
DRAGON KNIGHTS
DUKLYON: CLAMP SCHOOL DEFENDERS
DV June 2004
ERICA SAKURAZAWA
FAERIES' LANDING
FAKE
FLCL
FORBIDDEN DANCE
FRUITS BASKET February 2004
G GUNDAM
GATEKEEPERS
GETBACKERS February 2004
GHOST! March 2004
GIRL GOT GAME
GRAVITATION
GTO

GUNDAM WING
GUNDAM WING: BATTLEFIELD OF PACIFISTS
GUNDAM WING: ENDLESS WALTZ
GUNDAM WING: THE LAST OUTPOST
HAPPY MANIA
HARLEM BEAT
I.N.V.U.
INITIAL D
ISLAND
JING: KING OF BANDITS
JULINE
JUROR 13 March 2004
KARE KANO
KILL ME, KISS ME February 2004
KINDAICHI CASE FILES, THE
KING OF HELL
KODOCHA: SANA'S STAGE
LAMENT OF THE LAMB May 2004
LES BIJOUX February 2004
LIZZIE MCGUIRE
LOVE HINA
LUPIN III
LUPIN III SERIES 2
MAGIC KNIGHT RAYEARTH I
MAGIC KNIGHT RAYEARTH II February 2004
MAHOROMATIC: AUTOMATIC MAIDEN May 2004
MAN OF MANY FACES
MARMALADE BOY
MARS
METEOR METHUSELA June 2004
METROID June 2004
MINK April 2004
MIRACLE GIRLS
MIYUKI-CHAN IN WONDERLAND
MODEL May 2004
NELLY MUSIC MANGA April 2004
ONE April 2004
PARADISE KISS
PARASYTE
PEACH GIRL
PEACH GIRL CHANGE OF HEART
PEACH GIRL RELAUNCH BOX SET
PET SHOP OF HORRORS
PITA-TEN
PLANET LADDER February 2004
PLANETES
PRIEST
PRINCESS AI April 2004
PSYCHIC ACADEMY March 2004
RAGNAROK
RAGNAROK: BOXED SET COLLECTION 1
RAVE MASTER
RAVE MASTER: BOXED SET March 2004